Endorsements for

The Intentional Servant Leader: Premise and Practice

"For years, I have been hoping for a practical, how-to book on servant leadership. Linda Belton answered my prayers with her latest work, The Intentional Servant Leader. This book goes far beyond theory to the actual development of strategies and guides for those beginning the journey as well as those who have been on the path for years. From those teaching servant leadership in a classroom, to those who lead organizations steeped in servant leadership, this is a resource you will return to over and over. Belton has accomplished what we all need and want—the nuts and bolts of servant leadership."

—Mary J. Meehan, PhD, FACHE, Interim President, Seton Hall University; President Emerita, Alverno College; Board of Directors, Greenleaf Center for Servant Leadership; Board of Regents, Loras College; Board of Directors, Pieper Family Foundation

"Belton's exciting book combines her knowledge, experience, and intuitive foresight into a unique wisdom which is servant leadership. While many consider servant leadership a "soft skill", it is much more. In times of constant change it provides a business framework for agility and empowerment. Belton's presentation on the subject provides structure and practical application that anyone can take and apply to their business with effectiveness...and success. The book is a "Why to", "What to", "How to", and "When to" rolled into one concise offering. It is a must read for anyone wishing to enhance this life skill. A consummate work by Belton."

—Joe D. Battle, Director, James A. Haley VA Hospital & Clinics; Board Member, Tampa Innovation Partnership

"Linda Belton performs the alchemy of transforming the philosophy of servant leadership into the everyday operations of a leader. She has a knack for delightful turns of phrase that will ensure you remember the most important principles of servant leadership in action. The Intentional Servant Leader is both comprehensive and specific, sharing principles, stories, wisdom, and action steps from one of the nation's most experienced servant-leaders."

—Don M. Frick, PhD; Author, *Implementing Servant Leadership: Stories from the Field*, co-author, *Seven Pillars of Servant Leadership: Practicing the Wisdom of Leading by Serving*

"Linda's experience in a large, controversial organization has made her an expert on the "how to". Her authoring and applied knowledge make this book a great read, study, guide book, and teaching syllabus. This is her best work and is based on both the teacher of and practitioner of servant leadership."

—Richard R. Pieper, Sr., Chairman Emeritus, PPC Partners, Inc.; Past Chairman Greenleaf Center; Past President National Character Education Partnership (Character.org); recipient of the American Patriot of Character Award.

"This book is the embodiment of servant leadership. Linda Belton weaves together solid research and theorizing on leadership and organizational life with illustrative examples, rich activities, and many opportunities for reflection and action; all in service of drawing out the reader's thoughts and desires and facilitating their will and skill to claim servant leadership in their own lives. Her writing is elegant, accessible, and engaging. Every time a question would come into my mind, there would be a response that spoke to it. This book is a dialogue that I never wanted to end; a lovely guidebook for the journey of servant leadership."

—Loraleigh Keashly, Ph.D., Professor, Communication; Associate Dean, Curricular & Student Affairs, College of Fine, Performing and Communication Arts, Wayne State University

"If you wonder what it really means to lead as a servant-leader, read this book! Keep it near your desk where you can read and reread it, using its summaries, quotes and practices as your primary servant leadership reference for years to come."

—Virginia Gilmore, Founder Sophia Foundation, Fond du Lac, Wisconsin

"Whether you've recently discovered that your journey has a name, or whether you've been exploring servant leadership for years, this book is a must-have field manual for how to serve and lead. In plainly-stated style, Linda Belton has thoughtfully collected real-world reflections, questions, and practical actions that you can engage in, wherever you are. This book is a gift! I intend to keep it within close reach as a guide for when particular questions or situations arise, because there is always more to learn and the journey of the servant leader is more about striving than arriving."

—Robert Toomey, Ed.D., M.A. in Servant Leadership; Leadership Program Director, University of Wisconsin-Madison

*"Linda embodies servant leadership, and her insight is palpable. She has distilled simple truths from years of life experience, using practical, relatable examples and analogies. This book provides an important look into the anatomy of servant leadership, incorporating balance and connectivity to all relationships...both personal and professional. Readers will understand that it truly is **our** turn to serve, and the results can be transformational."*

—Linda S. Jeffrey FACHE, MS, Human Resource Development; Executive Officer (ret.), Communication and Organizational Development, VA Medical Center, Indianapolis; President, Indiana War Memorials Foundation/Indianapolis POW-MIA Council

"By exploring the paradoxical relationships between hands-on functionality and people-focused culture, here's a starting point to help you pursue a servant leader's journey no matter where you are in your organization.

"With a wide variety of questions, scenarios, and exercises, readers are challenged to examine their beliefs and behaviors and seek to find more meaning in their leadership choices."

—Phillip Anderson, Co-Program Director, Greenleaf Center for Servant Leadership

"Linda has earned the right to speak to us in the servant leadership community. We needed more approachable, practical, and encouraging advice. This book is it! I most highly recommend it!"

—Ken Jennings PhD, co-author of the international bestseller, The Serving Leader

The Intentional Servant Leader

Premise and Practice

A Symphony of Service

Linda W. Belton

ROBERT K. GREENLEAF
CENTER FOR
SERVANT LEADERSHIP

The Intentional Servant Leader:
Premise and Practice

Copyright © Linda W. Belton 2018
All rights reserved.

ISBN 13: 978-1-944338-09-1

Book design by Adam Robinson and Adrienne Belton

Published by The Greenleaf Center for Servant Leadership
133 Peachtree St. NE, Suite 350
Atlanta, GA 30303
www.greenleaf.org

*To those who have touched my life in an
extraordinary or abiding way:*

*Donna,
Chris, Terilee,
Janet, Stan, Randall, Don,
Faye, Lou Ann, Linda, Kent, Tom,
Steve, Tony, Harriet, Bud, Marge, Terése,
Dee, Kasey, Denise, Maureen,
Jo, Kelly, Leketha, Sue
& Rhonda*

Friends and Mentors all

Other books by Linda W. Belton

A Nobler Side of Leadership: The Art of Humanagement

A Nobler Side of Leadership: The Art of Humanagement
The Workbook

The First Shall Be Last: Servant Leadership in Scripture

A companion Workbook with additional interactive tools, activities, and resources is available for purchase.

Designed to accompany the book, the Workbook adapts the content to a learner-friendly format, where individuals and groups, on their own or with facilitation, can experience it at a more personal level.

For information about the Workbook or additional materials, please contact belton.leadership@gmail.com.

Contents

PART ONE

The Premise

Overture

SERVANT LEADERSHIP HAS BEEN AROUND FOR DECADES, SO I AM sometimes shocked at how many businesses, corporations, health care organizations, and academic institutions have not yet "discovered" it. Is that, I wonder, because there is a dearth of research and literature on the topic? Yet when I look it up I find thousands of books and hundreds of studies available at the click of the keyboard. There are some pretty weighty thinkers and authors out there who have covered the ground brilliantly, dedicated organizations like the Greenleaf Center, and even a cohort of Greenleaf scholars, all devoted to furthering the cause of servant leadership.

So:

1. What more is there to say? and,
2. Why haven't more organizations leapt on the concept?

I'll address the second question first.

There is no simple, single answer, but through my dealings with a range of organizations I have become convinced of at least a few possibilities:

- Servant leadership is countercultural. Being called a servant is simply not *de rigeur*. Thinking of others *first* won't get you where you want to go. Compassion is wimpy. Humility is not in the curriculum.

  Servant leadership turns *business as usual* on its head. So despite the data that substantiate an array of successful outcomes, it is in conflict with what our training and experience have taught us. It is hard to *unlearn* what has been drilled into us, or to *extinguish* behaviors that have been consistently rewarded.

- Servant leadership is not easy. I believe it is a commitment that has to be renewed every day, perhaps several times a day. There are risks—of being perceived as weak, of standing at odds with a boss or apart from colleagues, of facing misunderstanding or contempt, of being out–paced by the "climbers", and of recognizing that you may have to abandon a job to save your soul.

This list of risks sounds much like the potential side–effects on a bottle of aspirin! We are mindful of the perils, but they rarely happen and the benefits are worth it. That is surely the case with servant leadership, but they may not be exactly the benefits you signed on for. Instead of a quick trip up your career ladder, you get the satisfaction of boosting others up theirs. Rather than basking in public acclaim, you have the joy of wrapping your team in glory. Contrary to securing your own power, you accept the honor of sharing it with everyone else.

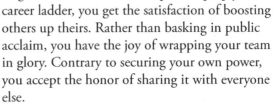

Servant leadership is not easy and even more difficult to undertake alone. Yet most workplaces are not structured to provide *community;* companionship along the way. And so we struggle along the path on our own, following the breadcrumbs and watching for guideposts …

• <u>The guideposts are few and far between, or they are written in a foreign language.</u> The hesitation I hear most often—even from people and organizations who genuinely subscribe to servant leadership—is that they don't know where to start.

The *what* of servant leadership is fairly straightforward, but the *how* is more complicated and comparatively personal. There is no checklist, recipe, or playbook. Each organization—in fact, each member of an organization—must tailor the practice to their own circumstances. Servant leaders arise from every level in the hierarchy and from every background and lifestyle, so our *applications* of servant leadership will not be mirror images of each other. If we are really internalizing the principles, that's the way it should be.

Nevertheless, the problem of *how* takes us back to my first question above: what more is there to say? *"How"* is the conundrum for which this book was written:

1. How do I transform the rhetoric of servant leadership into the everyday operations of leadership?

2. How do I personalize my implementation?

3. How does servant leadership look different in the way I carry out my responsibilities?

4. How will staff see me as a servant leader?

So, how do I begin?

The Intentional Servant Leader attempts to help individuals at all stages of the organizational continuum to answer those questions for themselves. Because every reader is not at the same level of mastery, **Part I** overviews what it is to be a leader, what it is to be a servant leader, how one serves with intentionality, and some myths about servant leadership. These are the basics, but with a bit of a twist.

There is a lengthy discussion of servant leader *charisms* in this section. Charism is not a word we typically use in organizations, most often applied in a theological context. Here I am construing it to mean both a special characteristic or aptitude and a special responsibility or obligation: *a gift and a promise*.

Part II presents the nuts and bolts of leadership—the specific duties and detailed functions; how they are typically performed in a traditional work environment and how they might be performed differently in a servant organization. It includes illustrative examples and strong practices that some organizations have adopted, as jumping–off places for your own ingenuity and imagination.

Where will you go from here? Each of these features augment the text in a way that makes it more personal and useful:

- *Practice Periods* are exercises to hone your skills

- *Contrasts: Traditional Organization v Servant*

Organization provide checkpoints to guide your progress in an *intentional* way

- *Make Your Own Kind of Music: Try This* offers some bold ideas for differentiating yourself as a servant leader
- *Thinking Between the Lines* are short essays that consider a particular leadership theme, but from an alternative angle

There are surely experts in servant leadership who are more knowledgeable, scholarly, and articulate than I. What I lack in those areas, I make up for in passion, persistence, and experience in the day–to–day crucible of complex and demanding organizations. By passing along my thoughts and impressions of servant leadership, I hope to stimulate the *hows* in your own mind, to whet your creative appetite for transforming your workplace, and to build "community" that nourishes us all on the journey.

SERVANT LEADERSHIP IS NOT A SOLO BUT A SYMPHONY OF SERVICE.

What Is a Leader?

You are a leader, somewhere in your organization's management hierarchy. You hire and fire, plan and budget, evaluate personnel and analyze data. You are accountable. At whatever your level of supervision, the buck stops with you. *You are followed because you are in charge.*

You are a leader. No one reports directly to you, but you are the pivot point for a critical program or office that has broad impact throughout the organization. While you cannot single–handedly carry out your function, you are responsible for ensuring that others do. *You are respected because you are knowledgeable.*

You are also a leader, in your community, your church, your social organization, or on your team. Using powers of persuasion and relationship, you help move people toward a common goal. *You are appreciated because you achieve results.*

You are a thought leader. People turn to you when there is a problem or a question, not because of any official position, but in response to your reputation and credibility. *You are effective because you have earned their trust.*

You probably are, have been, or will be each of these leaders during your life and career. You might use different skills and techniques in each iteration, but at some point and to some degree, you will exercise all the duties of management. You will hire, fire, discipline and promote; create strategic plans, tactical plans, succession plans, and financial plans. You will set up rules and regulations, policies and procedures. You will work with employees to establish a culture, priorities, and a set of company values. Co-workers, subordinates, team members, and colleagues will look to you as guide, model, and inspiration.

There are more than 200,000 leadership books in Amazon's catalog. Look at some of the titles and it becomes apparent that leadership has many definitions, descriptions, and directions. From "management by objectives" and "stay hungry, stay lean" to "leaderless groups" and "transformational leadership", there is a theory out there for everyone's taste.

Leadership theories and philosophies abound: are leaders born or made (trait or process theory)? Are you a transactional, transitional, or transformational leader? What model is best: Theory Y, Situational, or Level 5? Reams of information are available on all these concepts, each looking at leadership from a slightly different slant, each with its specific strengths and weaknesses, and each very illuminating in building a universal *gestalt* of leadership.

Fundamentally, a leader is someone who steps out to show the way, but there is more than one path and leaders can travel by divergent routes. Some are hands-off, others instill fear; some are authoritarian, others are participative; some lead from power, others from service. We'll consider that last one—the *servant–first*—in the next section.

Traditional models emphasize *leader–first*. They are based on power: personal power, organizational power, and positional power. Some of the characteristics of the power leader include (VANCOD, 2015):

- Drive to get to the top

- Highly competitive and independent

- Finds it important to receive credit for achievement

- Courts complexity

- Uses fear, intimidation, and splitting to get results; keeps people off–balance

- Focuses solely on fast action

- Relies mainly on facts, logic, and proof

- Controls the flow of information

- Spends more time telling and giving orders than listening

- Gains a sense of confidence and personal worth from building his or her own talents and abilities

- Sees supporters as a power base; uses perks and titles to signal to others who has power

- Speaks first and believes that his or her ideas are the most important; often dominates the conversation and bullies opponents

- Understands internal politics and manipulates them for personal gain

- Defines accountability by assigning blame (witch hunts)
- Bases decisions on what will win favor with the boss

Traditional workplaces encourage and reward these behaviors.

> NINETY PERCENT OF WHAT WE CALL 'MANAGEMENT' CONSISTS OF MAKING IT DIFFICULT FOR PEOPLE TO GET THINGS DONE.
>
> **PETER DRUCKER**

In the interest of fairness, there are some caveats to the list above:

✓ Power is not necessarily a "dirty word". *Power over* or *power against* can be depleting in an organization. *Power for* and *power with* can be, well, powerful!

✓ Traditional leaders are not all terrible, inferior, or evil! They come in many hues. If truth be told, you and I have operated from power and acted as traditional leaders many times. And without persistent attention and *intention*, we gravitate back: the recidivism rate is high.

✓ Traditional leaders can be good bosses and can get good results. I do believe, however, that without moving beyond the limits of traditional leadership, they cannot be *great* bosses and they cannot get *great* results.

Leadership is a sobering charge and an exhilarating opportunity. The nobler side of leadership can render us breathless and leave those we touch in a better place for our having touched them. Unexceptional leadership carries the risk of failure, of wounding lives or damaging organizations, and of rupturing our self–image.

We have the best prospects of preserving our wholeness when we seize new knowledge, embrace countercultural ideas, and add fresh tools to our management repertoire. It is then that we may possibly learn how to be the humblest and highest of leaders.

FAITH IS THE CHOICE OF THE NOBLER HYPOTHESIS. NOT THE NOBLEST, ONE NEVER KNOWS WHAT THAT IS. BUT THE NOBLER, THE BEST ONE CAN SEE WHEN THE CHOICE IS MADE.

ROBERT GREENLEAF

When Worlds Collide

IN ONE OF THE EPISODES OF THE SITCOM "SEINFELD", THE CHAR-ACTERNAMEDGEORGEISDISTRAUGHTABOUTTHEPOSSIBILITYTHATHISPRIVATE LIFEWILLINTERMINGLEWITHHISDATINGLIFE;INHISWORDS,THAT*HAPPY-GO-LUCKY GEORGE* WILL MEET *RELATIONSHIP GEORGE*.

Because he puts on his best self for his girlfriend, he does not want her to meet his other friends, with whom he behaves more naturally. He is nervous about all the funny but embarrassing stories his friends will tell. He worries that he'll have to share secrets of *private George* with the girlfriend (like PIN numbers) and humiliating things with the gang (like the couple's sappy pet names).

He rejects offers to double–date, torn about which *George* he would play with both sides at the same dinner table. He sees the situation as a dangerous split and goes to great lengths to keep his dual roles from intersecting. If this should happen, George laments, **worlds would collide**!

❧

George's dilemma is not so far–fetched and can be a familiar vulnerabil-ity in the work world. Traditional leaders sometimes experience lapses in authenticity; gaps between their self-concept on the job and in the rest of life; between who they have to be at work and who they really are.

❖ When I hear someone say they are in it for the paycheck, working for the weekend, or marking time until retirement, I know that *they have become disconnected from their work–spirit.*

❖ Leaders can become wrapped up in pleasing the boss (no matter how high we climb on the career ladder, we always have a boss). They make decisions in the best interest of the organization, but not necessarily in the best interests of employees or customers. *They have misplaced their conscience.*

❖ Some leaders distance themselves from those they supervise and those they serve. They stay busy with tasks at the expense of relationships. *These leaders have lost their sense of mission.*

❖ And a few leaders find that they have strayed so deeply into thickets of corruption or ethical abysses that the consequences are cast in stone and there is no redemption. *These leaders have hopelessly lost their way.*

Most leaders set out with grand motives and strong values. When the inevitable tests of character and will come along, it is easy to rationalize a questionable choice. "I can play around the edges and not fall off my scruples", we say.

• If I have to stretch the limits a bit in order to get elected, I'll do it. I can't change the system if I don't get in.

• If I admit my mistake, I may lose my job. I have a family to support.

• I'll look the other way, just this once.

The next tests are a little easier…until they cause us barely a ripple of disquiet and our integrity is scarred.

"Integrity" comes from the same root as "integrated", meaning "whole; undivided". Divided leaders become experts at compartmentalizing—holding their knowledge, beliefs, and feelings apart from their work lives. Remaining in this state of *values dissonance* takes a toll on the leader and the organization.

A business environment is not a social environment, but leaders must maintain their professionalism without compromising their wholeness.

- If you believe in the Golden Rule at church, you must live it in the workplace

- If you practice integrity in your community, then practice it at the office

- If relationships are important to you at home, they should be important to you at work

Don't make the mistake of isolating your "selves" from each other. You'll breathe easier, carry yourself more lightly, smile more often, and maybe find some peace.

When worlds collide, they become one.

What Is a Servant Leader?

LET'S START WITH THE SUPPOSITION THAT YOU ARE ALREADY A STUdent of servant leadership. If you pulled this book from the bookstore or virtual shelf, you probably understand the basics. You have likely read the essential works by Greenleaf, Keith, Sipe and Frick, Jennings, and Spears. If you haven't, they should be on your reading list.

Assuming all of that, this section will not rehash many of the elementals, except where necessary to develop a framework—rough out a silhouette—of the servant leader. We can add the particulars and fill in the features in Part II.

Overall, in contrast to the traditional leader, the servant leader: (VANCOD, 2015)

- Has a desire to serve others regardless of position within the organization

- Is highly collaborative and interdependent; gives credit to others

- Uses trust, respect, and compassion to build bridges and do what's best for the "whole"

- Strives to gain understanding, input, and buy-in from all parties on essential issues; understands that people support what they help create

- Uses intuition and foresight to complement facts, logic, and proof

- Shares big-picture information; coaches and mentors others by providing context and asking thoughtful questions to help them come to decisions by themselves

- Listens deeply and respectfully to others, especially to those with dissenting views

- Develops commitment across groups and toward common goals; breaks down needless barriers caused by hierarchy

- Invites others into the conversation and is able to build strength through differences

- Is sensitive to what motivates others and balances what is best for the individual with what is best for the group/organization

- Creates a safe environment for learning; ensures that lessons learned from mistakes are generalized

- Shares accountability; lets oneself become vulnerable

- Makes decisions based on personal integrity

> SERVANT LEADERSHIP IS CONTAGIOUS AND HAS A TRANSFORMING INFLUENCE.
>
> **FARLING, STONE, AND WINSTON**

ABC's of Servant Leadership

In a rapidly changing global environment, organizational performance is in the eye of the storm. Forces threaten from all sides: political insecurity; heightened consumer expectations; technological advancements; difficulty attracting and engaging employees; and resource challenges. At the heart of the chaos and complexity lies an inviolable corporate mission: to provide service. Regardless of who the beneficiary of that service may be, that is the mission to which organizations must remain true.

Based on the work of Robert K. Greenleaf, *servant leadership is not about a single style of leading: it is a philosophy and set of practices that overarches all styles of leading.* It influences how we hire and fire, plan and hold accountable, think and behave, relate and communicate (Belton, 2016). As a business executive and educator, Greenleaf conceptualized the servant leader as a person of integrity who leads an organization to success by putting the needs of customers, employees, and communities first, by sharing knowledge and power, and by helping people perform at their highest capacity.

Greenleaf (1970) defined the servant leader as a *"servant first,* who then makes a conscious choice to lead. That person is sharply different from one who is *leader first,"* with the perks and power that implies. The difference is both a matter of motivation and methods and, Greenleaf maintained, "manifests itself in the care taken to make sure that other people's highest priority needs are being served."

How is a servant leader recognized? Greenleaf formulated his *Best Test: Do those served grow as persons? Do they become wiser, freer, more autonomous, and more likely themselves to become servants? And what is the effect on the least privileged of society: will they benefit or at least not be further deprived?*

Edward Hess (2013) infers the extremes of servant leadership in this way: leaders–first seek and fall for the intoxicating powers of leadership; servants–first never forget what it was to be a line employee.

> THE LEADER-FIRST AND THE SERVANT-FIRST ARE TWO EXTREME TYPES. BETWEEN THEM THERE ARE SHADINGS AND BLENDS THAT ARE PART OF THE INFINITE VARIETY OF HUMAN NATURE.
>
> **ROBERT K. GREENLEAF**

Servant leadership is a critical organizational underpinning in times of change and uncertainty. Despite the highest of missions and the most gallant of aims, institutions cannot meet the challenges of the day without a foundation that supports them and permits them to shine.

For example, it's not good enough to think about customer service from time to time, or to pay attention to staff only when the annual employee satisfaction survey is due. It doesn't work to labor over the tasks at hand without attending to the organizational conventions that shape how we fulfill those tasks.

The leader's eyes must be on many things at once: quality, budget, diversity and inclusion, systems thinking, civility, ethics, psychological safety, succession planning, etc. Servant leadership helps to connect the dots, create a climate that produces results, and build a culture where service is the guiding principle.

Servant leadership forges a customer-conscious mindset; develops employees in place and prepares the next generation of leaders; encourages "big picture" thinking and foresight; generates an attitude of mutual respect and accountability; and enhances the bottom line.

While all the traditional management skills and competencies are required of the servant leader, there are some distinguishing qualities:

- ➤ Authentic humility: a regular practice of reflection
- ➤ Serving followers for their own good, not just the good of the organization, instilling a sense of collective ownership in the organization's success
- ➤ Concern for the wellbeing of all stakeholders—from customers, families, and staff to suppliers, contractors, and the community
- ➤ Emphasis on providing opportunities for growth and professional development; creating more servant leaders
- ➤ Leading by moral authority instead of relying on positional authority alone; inspiring followership

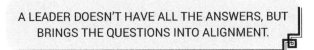

A LEADER DOESN'T HAVE ALL THE ANSWERS, BUT BRINGS THE QUESTIONS INTO ALIGNMENT.

Servant leader organizations are "webs of connection", giving the leader an advantage in:

- ✓ Understanding situations in their larger context
- ✓ Preventing unanticipated consequences and allaying crises
- ✓ Foreseeing impact/exercising foresight
- ✓ Maximizing resources and epitomizing results
- ✓ Serving colleagues and clients with reverence (Belton, Anderson, 2017)

℘

Servant Leader Outcomes

SERVANT LEADERSHIP SOUNDS LIKE A LOT OF EXTRA EFFORT. SO IS it worth it? Literature has linked servant leadership to a broad array of positive business outcomes and organizational citizenship behaviors such as (in brief):

- Creativity, collaboration, well–being of followers (Parris & Peachey, 2013)

- Service orientation (Wong & Davey, 2007)

- Helping behaviors (Erhart, 2004)

- Increased confidence in the job; perception of fairness (Walumbwa, 2010)

- Influence of/satisfaction with the supervisor (Laub, 1999)

- Innovation (Jaramillo, 2009)

- Individual and team effectiveness (Irving, 2007)

- Employee satisfaction and engagement (Cerit, 2009)

- Honest communication and trust (Hu and Liden, 2011)

- Virtuous constructs and organizational transformation (Patterson, 2003)

- Return on investment (Sipe and Frick, 2009)

A study of servant leadership and workplace perceptions (Figure 1) by the U.S. Department of Veterans Affairs, clearly demonstrates that as servant leader behaviors increase, workplace performance, workgroup psychological safety, satisfaction with the supervisor, and overall job satisfaction also improve. Merely the heightened *perception* of servant leadership (Y axis) results in a corresponding improvement, by quadrant from low to high, of those delineated characteristics (X axis).

Servant Leadership and Workplace Perceptions

Figure 1

Servant leaders get results. They obtain the resources necessary to support and expand the organization. They "grow" people strategically, understanding that when people grow, the capacity of the organization grows. When the organization's capacity grows, it can do things better, or do things it was unable to do before. Individuals benefit, the organization benefits, and those served benefit. When leaders focus on serving their colleagues and customers, they make the world a better place (Keith, 2013).

So a business case, a human resource case, and a customer service case can be established for servant leadership. I will go one step further and submit that there is also a personal case: servant leadership benefits the leader him/herself as well. While data are not yet available, there is ample reason to believe that those who practice servant leadership are more satisfied, more resilient, and less likely to experience burnout than their traditional counterparts; that the virtuous constructs of servant leadership—mercy, forgiveness, honesty, humility, and altruism—bring great reward to the giver as well as to the receiver.

Servant Leadership as Charism

Organizations have always had a love affair with charismatic leaders. We *want* to follow them; we are *happy* to follow them; we are *relieved* to follow them. The charismatic leader motivates us and makes us feel part of a movement. They are bigger than life.

Charisma is described as a personal magic that arouses exceptional loyalty and enthusiasm. We have many historical and contemporary examples of charismatic leaders. Some moved the world to righteousness; others left the world in stunning disarray. The charismatic leader can stir followers to meet his agenda, which is unquestionably in the best interest of the leader, and potentially in the best interest of the organization. But does that agenda benefit the followers and those being served?

A servant leader is more concerned about *charism* than *charisma*. The word charism is most commonly used in theological circles, defined as an extraordinary power or grace. In a secular context, it signifies a special power, virtue, or value which is used for the good of an organization or community. A charism is both a blessing and a responsibility; more than a karmic talent—a gift given primarily for the benefit of others. The servant leader builds the agenda on the best interests of individuals as well as the organization. *Charisma is at its peak when arising from a deeply-held charism.*

Service is a charism. Leadership is a charism. I believe that choosing to lead—*to lead first*—is a solemn pledge, and that by making this pledge the servant leader enters into a contract or covenant with the work community. You may never have thought about it with that level of reverence before, but servant leadership is not just another theoretical construct: it is an awesome commitment (Belton, 2017).

Any contract contains a number of special provisions, stipulating how the contract will be carried out and who will do what. These special provisions go beyond the parameters of traditional leadership. They are distinctive of servant leadership and uniquely effective to servant leadership, and they connect employer and employee in an uncommon relationship.

These special provisions are really the *charisms* of servant leadership: they profess both the principles I follow and the promises I make. I am not merely saying, for example, that I *believe in* the principle of primus inter pares, but that I will *practice* it; that I not only *have* integrity; but that I will *use* integrity.

Whether you prefer to call them qualities, special provisions, charisms, or promises, here are my top ten:

1. Service

This one should be self–evident, but the question is: who do servant leaders serve? The contenders are boundless. They serve the customer, the user of their merchandise or service, which could include anything from repairing a product to delivering health care. They serve their workers—hired staff, contractors, volunteers—by treating them with care and respect. They serve the organization by exercising stewardship and benevolence.

There is a famous scene from the movie "Five Easy Pieces" where Jack Nicholson goes to a diner and asks for an omelet, tomatoes, and a side order of toast. The waitress haughtily informs him that omelets come with potatoes, not tomatoes—**no substitutions**—and that they don't do side orders of toast. After a bit of a wrangle, Jack changes his order to an omelet and a chicken sandwich on toast—"hold the butter, hold the lettuce, hold the mayo—and then hold the chicken!"

What people relate to in this scene is that we've all been there. In this case, a business predicated on service has no concept of service.

Service can be as momentous as joining the Peace Corps and as modest as shoveling snow for an elderly neighbor. *No service is trivial service.* Moreover, because anybody can be a servant leader, the opportunities are infinite. Figure 2 shows some examples.

Every Day Examples of Servant Leadership	
• Listening	• Sharing credit for a job well done
• Giving others a sense of possibility	• Putting others' needs first
• Taking Risks	• Showing compassion
• Helping a team member	• Volunteering for an extra task
• Arranging an office food drive	• Accepting people where they are
• Being patient with a difficult customer	• Cutting an employee some slack during a personal crisis
• Standing up for a colleague	• Organizing a Habitat for Humanity project
• Remembering a co-worker's birthday	• Picking up trash from the floor
• Letting someone ahead in line	• Speaking truth to power

Figure 2

I have had some marvelous models of service. Both my son and my daughter have been restaurant servers at one time or another. (I love that the old terms "waitress" and "waiter" have been replaced with "server". *Serving* seems much more affirmative than *waiting on*.) From them I learned about serving cheerfully, with dignity, and with value–added: what little embellishment could be provided that is not required and not expected?

I have had the benefit of other models of service as well:

❖ A boss who ended every phone call with, "How else can I serve you today?" (and meant it!)

❖ A nurse who never left a bedside without saying to the patient, "Is there anything more I can do for you? I have the time." (even though she was rushed off her feet)

❖ A colleague who anticipated the needs of others, from going ahead to open a door to staying late to help a beleaguered staff member (one author calls this psychic pizza—delivering the pizza before it is even ordered!) (Goodman, 2009)

❖ The sales associate whose mantra was, "My customers are never satisfied, they are delighted!"

❖ The technician who, asked for help a hundred times a day, always responded, "It's my pleasure!"

Had to

Once we have defined for ourselves what service is, we then need to ask, "How do we serve?" Not out of self–interest, duty, or _noblesse oblige_. Servant leaders serve with humility, patience, joy, and generosity of spirit. They transform the drudgery of work into service.

Tall order. **No substitutions**.

2. Serving First

We have the basic idea of Greenleaf's hypothesis here, but let's dig a little deeper. Most of us reside neither at an extreme of leader–first or servant–first, but somewhere in–between or, more accurately, on a dynamic continuum.

> THE FIRST AND MOST IMPORTANT CHOICE
> A LEADER MAKES IS TO SERVE.
>
> **ROBERT K. GREENLEAF**

The summons to lead poses one critical moment of decision. Whether it is a position we have competed for or an appointment unexpectedly offered, we decide to accept it or reject it on the basis of *affirmation, pragmatism, or vocation.*

Affirmation:	We *accept* it because it affirms our stature and self–concept, or we *reject* it because the role is primarily a boost to the ego.
Pragmatism:	We *accept* it because it carries a salary increase and opens a door to further opportunity, or we *reject* it because that will never be enough to sustain us.
Vocation:	We *accept* it because we see the position as a calling, or we *reject* it because it doesn't reach that benchmark of service.

These appositions should be viewed as neutral and non–judgmental. To everything there is a season.

The decision to climb the hierarchical ladder or to stand in place for the present often reflects where we judge ourselves to be on the servant leader continuum. Sometimes we even decide to retreat. One corporate leader I highly respect stepped back from a prestigious, but bureaucratic position to assume an important, but lesser role where he felt he could serve better.

So, you say, you've already made that decision: your promotion or advancement was steeped in the highest motivation. Check off that box.

Wonderful, but before becoming complacent, recognize that the choice for servant leadership must be made over and over and over again. Faced with ethical dilemmas, we choose for or against servant leadership. Determining budget cuts, we opt for or against servant leadership. Dealing with employee mistakes, we stand for or against servant leadership. Building a corporate culture, we decide for or against servant leadership.

The servant leadership continuum is a fact of organizational life and situational leadership is indeed legitimate. Some situations call for more or less authority and autonomy; degrees of safety and security; and shades of accountability and compassion. There are also times when we are simply human and subject to backsliding or marking time.

Keeping the *servant–first* mantra at the edge of our consciousness guards against *unintentional* breaches of servant leader principles.

Kudos or Calling

A YOUNG MAN RECENTLY APPROACHED ME, ASKING FOR ADVICE ABOUT A CAREER MOVE. IT WOULD MEAN A PROMOTION, A SIGNIFICANT RUNG UP THE ORGANIZATIONAL LADDER. IT WOULD ALSO BE A HUGE RESPONSIBILITY, AND NOT IN HIS IMMEDIATE AREA OF EXPERTISE. AS EXCITED AND GRATIFIED AS HE WAS, HE QUESTIONED THE *RIGHTNESS* OF AND HIS *READINESS* FOR SUCH A STEP. IT WAS A BIG DECISION. HOW COULD HE BE SURE?

Promotion, power, paycheck, and position are on everyone's wish list, but, I probed, is there an opportunity to serve? To serve at a higher level, or to serve more broadly, or to serve more deeply?

Traditional leaders may be content with the "4 P's" above. This is characteristic of the *leader–first*. Those opportunities may be flattering, may feed the ego and the bank account, but I believe that without a deeper component, real fulfillment is always elusive, to be found in the next promotion or the next accomplishment—seldom in the *now*.

> THE SERVANT LEADER IS SERVANT–FIRST. IT BEGINS WITH THE NATURAL FEELING THAT ONE WANTS TO SERVE—TO SERVE FIRST. THEN CONSCIOUS CHOICE BRINGS ONE TO ASPIRE TO LEAD. HE IS SHARPLY DIFFERENT FROM THE LEADER–FIRST.
>
> **ROBERT K. GREENLEAF**

Servant leaders jump to the "service" question at the outset. They listen to their hearts to understand whether the new opportunity is indeed what they are being called to do. Is it the right place for them to serve? Is it the right time? Will it make the best use of their particular talents? Will the present organizational environment allow them to use those talents to elevate workers and the work itself? Is it attractive for the right reasons? Is it a wish or a charism?

We all encounter many career prospects in a lifetime. If we are honest, they aren't all the most beneficial for us or for the organization. Or the timing might be off, a great choice but for another day. Career goals are healthy, but they need to be suffused with discernment.

For thirteen years I held a prestigious and influential position as the leader of a multi–hospital health care system. I was responsible for almost 200,000 employees and a budget of nearly $1 billion. Then I was given an unparalleled opportunity to create an Organizational Health function at the national level. I would be able to spend my time teaching and talking about the cultural issues that make an organization thrive: civility, service, leadership, empowerment, etc.

All of my colleagues were supportive, but a few were also cautionary. In the new role, I would no longer have a large staff and budget to carry out the work. In fact, I would have to persuade and cajole for personnel and funding. These colleagues warned that without the position and its cachet, I would lose prestige and power. I would no longer be among the "elite" and my authority would be forgotten.

It took me nine months to reach a conclusion, continually weighing the pros and cons. I loved running a confederation of medical facilities, but this was a chance to instill corporate excellence from the ground up and from coast to coast. Accepting the assignment was a decision I never regretted. It was always much bigger than just a "job"; it was a passion.

Servant leaders rightfully see their work as a vocation, a mission, a crusade — a calling. Many of us experience the work as a battleground where struggles are replayed every day: struggles for authority and power, for recognition and voice, for principle and the highest good. Generosity confronts greed, justice competes with mercy, service challenges control, and stewardship clashes with self-interest. Work is the ground on which these nobler battles are fought, and servant leaders are the warriors who fight them (Belton, 2016).

My advice to the young man? If the opportunity is not a calling, enjoy the compliment, but think twice. Wait and prepare yourself. Be ready for the one that is.

3. Inverting the Pyramid

I have often used the image of power rolling downhill: by the time it reaches the bottom, there is little left. At the top of the pyramid in an organization is the boss. Some of the boss's power is absorbed by various tiers of supervisors, but it has mainly dissipated when it gets down to the rank–and–file. And what about the end–user? Where does the customer, client, student, patient—or whatever you call it in your environment—fall in the hierarchy? In too many organizations, they are nowhere to be seen.

Servant leadership turns traditional hierarchy on its head and in the process, empowers front–line staff and customers. *Servant leaders don't lose their power by sharing it.*

It is a special provision of servant leadership that leaders do not need to be in official positions of authority. They may be anywhere—or nowhere—on the organizational chart. These are the people who are willing to step out and lead the way, even in a small niche of service. These are the informal leaders who have earned the respect and trust of their colleagues.

One health care manager I know identified informal leaders from each level of the pyramid and every professional category. She kept them extraordinarily well–informed, regularly picked their brains, encouraged them to liaise across hierarchical lines, and authorized them to speak on her behalf. By doing this, her leadership was strengthened in every corner of the organization.

Servant leadership in today's business climate demands our full participation. Every one of us is invited to lead and none of us can RSVP our regrets. *We are all leaders, all the time.*

> SERVANT LEADERS ARE NOT ALWAYS PEOPLE OF POWER,
> BUT THEY ARE ALWAYS POWERFUL PEOPLE.

4. Primus Inter Pares

One practical way the servant leader can invert the pyramid is through the charism of *primus inter pares*. This principle of "first among equals" disperses the power by decentralizing decision–making and building consensus. It listens to ideas and opinions, hears disagreement, and welcomes respectful admonition. It teaches the team to contribute to the process *and* the solution: in essence, to become servant leaders themselves.

Primus inter pares is a significant departure from the traditional leadership model. It overlooks rank and hierarchy, status and title, allowing great ideas to emerge from below, and sharing credit for the success of the collective effort.

Servant leaders never relinquish responsibility: the leader is *always* accountable, however the attention is less on pecking order and formal designations, and more on empowering the team.

Servant leaders seek consensus at every opportunity. Consensus is not decision-making by committee, or managing by vote, or kneading an issue until everyone capitulates. Building consensus, where that is possible, is just good common sense. People who invest in a decision are more likely to support it or at least not sabotage it. Consensus–building is consistent with servant leadership. It helps to buy trust and good faith for those times when a leader must produce a speedy, unilateral decision.

Servant leaders don't hand off their authority, they simply offer others a seat at the table. In most work environments, a seat at the table is *prime real estate*: an earned privilege, a perk of increasing responsibility, and a badge of acceptance into the inner circle.

In the servant organization, leaders share that honor widely. They invite those on the sidelines to join at the table. They offer everyone who wants it a seat at the table. They include and welcome all comers, but not indiscriminately. Thoughtful and informed membership is the price of admission.

To me, *primus* evokes an aura of inclusiveness and multidisciplinary participation. I imagine a collection of people from different backgrounds and life experiences, professions and trades, labor and management, seasoned and novice, sitting around the decision–making table. Servant leaders understand the wisdom of gathering members who are not merely clones of themselves; who will push and challenge and broaden the discussion. Think for a moment: if you could invite a wildly unconventional guest to your table, who would that be? What new dimension would they bring? What is stopping you?

When leaders understand that their role is not to dominate, but to orchestrate, a fresh perspective on team emerges. The maestro doesn't compose the music, he synchronizes disparate sounds. Where the players see only their own fragments of the piece, he is privy to the entire opus. From his position on the stage, he is reminded that it is the diversity of instruments that brings life to the work. And he knows that without them, he would be conducting to an empty auditorium. The leader is not the sovereign of those he leads, but their servant (Belton, 2017).

5. Humility

Humility has gotten a bad rap. We learn lessons in humility from an early age. We are taught not to boast or brag; not to be proud or put ourselves forward. Parents take pains to make sure their children don't get conceited.

Later, if we're not careful, we become prey to the "aw shucks" genre of humility: fawning and submissive, going along to get along, deflecting compliments, shrinking from attention, refraining from speaking up or accepting responsibility—in metaphorical terms, hiding our lights under a bushel. In striving for selflessness, we lose our sense of self.

Humility Is ...	Humility Is Not ...
Robert *Greenleaf* defined *humility* as the ability to learn from and gratefully receive the gifts of the less powerful (Greenleaf, Spears, 2002)· I would add that servant leaders not only gratefully but *gracefully* receive those gifts. Humility is one of the distinguishing traits of a servant leader, and a special provision of the servant leader covenant. The servant leaders I know are genuine, authentic, and unassumingly confident. They have found legitimate ways of taking on commanding roles without being self-important. They defer praise or redirect it to the team; share their expertise freely; communicate candidly to engender trust; step back to let others practice leading; and are loyal followers themselves.	• ... Self-deprecation, abasement, false modesty, or obsequiousness. We mistake innocent eagerness or excitement with arrogance. We confuse humility with humiliation and simplicity with shame. We have it backwards. • ... Timid leadership—the manager who leads from behind, whose opinions and decisions change with the political winds, who hides from accountability, or grandiloquently shoulders all the blame. That is not humility: it is hubris. • ... Taught, understood, or rewarded in the traditional model of leadership. There is no college course in humility. In the work environment, true humility is an endangered species, regularly mistaken for the fictions above. Humble leaders aren't as immediately visible as their more aggressive counterparts, who may, frankly, have an edge in vying for the big promotions and bonuses in the short run. In the long run, however, servant leaders outpace and outlast the traditional competition.

Humility in the work world can be an undeniable challenge; it is even hard to talk about. Work is competitive. We are supposed to outperform colleagues; to tout our achievements; and to take credit for the accomplishments of our team. In every interview, progress appraisal, or test of skill, we're expected to outdo our co-workers and broadcast our great successes. For those of us who cringe at blowing our own horns, those situations make us squirm.

Servant Leaders combine humility with determination. They lead from their competence rather than their position. There is both humility and courage in conceding that they don't know, asking for help, acknowledging mistakes, and even admitting they are afraid. Humility is an "unprotected" place, and the leader's exposure teaches colleagues and co-workers how to survive their own human flaws as well.

Servant leaders recognize their abilities and are generous in sharing them; they are open to new ideas and new ways of doing things. They take responsibility for outcomes, acknowledging their contributions to the team's successes, but also to the team's failures. While humility may be quiet, it is not weak. While it may be vulnerable, it is innately powerful. While it shows deference to others, it cherishes its own spirit.

Traditional leaders see humility as a frailty, but servant leaders know it is a strength. They are grateful for their gifts, for opportunities to help and to let others help them.

Humility consists of accepting the role and the charge we have been placed here to accomplish. It is a stamp of humility to accept the designation of *servant*. Servant leaders shine brightly and ignite many other lights along the way.

6. Integrity

I remember hearing an executive team member contesting his colleague's controversial decision. Rather than explaining his rationale, the colleague snapped back, "Are you questioning my integrity?" Disagreement, concern, and questions are not necessarily attacks on integrity—they are due diligence. Nevertheless, the word *integrity* has become loaded with ambiguity and innuendo.

We all like to think of ourselves as persons of integrity. There is something moral and upright in that. Integrity is a "given" in most schools of leadership thought and appears in many companies' mission statements. But do we really understand what integrity means?

Sources define integrity as a firm adherence to a code of values; incorruptibility; a quality of being complete, undivided or unbroken; and truthfulness in words and actions. Using these descriptions, I see integrity as a multi-layered characteristic of servant leadership. The person of integrity is best portrayed as *honest, whole, and holistic.*

Honest

Honesty is the tip of the iceberg, perhaps the most fundamental degree of integrity. But honesty is about more than not being untruthful. It rules out obfuscation, selective withholding, mental reservation, or half–truths. There can be no crossed fingers! Honesty involves consistency—from one person to the next and from words spoken to deeds done. Honest leaders are transparent, guileless, and sincere. Servant leaders model the message in their communications, their policies, their budgets, their ethics—in every leadership task.

Whole

We said earlier that "integrity" comes from the same root as "integrated", meaning "whole or undivided". Contemporary leaders have become adept at compartmentalizing: they learn to rationalize weighty decisions in order to live more easily with them. For example:

"By making massive layoffs, I'm protecting the future of the company." Or, "I'm not doing anything every other leader doesn't do." Or, "We won't have room for you in the reorganization, but don't take it personally."

Of course leaders have to make difficult decisions, but when they become too comfortable—when there aren't a couple of sleepless nights—it's time to check whether their wholeness is intact.

Holistic

So what's the difference between "whole" and "holistic"? The nuance here is that servant leaders are not only integrated, but multidimensional. They bring their bodies and minds to the work, their intellect and imagination, their souls and their spirits. They are relational, familial, and economic beings.

They give permission to their employees and colleagues to be multidimensional as well. They allow the data clerk an opportunity to teach and the caregiver a chance to plan; the engineer a moment to create music and the waitress an occasion to design a website. Servant leaders are not content to bring less than 100% of themselves to the job, and expect—allow—the same from their associates.

_ntegrity is risky behavior and institutions have been known to punish people for leading integral lives (Palmer, 2004). I recall a situation where a distinguished physician was courted by a prominent organization to transform the culture. The physician was promised a free hand in making changes, and generous staff and budget support to accomplish the task. The physician accepted and set out with enthusiasm, only to find the resources mired in bureaucratic delays and her plans thwarted at every turn. The physician felt that her integrity was compromised and over time, this led her to a real sense of moral distress: anger at being impeded in doing what she was hired to do, and a pang of personal failure in not meeting her commitment.

Servant leaders find it debilitating to exist in moral distress or values dissonance for long, and do whatever is necessary to reunify their ideals with their behaviors, even if that results in hardship, retaliation, or loss of the job.

Servant leaders *grow trust* by demonstrating integrity in its deepest sense. They are known and *experienced* as dependable, reliable, steadfast, and trustworthy.

> THE ONLY SOUND BASIS FOR TRUST IS FOR PEOPLE TO HAVE THE SOLID EXPERIENCE OF BEING SERVED BY THEIR ORGANIZATION.
>
> **ROBERT K. GREENLEAF**

7. Stewardship

An entrenched executive once told me, "I don't want to be called a servant or a steward. I rose far above that when I became accountable!"

The idiocy of that sentiment would almost make me chuckle, if it weren't so sad. The discomfort many leaders have with what they consider "soft" terms is often palpable. "Stewardship" is a little edgy to managers, whereas "accountability" is a concept they can get cozy with.

But accountability carries baggage, often being linked with censure or blame. Not a week goes by that I don't watch a Congressional hearing where a politico is demanding accountability of some government operative. Accountability has come to mean firing, shaming, head–rolling, etc., even if that is not the most pragmatic solution.

My friend Donna's father was hospitalized for a treatable condition, but died there from a medical error. The resident caring for him did not recognize an unrelated complication, and because it was not diagnosed correctly, the steps that could have saved the patient were not taken.

Donna needed to hold the hospital accountable. She could have demanded the resident be fired. She could have sued the medical center. She could have gone to the media or her congressperson. She could have done all of the above.

Instead she spoke with the president of the organization who apologized for the lethal error. He assured her that policies would be changed and clinical personnel trained to identify and treat the rare disorder in the future. It would not, he acknowledged, bring her father back, but would prevent others from a similar tragedy. The resident would have to live with his mistake, a hard, but indelible lesson learned. My friend accepted this course of action.

This was a case where suing, firing, or shaming would not have been the most beneficial solution. The physician, the hospital, and the corporate president were indeed held accountable, and they accepted accountability in a way that was sensible, constructive, fitting, enduring, and honored the memory of my friend's father.

In so many environments, accountability has become synonymous with fear, and when leaders are fearful, they circle the wagons, cover themselves, and don't always do what is best for the organization. The essential leadership function of accountability has been tainted.

Accountability is a state of mind. Accountability motivated by fear is unproductive and unethical. Accountability arising from stewardship and compassion is powerful.

Failures in accountability are really breaches of trust: layers of oversight are then built to bridge them. What this means is that if we don't follow through, if we don't work to our "optimum", or if we fail the organization, we actually *invite* micromanagement.

Stewardship *is being accountable for the right reasons.*

Where accountability is motivated by extrinsic factors; stewardship is driven by intrinsic values. Stewardship comes from a deeper place. Good stewards are the guardians of something entrusted to their care.

Stewardship makes something more than it is. It is not enough to conserve or oversee what is given into our custody: stewards return it with increase.

Servant leadership is about understanding the human impact and corporate consequences of one's actions and decisions. Stewardship is about lifting the organization to a better state, an attitude wholly congruent with servant leadership. The role of caretaker, of making *more* of the assets under their control, is an easy burden.

The *servant-first* is comfortable with working to meet other people's highest priority needs and enculturating a service orientation.

Creating More Servant Leaders

I'm not sure that "growing" new servant leaders is generally considered under the category of stewardship, but it may be the most important obligation of stewardship. Servant leaders are duty–bound to develop co–creators and co–owners of our organizations, and to cultivate a sense of shared ownership.

Accountability is doing what you are supposed to do because someone expects it of you. Ownership is doing what needs to be done because you expect it of yourself. Ownership is possible when personal values are congruent with organizational values. Those values motivate behaviors that drive outcomes. Servant leaders are missionaries, constantly striving to win new converts by repeating the message, giving opportunities, stimulating employees to stretch and mature, leveraging inclusion and diversity of thought, and above all —by *living the model*. It is all about the planting, the nurturing, and the reaping.

It delights me to witness acts of stewardship in any area of life: the artist who doesn't merely draw pictures, but touches spirits; the teacher who goes beyond the lesson plan to open minds; the nurse who finishes her tasks and sits with a dying patient; the lawyer who works pro bono; the groundskeeper who chops down one tree and plants two; the food service worker who adds a flower to a patient's tray; or the business executive who becomes a servant leader. These are people who go beyond the basic expectations of their circumstances and ennoble them.

Servant leaders are stewards of an organization's human & financial resources, its temporal and material resources, its culture and environment, its reputation and public persona, and even its future stability and resilience. Some of those are no–brainers. Who would not expect the leader to use employees, budget, and supplies wisely? But what about the others?

Stewardship of time demands that it not be squandered on pointless meetings, futile pursuits, or political games. Being stewards of the culture entails fostering a climate of service by intention, not default. Stewarding its image and standing in the community secures the organization's viability and resistance to social or economic stressors.

Servant leaders are conscious that they are *interim proprietors* and use everything under their aegis for the highest purposes of the organization. At the end of their tenure, they relinquish an organization *with dividends*.

Accountability extends to what we owe society, the organization, those we serve, and each other—not because we are afraid of the consequences, but because we have clear priorities, an inherent mission, and moral courage.

Servant leadership is a platform for accountability *and* service in organizations that have caring at their core. Stewardship is leaving the place better than you found it. It is the act of building a legacy, one empowered thought and one audacious deed at a time.

8. Moral authority

We all have a lifetime of experience at being led. Many of our leaders hold power by virtue of their position: they have been hired or elected to lead. Sometimes followers have a say in those decisions, but often they don't.

There are other leaders who hold power by capturing our imagination, loyalty, and trust, whether or not they are in official positions of authority. Those are the leaders we get in line behind.

Some people are appointed to lead and some are "anointed" to lead.

Moral authority is a quintessential and distinguishing characteristic of servant leadership. It is also a sensitive one, sometimes causing traditional leaders to fidget in their seats. The word "moral" is the sticking point, especially if it is understood as religion, religiosity, or the promotion of a particular creed.

More accurately, moral authority hinges on the leader watching his own internal compass— living up to his own moral code—not on moralizing or preaching to others. Servant leaders find and follow their own "true north", so they have a reliable starting point and a fixed destination.

Moral authority is the capacity to convince followers of how the world *should be* and *could be*, and to persuade others to follow in the absence of formal control. Moral authority is conferred upon someone who is exceptionally respected for their character, conduct, and knowledge.

Figure 3 shows the comparison:

Positional Authority	Moral Authority
Command and control	Shares power
Who messed up?	Glitch hunts, not witch hunts
Climate of fear	Culture of accountability
End justifies the means	Messages, mentors, and models
People are tools	Builds community
Demands loyalty	Inspires followership

Figure 3

Moral authority is not tied to rank or status, but to service. I know of no other leadership philosophy that opens its arms to anyone wanting to lead.

Subordinates and co-workers recognize in this leader something beyond hierarchy; something compelling; a presence that draws them in; something worthy of being followed. Loyalty is not demanded nor even solicited: it is given unreservedly—and it is reciprocated. Because the leader with moral authority is followed willingly, the hammer of control is put aside. Or perhaps the hammer of control is put aside because the leader is followed willingly. People follow this leader not by command, but by *choice*.

Leaders with moral authority are coaches, mentors, and guides. When something goes wrong—and it will—they engage in systems fixes, not scapegoating: "glitch hunts, not witch hunts". They teach by messaging and modeling, in perfect alignment; and they develop communities of support. Leaders with moral authority inspire trust.

Trust is a fundamental aspect of moral authority—in both directions. Servant leaders earn trust by sharing power and setting people free to serve. They do what they say and say what they do—no surprises or keeping staff off balance. They ensure an environment of psychological safety.

Everything the leader says and does leaves a mark. Leadership based solely on positional authority may inflict wounds and leave scars. Leadership based on moral authority creates an indelible imprint. Organizations can make people obey, submit, or conform in one guise or another, but they cannot force anyone to follow. Followership comes from the heart.

9. Foresight and Reflection

I'm not sure which comes first—foresight or reflection—but I think of them as two sides of the same coin. They are both special provisions of servant leadership which, translated into traditional "management–ese", would be forecasting and evaluation. But forecasting is not foresight and evaluation is not reflection.

Forecasting has to do with calculated guesswork.

- If revenues are $___ today, what will they be next fiscal year?

- If the client base increases by 20%, how many new full–time equivalent staff will be needed?

- Given the current rate of growth, when will we need to expand our facility?

Foresight is more visionary and intuitive. It is closely associated with systems thinking, where the leader scans the environment from 30,000 feet in order to detect patterns and relationships.

- How will new trends in technology affect the industry?

- If customers want this today, what might they be demanding in five years?

- What could be the unanticipated consequences of this decision down the road?

According to Robert Greenleaf, "Foresight is the only lead a leader has." He goes on to speculate that when events start to force the leader's hand, he is no longer leading, but reacting (Greenleaf, 1970). Foresight is not a parlor trick, but it does require some imagination and acumen, an instinct for the "big picture", and a finely–tuned sense of the possible.

In sports terms, foresight is "skating to where the hockey puck will be." This requires a bit of intelligence about a broad field of factors— enough to conjecture a potential outcome, the significance of that outcome, and what could be done to improve upon that outcome. The servant leader must be comfortable with complexity, accept the unknowable, and exercise a little conviction to bridge the gap.

How many times have leaders thought, "If only I had known that!" We are all susceptible to Monday morning quarterbacking or hindsight. "If I knew then what I know now!" I believe those are cues for the servant leader to hook up his antenna and sharpen his reception. Foresight is not a game of chance, but an ethical obligation owed as stewards of the organization's future.

And here's the flip side of the coin: **foresight often arises from withdrawal and deep reflection**.

In the contemporary work world, reflection goes against the grain. "There just isn't enough time". "I have more important things to do." "This is reality; I can't be caught daydreaming". Important considerations, surely, but servant leadership sees reflection as *imperative*. So what do we need to do to factor reflection into our workday? How can we teach others the value of reflection?

First of all, reflection is different from assessment or evaluation. We do a lot of that in business. We assess and evaluate our employees, our progress, and our results. We are obsessed with measurement. But that measurement is essentially external and concrete, based in metrics.

Reflection has no metrics; it is internal and imprecise. Evaluation and assessment measure against criteria, but reflection measures against values and behavioral ideals. "Reflect" is a verb—an action word. Hoping for a break in the day to reflect isn't good enough. We need to make it *intentional*. It is necessary to plan for reflection, carve out a space and a time for reflection, and hold it *sacred*.

While the major excuse for side–stepping reflection used to be time, it is now running neck–and–neck with technology. Technology is never the time–saver it is trumpeted to be. Technology just allows us to do more in the same amount of time. It revs up the organizational pulse and accelerates the speed of life.

To reflect, one must withdraw and to withdraw, one must disconnect—briefly and regularly—from the gadgets and social media. When we let our digital devices control us, they become electronic shackles. Withdrawal is stepping back in order to move forward more deliberately.

The rationalizations of time and technology, while legit-imate, may also conceal a deeper defense mechanism. Reflection is uncomfortable work. It forces us to examine the *hows* and *whys* of our actions; and to face our *outtakes* and our *mea culpas*. It is no surprise that many of us would rather prepare a budget, weather a reorganization, or manage a crisis than plumb our inner depths.

Withdrawal and reflection are not merely private pursuits, they enhance the effectiveness of the team, and this is where the leader can instruct organizational performance. And how much is enough? Sometimes a prolonged retreat is called for; often a meager fifteen min-utes will suffice. Teams and other workgroups need systematic opportu-nities to consider their shared activity.

High functioning teams are conscious and responsive. They rec-ognize that teams elevate their performance by continuously reviewing their purpose and methods, role clarity, communication, and business practices. They ask themselves and each other in an ordered process:

- Who needs to know what and when?

- How do we handle conflict when it occurs?

- How will we collaborate and make decisions?

- How will we hold one another accountable?

- When and how often will we take time to reflect on what is working well and what isn't?

- What will that look like?

- What will we do with the insights gleaned from our reflection?

- How will we thoughtfully set new goals and reinforce our successes?

The sustainability of the team's *reactions* to their reflections will be related to the team's sense of cohesiveness and their quality of relationships. The *impact* of the reflections depends on their ability to take action based on their insights.

Servant leaders understand that reflection brings quantifiable advantages. It helps them to gain perspective and absorb complex information, produce creative thoughts and ideas, defuse emotionally charged situations, and make wiser decisions. It brings awareness of and harmony with a greater consciousness.

Reflection is not a punishment or a penance. It is honest scrutiny from a safe distance. Withdrawal and reflection are where the struggles are brought to peace and the obscurities are brought to light. Foresight uses the intuitions won to anticipate and enrich the future.

> TIME SPENT IN SELF-REFLECTION IS NEVER WASTED
> – IT IS AN INTIMATE DATE WITH YOURSELF.
>
> **DR. PAUL TP WONG**

10. Relationships and Community

Faye was a department head struggling to be a servant leader. Her heart was in the right place, but she felt constantly pulled in other directions by the turmoil around her. Her schedule was packed with meetings, deadlines, and the inevitable crises, so employees needing help, counseling, or (heaven forbid!) coaching had to go to the back of the line. Because every decision was a critical one, Faye seldom had the luxury of seeking input from her staff. It was no surprise to her when the employee satisfaction and customer service ratings started to droop. And that precipitated a whole new round of complications—a vicious circle.

In a fast–paced, task–oriented world, people become distractions and relationships are seen as interruptions. In a servant leader environment, people are the focus and relationships are the *raison d'etre*. Real power in organizations is not derived from position, the number of staff supervised, or the budget dollars controlled: *real power comes from relationships.*

My personal motto is, "All things connected," and that is never truer than about people. We are never in relationship alone; we are always *in relationship with.* The very term implies connection. It is a convergence—a meeting point—with some common interest.

Relationships can be superficial and short-term or intense and enduring. We might relate tangentially as co–workers, deliberately as friends and allies, or magnetically as ideological soul–mates. Our aim in relating may be to get a job done, to give or receive support, or to be part of a higher ambition.

I am often astonished when a speaker at a conference says exactly what I have been thinking—what my heart tells me is right, but society disparages. Or when I am the presenter and participants are so touchingly grateful that I somehow affirmed what they knew to be true, but were afraid to voice in their workplace.

How many of us are there who, immersed in traditional organizations, think the "heretical" thoughts of servant leadership? Which of us, struggling in a business climate of self-interest, are drawn to commit "treasonous" acts of service? *We are all alone in this together;* the journey of intentional servant leadership is simply too arduous to be undertaken on our own.

Relationships in healthy organizations are like webs of connection, relentlessly and optimistically reaching out to forge linkages, develop synergies, and form community. One thread searches for another and they create nodes of association, multiplying exponentially.

There is scientific basis for community in the principle of quantum entanglement, where the impact of sub–atomic relationships transcends time and space. Virtual teams and colleagues can similarly be connected in unanticipated ways. Thoughts and ideas become "quantum property". We sometimes call this synchronicity.

Cellular biology teaches us that when equivalent cells (e.g. heart cells, liver cells, kidney cells) work *in community* toward a shared purpose, they are more successful than in the competitive "survival of the fittest" mode.

Community is the goal and the end result of relationships. It acknowledges a kinship that is nourished by like minds. Community can be in physical proximity or in virtual space. Some organizations provide communities of support such as servant leader "encouragement groups" or "CREW" cohorts (civility, respect, and engagement in the workplace).

But for lone servant leaders in unreceptive workplaces, a virtual community may be their closest source of sustenance—perhaps even a lifeline. Just knowing there is a sympathetic listener on the other end of a telephone or wise counsel at the press of a "send" button, can lighten our spirits and renew our determination.

Community helps us as individuals. It makes us stronger, bolsters our resolve, and reminds us we have companions along the way. More importantly, it helps us as a group, accumulating new knowledge, magnifying our experience, and promulgating an ethos of servant leadership. This kind of community knows no limits. In relationship or in community we are never alone. All things are connected.

So there we have it: ten charisms that make servant leadership a blessing and a responsibility; ten special provisions that make it a contract; ten commitments that make it a covenant.

Servant Leader

	MYTHS	TRUTHS
1.	"Servant leadership is weak leadership."	Servant leadership is not for the faint–hearted. It requires strength of self–mastery, strength of action, and strength of relationships.
2.	"I have to be tough; decisive."	Yes, but you don't have to go it alone. Offer others a seat at the table.
3.	"People must be treated uniformly – you can't set precedents."	Fair and just doesn't mean lock-step. Servant leaders appreciate that people have different needs in the workplace and try to meet them.
4.	"Leaders have to maintain boundaries."	In the words of the Eagles, *"Come down from your fences; open the gate."* (Henley & Frey, 1973)
5.	"My people are paid well. I don't have to thank them."	The old saying about this is, "Every dog needs a pat on the head." Servant leaders can do better than that: "Gratitude breeds commitment."
6.	"I can't be a servant leader if my supervisor isn't one."	Servant leadership is top–down, bottom–up, and side–to–side. Don't wait for the memo!
7.	"Everyone has to pay their dues; earn their way up the pyramid."	Servant leadership turns the pyramid upside–down.

	MYTHS	TRUTHS
8.	"Trust, but verify."	Micromanagement is a clear message of distrust and a vain struggle to control. Control is an illusion.
9.	"The term *servant* is offensive. I can't be subservient <u>and</u> an effective leader."	Understand the difference between service and servitude. Servant leadership is a deliberate decision to serve.
10.	"Tell staff only what they need to know, only when they need to know it."	Servant leaders share information freely and transparently. The more employees know, the greater their engagement. There are no secrets in most organizations!
11.	"It's desirable to keep staff a little off balance. You shouldn't become predictable."	People work best in a psychologically safe environment. Keeping them on the edge is actually a form of exploitation.
12.	"You can't practice servant leadership in a government agency."	Government employees and elected officials are, after all, public servants.
13.	"Leaders have to create a burning pier in order to carry out unpleasant decisions."	Leaders should give staff information and help them understand. Make them allies.
14.	"Do whatever it takes to get elected/selected because you can't do good things if you don't get in."	The ends do not justify the means. If a candidate's ethics and integrity are that fluid, he probably shouldn't get the job.

	MYTHS	TRUTHS
15.	"Past behavior is the best predictor of future behavior."	Maybe, but when we hold people to their pasts, they cannot be made new in the present.
16.	"Everybody resists change."	Employees support change that makes sense and is communicated clearly. People who have to live with the change should be involved in the change.
17.	"When something goes wrong, a head has to roll."	That is not accountability—it is retribution. Accountability and mercy travel together.
18.	"I can't afford to let my feelings and vulnerabilities show."	Leaders are people too. When they share emotions appropriately, they give staff permission to experience honest emotions as well.
19.	"Management will always have natural adversaries. A We/They mindset is an absolute."	In a healthy organization, We/They are always Us.
20.	"Don't take it personally—it's just business."	Whenever you hear that beware: an abuse of power is about to take place. Servant leaders take their power very personally.
21.	"The leader has to know everything, or pretend she does."	Servant leaders can admit they don't know, then give someone else a chance to shine.

	MYTHS	TRUTHS
22.	"Ethics are relative."	Ethics is doing the right thing when nobody is looking.
23.	"You cannot be people–centric and maintain high standards."	The correlation between performance, engagement, and how employees are treated is compelling. Employee satisfaction drives customer satisfaction and loyalty (Hess, 2013).
24.	"Unless you watch employees like hawks, they will take advantage."	If leaders create the right values and culture, ordinary people will do extraordinary things.
25.	"When you've checked off all the boxes, you can consider yourself a servant leader."	You're not a servant leader until others see you as one.

What is an Intentional Servant Leader?

FROM QUANTUM PHYSICS WE KNOW THAT SUBATOMIC PARTICLES react in the way the observer *expects* them to. From management performance theory we learn that what we measure gets better. The inverse is also true: when we take eyes off them for a moment, subatomic particles will react at random and performance will fall prey to entropy. What do you expect in your organization? What do you measure? On what do you focus and to what do you pay attention? What happens when you shift your focus to something else? The lesson here is that things don't just happen; *they flow from intention.*

What exactly does it mean to be an intentional leader; an intentional servant leader? The words that capture this best for me are:

Deliberate: Having a well–thought–out plan or framework, realistic strategy, coherent rationale, and articulated values; working from a blueprint instead of a cocktail napkin

Purposeful: Being mindful of the framework, vigilant to distraction and digression; alert and responsive to perceptions, impressions, and emotions; in sharp relief

Conscious: Aligning every word, decision, and action to the context of the framework; ensuring congruence with the stated values; constant, steadfast and unwavering

One well–known leadership pundit expresses concern about being intentional, suggesting that setting explicit goals or having an exact plan is restrictive—closes us off from achieving unimagined results. If, for example, the leader states an intention or objective for a meeting, will conversation in another direction be stifled; will inspiration or creativity be limited? I agree with her, so let's add another descriptive word to our definition:

Receptive: Remaining amenable to diverse thoughts and ideas; inviting feedback and constructive conflict; accessible and approachable; open to the stirrings of higher consciousness

Viewed through a single lens, these descriptors conjure up an image of intentional leadership as **orchestration**.

Let's think about that analogy. The composer hears the music in his head. He knows what it will sound like before a note is ever writ-ten on paper. Harmony and synchrony are his muses. He understands the rubrics of musical arrangement. As the movements course through his mind, he instinctively brings in the strings here and the reeds there. This melody requires a horn and now the tympani enter to accentuate a passage. They weave together seamlessly. He eagerly scans the cohesive score, monitors the pace and the intensity, and viscerally feels the composition—all of this in his head! He knows that when the piece is performed, the players will rise to shouts of "Encore!" barely aware of the composer.

This is how I visualize the competent servant leader—coach of the team, choreographer of the dance, director of the play; working from intention to orchestrate the work through others. He designs the interaction and creates the chemistry, but allows the group to make it their own.

Intention is created at three levels: thought, behavior, and beliefs, all of which must be compatible and attuned to each other.

Intentional leaders move an organization forward by balancing:

✓ What they'd like to do and the capacity of the organization to do it

✓ What the environment will sanction or prevailing norms will support

✓ What is compatible with personal, professional, and organizational values

When those aspects do *not* come together, the leader has three choices:

1.) Devolve to *laissez faire leadership*, letting the organization go where it will:

    This may be tantamount to giving up. If the organization does move forward, it is a stroke of luck or an act of providence

2.) Become an *interventional* leader, forcing the leader's agenda on the organization:

    Eastern leadership philosophy teaches that the wise leader does not intervene unnecessarily, even when it seems that powerful intervention should be exercised. Making people do what you think they ought to do, even if the intervention appears to succeed, is no cause for celebration. It may foster deeper resistance, resentment, and sabotage (Heider, 1985).

3.) Or, work within the framework to modify the *authorizing environment*, shaping and molding the organization, and preparing it to move forward:

    Organizations are constantly juggling their internal capabilities (what we have the capacity to do), against predominating social conventions (what society will allow us to do), then weighing the results in terms of corporate values (what is the right thing to do).

    Outside a very limited zone of congruence where those three factors converge, leaders engineer the give and take, stretch and relax, to and fro of evolving boundaries to bring the organization and the environment into state of readiness. Working within that framework to ensure an authorizing environment may take a bit longer, but it will position the organization for transformation. Servant leaders have the ability and influence to navigate such change.

Intentional servant leaders understand their impact and are humbled by it. They see their influence circulating in ever–broadening spheres:

Personal

Influencing at the point of service

Professional

Influencing at the point of organizational performance

Social

Influencing at the point of the community

Intentional servant leaders recognize their profound responsibility for the ripple effects they create. They are sentinels of their own thoughts, behaviors, and actions, always monitoring whether they are **deliberate, conscious, purposeful, and receptive.**

That takes intentionality to a different level. The servant leader not only ensures an intentional path for the organization, but also for him/herself. Reflection, meditation, team de–briefing, self–assessment, and gut–checking are some tools to keep us honest. And needless to say, they are not done haphazardly, but regularly and by design. How do you keep your intentions on track?

YOU CAN LIVE YOUR LIFE OUT OF CIRCUMSTANCE OR OUT OF VISION.

WERNER EHRHARD

At a casual get–together, a friend was in conversation with a group of people about an avant-garde idea. "Would you ever do that?" posed one of them. "What would people think?!" another replied. "Do you really care what people think?" inquired a third. The friend's immediate and fierce response was, "Of course not!"

I had to consider for a moment what my answer to that question would have been. "Of course not" is the fashionable answer in our culture of individualism. To care what others think is a sign of dependency and weakness. I was raised not to be at the bidding of other's opinions.

Yet in my heart I recognize that every thought, word, and behavior is a teaching moment. I see every interaction as an occasion to lead; a chance to implement what you believe, and demonstrate who you are. This is not caring what people think in the "wanting to fit in" or "keeping up with the Joneses" mode. Perhaps caring what people think in this sense arises from wisdom, humility, or compassion. Perhaps that is the central point of *intention. Intentional servant leaders have a responsibility to care what others think.*

Servant leaders don't sit back and hope that the greater good will happen: they energetically strive to bring it to fruition. Anything that is not in alignment with that intention falls away. Intentional servant leaders are trusted helmsmen, setting the organization on course toward an optimistic future.

Vision for memories, created by adventure looks like circumstance but planned

A Personal Note on Intention

The word "intention" is used fairly frequently these days. When someone says, "You did that intentionally!" it usually implies some harm done deliberately and gleefully. Intention can connote a deep desire or prayerful petition. Or it might be a lazy wish with no real action behind it. We've all heard where the "road paved with good intentions" will lead us! Some people interpret _intention_ as a form of actualization or wish–fulfillment: "If I visualize my intention, I can create it."

We can have good intentions, bad intentions, prayerful intentions, selfish intentions, magical intentions, failed intentions—and we all do.

So what does intention mean to me in this context? It is profoundly personal, a hope and a purpose that comes from the heart; a sacred trust meant to further _the good_. It is not cast in concrete because I intend it. It charges me to leave space for the intentions of others that may or may not correspond with my own. It reminds me constantly that there is an _Intention_ greater than mine.

This _intention_ is not an arrogant imposition of my own will upon others; it is a humbling acknowledgement of my leadership imperfections. It is what I would like to happen and what I would like to be, until it meets full force the intentions of my family, my colleagues, the workplace, and the universe.

My intentions are meant to guide me, not to strong-arm you.

My struggle is in following ideology with action. I can theorize well, know what the right moves are, and understand what constitutes good leadership. But the pressures of the work environment and my own flaws often get in the way, and I fall short of my expectations of myself. When I do that, I cannot lead others well; I cannot fulfill that sacred trust.

Very simply, intentionality is my prime motivator. I might hope to do many great and wonderful things, but without the purposefulness of _intention_, they flounder. Intentionality is the consistency of thought and action that makes serving more than merely accidental or incidental. It is _the work behind the wish_ to become a worthy servant leader.

Setting out on the Journey

SERVANT LEADERSHIP IS MORE A JOURNEY THAN A destination. Most organizations have not "arrived": they are *works in progress*. There is no pre–programmed formula for the journey, but we will explore many specific applications and best practices later in this book.

Meanwhile, my own experience has suggested a few essential steps that can begin moving an organization methodically in the right direction:

1. Generate interest; raise awareness. Talk about servant leadership. Identify examples of it in everyday practice. Mention it in meetings and town halls. Schedule servant leadership events. Include it in newsletters and written materials. Get everyone involved.

2. Educate both current and developing leaders in servant leader principles. Teach all employees about their role in a servant organization and help them discern their personal contribution to a mission of service. *Everyone* in the organization is a caregiver, if only in that we care for each other. *Everyone* can be a servant leader in their niche of service.

3. Leaders are the primary models and messengers of servant leader behavior, which is then replicated throughout the organization. Language must consistently reflect the principles of service. Review policies, budgets, position statements, employee memos, performance appraisals, customer correspondence, public reports, marketing materials, etc. through the microscope of servant leadership.

4. Provide self-assessment opportunities. As one example, the Veterans Health Administration developed an online 360 degree instrument (McCarren, et al, 2016) based on the "Seven Pillars of Servant Leadership" (Sipe & Frick, 2015) to help leaders assess their servant leader competencies and develop plans for personal growth.

5. Measure organizational outcomes, but allow time for culture change to take root. Consider creating a servant leader index or balanced scorecard that cross-references supervisory outcomes, workgroup effectiveness, and external quality metrics. Include questions in employee satisfaction surveys that gauge servant leader behaviors.

6. Integrate servant leadership into other corporate programs and priorities to avoid a "flavor of the month" mindset and to survive leadership turnover. Build it into human resource processes, performance objectives, information and communication systems, customer service programs, etc. Weave it into the fabric of the organization.

7. Sustain the effort over time. Without a plan to support and grow the culture, it will succumb to neglect or attrition; it will yield to entropy. Be *intentional* about sustaining it. What you are seeking is more than individual servant leaders: it is a *servant organization.*

8. Watch for landmarks of success. You'll know you've made headway when servant leadership is no longer a program, a project, or an initiative, but the *way we do business.*

THE PRACTICE OF SERVANT LEADERSHIP PLACES THE GOOD OF THE LED OVER THE GOOD OF THE LEADER.

J. A. LAUB

A Nobler Side of Leadership

LEADERSHIP IS A PERSONAL DECISION TO SERVE. SERVANT LEADER-ship does not replace traditional management functions, but it shapes how they are performed. Servant leadership doesn't always make things easy or comfortable. It often defies us to think and act differently. Servant leaders will make mistakes, but they are less likely to be derailed by unethical or unaccountable behaviors.

It is surprising that servant leadership is not the predominant business model in today's corporate world. Service and leadership seem to be such natural and vital partners. I am often astonished to find distinguished companies, centers of learning, and health care systems that are not even familiar with servant leadership. More disappointing still are those that call themselves servant leader organizations and are anything but. In a perpetual state of crisis, chaos, and change, the business part of organizations and the mission part of organizations sometimes fail to intersect.

Servant leadership calls upon all managers, employees, and stakeholders to become "co–creators" of the organization. It sets ambitious, but attainable, standards for meeting the critical challenges of contemporary organizations, while honoring the humanity of everyone they touch.

Servant leadership is not naïve or unrealistic. It acknowledges and grooms us for the hard realities of corporate life. But it doesn't stop there: it points the way to success by affirming the highest values that make work a calling.

It is good to remember that service is not a by-product of leadership: *it is the whole point.*

A NEW MORAL PRINCIPLE IS EMERGING WHICH HOLDS THAT THE ONLY AUTHORITY DESERVING ONE'S ALLEGIANCE IS THAT WHICH IS FREELY AND KNOWINGLY GRANTED BY THE LED TO THE LEADER IN RESPONSE TO, AND IN PROPORTION TO, THE CLEARLY EVIDENT SERVANT STATURE OF THE LEADER. THOSE WHO CHOOSE TO FOLLOW THIS PRINCIPLE WILL NOT CASUALLY ACCEPT THE AUTHORITY OF EXISTING INSTITUTIONS. RATHER, THEY WILL FREELY RESPOND ONLY TO INDIVIDUALS WHO ARE CHOSEN AS LEADERS BECAUSE THEY ARE PROVEN AND TRUSTED AS SERVANTS.

ROBERT K. GREENLEAF

The Power of Community

OVER THE PAST FIVE YEARS, I HAVE BEEN A MEMBER OF AT LEAST twenty "communities". Some were by virtue of my job, some by location, and some out of special interests. We might be members of the academic community, the scientific community, the retirement community, the medical community, the Jewish community, the Veteran community, the Atlanta community, the theater community, the online community, and on and on.

We use the term community loosely. For example, my <u>homeowners association</u> calls itself a community. It is rife with rules and regulations, and in all my time there, I have never felt particularly welcomed. The only common denominator among the members is proximity, and proximity is not enough. So for me, this is not a community, but simply a neighborhood.

My <u>work organization</u> also calls itself a community. In many ways it truly is. I have been supported by and accepted into the group. When individuals are in difficulty, experience major life events, or have reason to rejoice, the community is there. It has common goals and experiences that bind the members together.

My organization, however, has the power to fire me at will, or to make such changes in my work life that it is untenable to stay. It is accountable and responsive to a powerful higher body that is perpetually at loggerheads with the work community, and whose rank supersedes the work community. Therefore, this community will only defend its members to the point where the higher body steps in. When that occurs, and it is often enough, the community disappears, at least until the crisis has passed. Even though it's positive most of the time, it can never feel completely safe. This is a community with strings.

I am also affiliated with a <u>religious community</u>. These are women who are joined by faith and vocation. They have elected to live, eat, work, and worship as a community. I am drawn to them because of that, but I am not one of them. I share their beliefs and their ethic, but I am peripheral to their way of life. I am with them in spirit daily, but in body, almost never. For me, inaccessibility is not an issue, because the deeper connection transcends place. This community is more satisfying than the neighborhood and work communities, yet the sense of belonging will always be by definition second–tier.

> ONE OF THE MOST IMPORTANT THINGS YOU CAN DO ON THIS EARTH IS TO LET PEOPLE KNOW THEY ARE NOT ALONE.
> **SHANNON L. ALDER**

Let me tell you about another community. We called it the CREW Community. CREW—Civility, Respect, and Engagement in the Workplace—began as a program to facilitate more honest, accountable, and rewarding relationships between co–workers and with their supervisors.

The premise was simple; the practice was anything but. Yet the initiative was so effective that more and more work groups gravitated to the training. In the course of ten years or so, thousands of people took part. We sponsored regular refresher sessions because participants clamored to come back together, to reconnect and recommit—a sort of CREW booster shot.

Over time, they developed a sense of community, not based on location—they were spread all over the country, not even based on their jobs—they were at all levels of the hierarchy and in widely–divergent organizations. What they had in common were a goal, a foundation, an experience, an identity, and a commitment.

Despite distance, they reached out to each other for encouragement, information, ideas, and empathy: "I know what you're going through," or "I've been there and here's how I handled it." This is a group that wore the mantle of community lightly and by choice.

So community has many connotations:

- a group of people living in a particular area
- a "band of brothers" we lean on when times are tough; who are there for us when we need love, support, and encouragement
- social, religious, or occupational associates sharing common characteristics or interests
- a body of persons of similar professional pursuits scattered through a larger society
- having comparable character, values, and identity

- an attachment or feeling of belonging among like–minded people.

Humans are made to live and work with others; we are social beings intended to exist within communities. Communities are meant to kindle in their members a sense of self-discovery and group connection, embolden them to express their beliefs and opinions in a "judgment–free zone", and to build relationships with others. They have a tangible impact on individual self-awareness and fulfillment.

Positive experiences with communities allow individuals to feel more connected to their environment and the people in it, facilitating self-reflection and exploration of core values and beliefs.*

Servant leaders are "born" to community. They hold similar work values and common goals. They foster a feeling of genuine connection among members by providing opportunities for interaction. They set a climate of respect, allowing everyone to feel heard, knowing that when people speak their minds they are more likely to be bonded to the community.

Servant leader communities are not rule–bound or managed from a pinnacle. Everyone is expected to step up and lead at the suitable time: leadership in community is shared. And they celebrate community traditions: their roots and origins, their philosophy and purpose, their milestones and successes, and their legacies.

A servant leader community is not a crowd, a clique, or a cult. It is not dependent on proximity, structure, or management imprimatur. It offers an uncensored milieu for working out what servant leadership means in our daily lives, with the support and goodwill of fellow travelers. Leaders who smooth the way for community are heroes.

I recall the sentiments of one servant leader community member, "What a relief that I don't have to do this alone!" Maybe that sums it up best.

A COMMUNITY IS LIKE A SHIP; EVERYONE OUGHT TO BE PREPARED TO TAKE THE HELM.

HENRIK IBSEN

*positivepsychologyprogram.com

Practice Period

More – Same – Less

Everyone has strengths and opportunities for improvement. With what you now know about servant leadership, how can you progress as a servant leader *intentionally*?

Think about what you could do more of, less of, and the same as you are doing now—in order to improve your servant leader performance. You can do this individually or in a group.

On separate post–it notes, write the things you could do <u>more of</u> to be the best servant leader. Note behaviors that are within your control and be specific, e.g. I could communicate more with staff, share credit more generously, or spend time in reflection.

Next write what you could do <u>less of</u>, e.g. micromanaging, unilateral decision–making, or placing blame.

Then write what you would do <u>the same</u>–what you feel you are doing well now, e.g. making rounds in the organization, celebrating small successes, or soliciting feedback.

Designate three areas on the wall as "More", "Same", and "Less" and post your notes under the appropriate heading. Can you identify any themes? Do they fall into categories, like communication, control, or relationships? If you are in a group, do any larger themes become apparent?

What did you learn about yourself in this activity? How can this information enhance your progress as a servant leader?

How can you achieve more, the same, or less of the actions you identified? What will it take, how will you proceed, and how will you know when you get there?

References

Alder, S. www.goodreads.com/quotes.

Belton, L. (2016). A Nobler Side of Leadership: The Art of Humanagement. Atlanta: The Greenleaf Center.

Belton, L. (2017). The First Shall Be Last: Servant Leadership in Scripture. Bloomington: Westbow Press Division of Thomas Nelson & Zondervan.

Belton, L. & Anderson, P. (2017) Servant Leadership and Health Care: Critical Partners in Changing Times. Arkansas Hospitals. Winter Issue. 17-20.

Block, Peter. (1996) Stewardship: Choosing Service Over Self-Interest. San Francisco: Berrett-Koehler Publishers. www.leadingtoday.org/ Book Review.

Cerit, Y. (2009). The effects of Servant Leader behaviors of school principals on teachers' job satisfaction. Educational Management Administration and Leadership, 37 (5), 600-623.

Drucker, P. (1954). The Practice of Management. New York: Harper Business.

Erhart, M. G. (2004). Leadership and Procedural Justice Climate as Antecedents of Unit Level Organizational Citizenship Behaviors. Personnel Psychology. 57, 61-94.

Erhard, W. (2017). www.wernererhardinfo.com/blogs3.html

Farling, M.L., Stone, A.G., & Winston, B.E. (1999). Servant Leadership: Setting the stage for empirical research. Journal of Leadership Studies. 6, 49-62.

Goodman, J. A. (2009) Strategic Customer Service. New York: AMACOM.

Greenleaf, R. K., & Spears, L. C. (2002). Servant leadership: A journey into the nature of legitimate power and greatness. Mahwah, NJ: Paulist Press. 320.

Greenleaf, R. K. (2009). The Institution as Servant. Westfield, IN: The Greenleaf Center for Servant Leadership. 16.

Greenleaf, R. K. (1970). The Servant as Leader. Atlanta: The Greenleaf Center for Servant Leadership. 15, 16, 27.

Heider, J. (1985). Tao of Leadership. New York: Bantam Books. 61.

Henley, D. and Frey, G. (1973). Desperado. Cass County Music/Red Cloud Music.

Hess, E. (2013). Servant Leadership: A path to high performance. Washington Post.

Hu, J. and Liden, R.C. (2011). Antecedents of team potency and team effectiveness: An examination of goal and process clarity and servant leadership. Journal of Applied Psychology, 1-12.

Ibsen, H. https://en.wikiquote.org/wiki/Henrik_Ibsen

Irving, J. A. and Longbotham, G. J. (2007). Team effectiveness and six essential themes: a Regression model based on items in the organizational leadership assessment. International Journal of Leadership Studies, 2 (2), 98-113.

Jaramillo, F., Grisaffe, D. B., Chonko, L. B. and Roberts, J. A. (2009b). Examining the impact of Servant Leadership on salesperson's turnover intention. Journal of Personal Selling and Sales Management, 29 (4), 351-365.

Keith, K., (2013) Growing to Greatness through Servant Leadership. Today's Manager: Issue 1, 1.

Laub, J. A. (1999). Assessing the servant organization: Development of the servant organization leadership assessment instrument. Dissertation Abstracts International, 60, (02), 308.

McCarren, H., Lewis-Smith, J., Belton, L., Yanovsky, B., Robinson, J., and Osatuke, K. (2016) Creation of a Multi-Rater Feedback Assessment for the Development of Servant Leaders in the Veterans Health Administration. Servant Leadership: Theory and Practice, Vol. 3, (1), 12-51.

Palmer, Parker. (2004). A Hidden Wholeness; San Francisco: Jossey-Bass. 16, 20, 31, 55, 76-77, 168.

Parris, D. L. and Peachey, J. W. (2013). A systemic literature review of Servant Leadership Theory in Organizational Contexts. Journal of Business Ethics, 113, 377-393.

Patterson, K. (2003). Servant Leadership: A Theoretical Model. Dissertation Abstracts, International, 64 (2), 570.

Sipe, J. W. and Frick, D. M. (2015). Seven Pillars of Servant Leadership. New York/New Jersey: Paulist Press.

Schwantes, M. (2017). Leadership From the Core. www.25 Unique Leadership Quotes to Inspire and Motivate

10 Qualities of Positive Communities. www.positivepsychologyprogram.com.

Walumbwa, F. O. (2010). Servant leadership, procedural justice climate, service climate and organizational citizenship behavior: a Cross-level investigation. Journal of Applied Psychology, 95, (3), 517-529.

Wong, P. (2017). www.Quotepixel.com

Wong, P. and Davey, D. (2007). Best Practices in Servant Leadership. Paper presented at the Servant Leadership Research Roundtable, Regent University, Virginia Beach, VA.

VA National Center for Organizational Development. (2015). Servant Leadership Development Guide.

PART TWO

The Practice

Opus: Allegro Animato

Now let's pick up the pace; animate the practice. It is one thing to ponder a composition: it's another to perform it. This is the work of servant leadership.

I am fortunate at this point in life to be able to review my own and others' performance from a safe distance. I now get to take the long view, to assess what I could have done better, what I would improve in the next incarnation, and to appreciate the wins. I can sit in gentle judgement of my peers, colleagues, and bosses who have offered remarkable lessons in leadership—both good and bad. They have been effective, abysmal, talented, flawed, honorable, unscrupulous, compassionate, cold, generous, arrogant, wise, and inspired—and I have learned from them all.

I can also, in retrospect, recall the consummate organizations and the gurus toward which I have gravitated—kind of work–ethic soulmates—who demonstrated a different path and attracted me to roads less traveled. These are the voices that stirred me to lead by the heart instead of the rulebook, to follow my instincts and imagination, to be true to the mission without and the source within.

That said, performance is what it's all about—where the rubber meets the road. Whatever their philosophy, leaders forget that at their peril. There is a plethora of performance measures and management metrics, but intentional servant leaders remember that those are not the ultimate goals—they are the basics, the minimal standards.

The performance of a servant organization doesn't end at the numeric scores, it begins there. It goes on to encompass what leaders do and how they do it; what they say and how they say it; how their decisions affect others; how their words and deeds align; the ramifications of their actions and omissions; and the totality of their outcomes. When we do the right things, the metrics just happen. Servant leaders don't practice merely from altruism, but because *it works*.

In Part II we'll put *premise* into *practice*. We'll look at specific functions of leadership, which I have categorized into seven sections. Some functions could legitimately appear in more than one section, so I've made some executive decisions there! We'll also call upon those gurus and organizations that have found creative, often courageous, ways to put service into practice. The aim is to juxtapose traditional leadership with servant leadership in a very deliberate way.

Some of the examples and suggestions may not be pertinent to your field or would need to be adapted. Some may simply seem too hard and not worth the risk. Then allow them to pique your curiosity and stimulate your imagination: find your own practices, the ones that reflect the leader you want to be.

With planning, forethought, and foresight, leaders can be intentional about transforming their sphere of influence—no matter how large or small—from a power model to a service model. That transformation can be at once challenging and rewarding, maybe a bit scary, but satisfying.

Servant leadership is always a choice.

How will my daily practice identify me as a servant leader?

> THOSE WHO SAY IT CAN'T BE DONE SHOULD GET OUT OF THE WAY OF THOSE WHO ARE DOING IT.
>
> **CHINESE PROVERB**

Tune–Up

A new policy directive is issued. You are concerned about how it will affect your department and how your staff will react. Which answer best reflects servant leadership?*

1. "Corporate is making us do this, so hop to it."

2. "I think we all have some concerns about this policy. Let's talk about how we can make it work here for our clients. Then if you have ideas to improve the policy, I'll present them to leadership."

3. "This policy will generate a lot of complaints. Then they'll see how foolish it is."

In a *symphony of service, administructure* is like a piano. Privy to the entire score of music, it holds the composition together.

Every organization needs a framework: what are the parameters within which we do business? How will we know if we have fallen short or exceeded our mandate? What standards will guide our work? If priorities conflict, how will we choose? What benchmarks will chart our progress? How will we balance immediate needs against projections for the future?

The structure of an organization consists of, at a minimum:

✓ Mission
✓ Vision
✓ Values/Principles
✓ Laws/Regulations
✓ Policies and Procedures
✓ Strategic Plan
✓ Priorities
✓ Performance Expectations

*   ANSWER: 2

Structure is an administrative tool meant to bracket or *parenthesize* the work. It is not the be–all and end–all of the work, but an *exoskeleton* that gives form to the work. Traditional organizations often make more of the structure than it is, losing sight of the living and dynamic organism within. They focus on the frame instead of the masterpiece it holds.

If structure is the bones of an organization, administration is the skin—the *integument*—that covers the body of work. The skin functions to protect, absorb environmental assaults, and regulate the internal climate. As part of the peripheral nervous system, the skin is constantly receiving and responding to various types of stimuli. It is resilient and a bellwether of overall health. In its most fundamental form, administration is the well-designed integumentary system of an organization.

Administration is sometimes confused with structure. It does not mean to do paperwork, or to oversee, to detach oneself from the frontline, or hunker out of the line of fire. There is no "administrivia". The word "administer" comes from the Latin *administrare*, meaning **to serve**. An *"administructure"*, then, is the organizational anatomy that makes it possible for service to be rendered.

Mission

Mission statements should be simple, comprehensible, unambiguous, and describe the reason the organization exists. We all know this, yet finding succinct and repeatable mission statements in the field is a rarity. What is your mission statement like? Can every employee recite it, understand it, and apply it to their work?

A good mission statement can draw the right applicants to your Personnel Office. If it is accurate and truthful, not just perfunctory and politically correct, candidates will self–select, saving you much of the hassle of the recruitment process. For example, a publicly–traded company may have as its mission statement, "To make the best return for our stockholders"; the U.S. Department of Veterans Affairs, "To care for him who shall have borne the battle…"; or a hospital, "Patients first". The mission statement will draw people who are enthusiastic about the objective and discourage those whose goals are not congruent.

Being explicit about mission informs your strategic plan, budget, and business/product lines. It guides priority–setting and operational decision–making. It also tips off the decision–making public about whether they should patronize your company.

Mission is the foundation on which the organization rests. I know an agency whose mission shifts every time a new Director is hired. Mission statements are meant to be more permanent than that. It is the founder of an enterprise or its governing body that generally determines the mission. In a government agency, that governing board is often a legislative group.

Specificity is important in defining the mission. For example, does your organization cater to a particular customer? Is its purpose education, service, information, research, or development (fund–raising)? Many boards have not distinguished that for themselves, trying to be all things to all people. Without working through that process, the mission floats from one function to another, never quite meeting anyone's needs, confusing the players and wasting precious resources.

Servant leaders may involve a universe of players in deliberating on the mission, but not for the purpose of gratuitous change. Mission does not drift with the tide. It remains stable over time, although the methods for fulfilling it may evolve. Any significant departure from the primary mission beyond simple tweaking requires considerable retooling of the established corporate "machine".

Mission is what the organization stands for; it articulates the corporate culture and gives it identity. It permeates the organization. Company sub–units will shape their secondary missions as "fractals" of the original, while remaining in step with the larger mission. Customers and staff come for the mission and, despite minor failings or flaws in service, they stay for the mission. The intentional servant leader uses this as a compass point, ensuring that people, programs, and priorities remain in steady alignment with the mission.

Vision

One part foresight, one part ingenuity, and one part optimism. Any leader can be a visionary by scanning the horizon, imagining "what if", and exercising confident realism (or realistic confidence!). Vision is not pie–in–the–sky; it is based on *predictive plausibility.* Where mission is not a group project, vision often is. Servant leaders can engage staff and stakeholders in a participative process where they not only help to conceive the vision, but are motivated by it.

How do they take the mission and project it into the future? How can they apply the mission to unanticipated markets or in ways not dreamed? What is the highest calling of the organization?

The term "vision" is apropos. "Seeing is believing" or "What you see is what you get" are not just clichés. Think about it! If an organization can envision a future, they may be able to attain it. If they can't envision a future, they surely won't. No organization concocts a vision statement that forecasts failure. Working together on a vision promotes buy-in. It is inspirational. It stretches people, arousing their best instincts and highest energy.

But vision is not accidental. It is developed thoughtfully and *intentionally* through reflection and action planning. Figure 4 shows a sequence of questions used by one organization to build a vision and employee commitment to the vision.

Build a clear and compelling vision

- What is the future state that we are trying to create?

- Do all staff share this vision?

- Do staff understand the connection between the tasks they are assigned and the vision or big picture?

- How can the leader help make that connection clearer?

Figure 4

The third point above transitions the vision from a document on a shelf to a behavior; a way of life. It is the step that moves a group from pondering a composition to performing it.

I often speak of a housekeeper I met while making rounds at a health care facility. When I asked him to describe his job at the medical center, he avoided eye contact and replied, "I mop the floors." Months later, after he had been involved in several culture–building initiatives, I saw him again. This time he approached me and said proudly, "My job at this hospital is to maintain an infection–free environment." This man now clearly understood the connection between his assigned tasks and the mission and vision of the organization. It was a remarkable moment.

Likewise, every employee needs to consider *specifically* how they will put the mission and vision into action. Leaders at all levels can help them do this. The supervisor of a counselling center walked her staff through the application of the mission and vision to their clientele. They identified the principal concerns they dealt with every day: issues of alcohol and drug abuse, stress reduction, PTSD, suicide prevention, grief counseling, and work/family balance. As a group they determined how they could be client–centered in their service (mission) and holistic in their approach (vision).

A government Office of Regulation and Compliance took a different, but equally effective tack, pinpointing its major obstacles to meeting the mission: constant unpredictable change, resource challenges, limited autonomy, leadership turnover, and customer demands. They concluded that *working to the mission* would actually help shatter the obstacles and planned how that would be done. They adopted as their vision "to be recognized as a servant office"—a tall order for a group of inspectors!

A servant leader's greatest contribution in this regard is as a "midwife", helping each office, each professional discipline, and each individual discover the relevance of mission/vision to their own practice. It doesn't get more intentional than this.

> VISION WITHOUT ACTION IS A DAYDREAM. ACTION
> WITH WITHOUT VISION IS A NIGHTMARE.
>
> **JAPANESE PROVERB**

Values/Principles

Many organizations have Values Statements. Values are characteristics or qualities that the company finds intrinsically desirable or worthy. A values statement describes what the organization believes and how it will behave.

Principles, on the other hand, arise from widely accepted laws, doctrines, or assumptions. Values and principles are terms often used interchangeably, but there is a subtle difference. Values are deeply held beliefs, personal and subjective, whereas principles are more closely related to objective codes and standards.

Professional bodies typically follow principles. For instance, Generally Accepted Accounting Principles (GAAP) are a common set of auditing standards that companies must follow when they compile their financial statements. Lawyers and courts use principles of jurisprudence. The American College of Surgeons follow such principles as:

- Informed consent
- Do no harm (also an ethic)
- Continuous medical education
- Conflict of Interest
- Patient Privacy and Confidentiality

Groups may support sets of principles as well as values statements. One Organizational Health department (VANCOD, 2012) uses principles of psychology, but declares as its *values*:

- Civility
- Respect
- Engagement
- Service
- Excellence
- Compassion
- Passion
- Integrity
- Relationships
- Innovation

One can pick out the slight differences. Perhaps this is a significant, but not important distinction, except to understand that the emotional attachment to values may be greater than to principles. People are wedded to their beliefs.

There is much written about company values. Values statements should ideally function as the operating instructions of the company, but this rarely happens because they don't point out what's unique about the firm. Many values have become buzzwords. In fact, one author recommends that descriptors like integrity, teamwork, fun, authentic, and customer–oriented be banned from corporate values statements. I would not go that far, but if you decide to use them, it's essential to have a common understanding of their meaning, and to specify what is distinctive or unique about those values in your environment.

Your organization's values must embody what makes your company inimitably "you"—what makes it stand out from others. All fast-food restaurants must include values of speed and convenience; all software makers must value reliability and ease of use. A good values statement will communicate how *this* fast-food restaurant and *this* software developer stand out from the others. It conveys the attitudes and beliefs they want employees to hold, translates them into specific actions, and shows how they will produce the desired customer experience (Yohn, 2018).

Complicating matters, individuals don't have just one set of values, e.g. their personal and professional values may not always align. They may clash with the values of their colleagues or direct–reports. The emotional impact is such that when there is concurrence about values, it feels like a tightly–knit club; when there is not, or when a member breaches the value, it feels like betrayal.

Lastly, values must be made visible. No matter how skillfully leaders generate the values statement, how participative the process was, or how expertly it is socialized, it must be reflected in the leader's actions. There is nothing more embarrassing than having an employee point out that your latest policy decision does not mesh with the organization's official values! A values statement is not a "one and done" proposition; it must be affirmed every day. If the leader cannot do that consistently, it is better not to have a values statement at all.

CORE VALUES ARE THE DEEPLY INGRAINED PRINCIPLES THAT GUIDE ALL OF A COMPANY'S ACTIONS; THEY SERVE AS ITS CULTURAL CORNERSTONES.

PATRICK M. LENCIONI

Value Flags

This activity is helpful to expeditiously develop a new team, or to deepen the commitment of an existing team.

Ask each individual to create a list of personal values important to them in the workplace. Then ask them to narrow the list to 3-5 values. Instruct them to draw a visual representation in a personalized *value flag*. The idea is for the person to be as creative as possible, using no written words.

Once completed, each participant will display their value flag. Allow others on the team to try to guess at the values depicted, then have the presenter explain the flag and how they live those values in the workplace. When everyone has presented their flags, engage the group in discussion:

- Are there any common themes?

- What differences did the group notice?

- How can common values facilitate our work as a team?

- Was there anything that surprised you?

- What does our team aspire to become?

- How might sharing values with your co–workers change your perception of each other? Of your work environment?

- Are there any values that are missing that we need to incorporate into the work environment?

Rules

Rules in any form are meant to generate standardization and compliance. They do not propagate an environment of innovation and trust. So while rules are necessary, they must be balanced with common sense, wisdom, and compassion. Organizational rules come in different flavors.

Laws and Regulations are for the most part inviolate. Servant leaders understand the laws to which they are bound. Regulations may not be as constraining and, depending on the source of the regulation, might be altered. One agency followed a bookkeeping practice years after it was outmoded because it was a "regulation". When someone finally checked, they found that the regulation had been imposed by a long–retired CEO; it was not mandated by any external agency. Often companies follow regulations unquestioningly, not realizing a regulation was internal and therefore permissible to be changed. Servant leaders know what is and what isn't under their jurisdiction.

Professional Certifications and Licensing Standards regulate the qualifications and practice of many occupations, the safe operation of equipment, cautious handling of drugs and toxic materials, etc. These standards are meant for the protection of employees, consumers, and the public. Some reach the criteria of law or regulation, and others are required by professional accrediting bodies. Since servant leaders are not looking to cut corners on safety and quality, they remain current on these standards, can explain to others why they are important (not just to satisfy a licensing requirement), and build systems that take the complexity out of meeting them.

Policies and Procedures are where leaders have the most latitude. I believe that when it comes to policies, _less is more_. Most organizations boast reams of policies—have _policy tomes_—documenting every step of every procedure and every behavioral possibility. They are constructed with the bricks of one person's failure, on top of someone else's shortcoming, added onto another's slipshod work; they are mortared with disappointment, disaster, or control: "_we're never going to let this happen again_".

To be sure, policies and procedures often reveal hard lessons, and can be one mechanism in a learning organization. Or they can ensure uniformity in research–driven standards of practice. But let's face it: if the policy book is too dense or complicated, who reads it? If it is stored on a shelf somewhere, who can find it? If it doesn't make sense to the user, who will follow it? If is it outdated or obsolete, _should_ anyone follow it?

So the servant leader needs to be judicious, creative, flexible, trusting, and consistently reflect the philosophy.

- Judicious – what needs to be detailed for posterity and what obscures it

- Creative – how to display policies and procedures in a friendly, accessible, and just–in–time format

- Flexible – which policies are directives, which are guidelines, and which can be prudently adapted

- Trusting – where can general policy framework be set, allowing staff to work from their inherent inclination toward excellence

- Consistent with servant leader philosophy – in retrospect, does the verbiage, tone, and goal of the policy echo the principles that I preach?

I was intrigued years ago to find an organization that limited its policies to a handful. "These are the critical parameters of employment here. We trust our staff to live up to them." This was a privately–owned company, for whom such an approach elicited bright, independent applicants. It did not take a parental or micromanaging stance, but treated staff as self–motivated adults, and it worked for them.

Other organizations, especially more highly–regulated ones, may not have the luxury of a "policy pamphlet", but can still respect the thoughts above. A case in point: hospitals applying for accreditation after 2010 were required to establish a Civility Policy, to include a definition of incivility and a process for reporting it. On the minus side, it was the typical knee–jerk reaction to incidents of bullying, intimidation, and temper tantrums sometimes found in stressful professional environments. On the plus side, it was an opportunity for leadership to implement a zero–tolerance policy for those behaviors, and to promote a value of civility in the workplace.

I was able to review quite a few of those policies, all of them different. Hospital A's policy was thirteen pages long, ten of which were lists of potential uncivil behaviors—eventualities most people would never even think of—detail by excruciating detail. The rest was a multi–level disciplinary procedure to be invoked if the policy was violated. The policy's author concluded by adding that employees would also be held responsible for any infraction not on the list. He told me that his biggest concern was that if an uncivil behavior was not mentioned, staff would engage in that with impunity, and tie him up in due process complaints.

Hospital B's policy was two–and–one–half pages in length. It defined civility as "treating each other as we all want to be treated, even during moments of stress." A simple, unlayered process was put in place, but noted that due to the maturity and propriety of staff, its use was expected to be minimal.

Which policy best meets servant leader principles? Hospital A dwells on the negative behaviors—incivility—in a vain attempt to control every manifestation. People *will* look for the missing item in this list! It becomes a dare! This policy establishes a remedy that is onerous and sends a message that leadership *expects* staff to do the wrong thing.

Hospital B emphasizes the positive—civility—conveying a message of confidence and trust. It does not treat personnel as children, but with respect, and believes they will treat each other with respect in turn. Clearly, Hospital B is the winner and its prize is a staff intrinsically motivated to observe the policy.

I have discovered other best practices related to policy formation. Electronic variations address issues of accessibility: key words entered bring the correct policy or procedure up on the screen in seconds; and policy changes are displayed broadly and timely on electronic message boards. In one company their bi–annual policy review not only assesses for accuracy and out–dates, but for "unfriendly" or confusing language, and offers suggestions for how to improve the policy through a servant leader lens.

What about your policy and procedure function: do you have a "policy tome" or a "policy pamphlet"? Glance through your organization's policy manual with the next orientation/onboarding class. What do you see? What do your new employees see?

The Company Bible

I believe that we learn better how to follow rules than to lead. Traditional leaders can be great at following rules, or at least making sure that everyone else follows them. It takes a bit of courage and humble self–assurance to color outside the lines. It's safer and more comfortable to manage in lock–step. We are a rule–bound society.

One organization I worked for used the term "guidance" instead of "directive" or "mandate". It may actually have meant the same but, euphemism or not, I liked the way it sounded. It was not heavy–handed, but respectful; a wise and expectant recommendation.

My well–used edition of the Bible feels like that—the guidance of thoughtful, sagacious mentors. As "commandment", questions and disputes are thwarted. As "guidance", I can mull it over, test it, and see it with fresh eyes. Working our way from Old to New Testament, it is apparent that laws/regulations/policies changed over time. "Thou shalt not" warnings evolved to "Thou shalt" encouragement.

The Bible may not be your holy book, but we all have one: a text or writing somewhere that marks our path.

The Company Bible was one firm's pet name for its Policy and Procedure Manual. This manual displayed literally hundreds of "commandments", all written in stone. People joked about being called to a "Thou shalt not" meeting; rewards and recognition were affectionately labeled, "Thou shalts."

Some laws deserve to be written in stone, but most company rules and parameters—budgets, performance standards, and other "sacred texts"— should really be seen as guidance. If you can't concede that, at least consider how much of it *can* be. Giving people direction every step of the way discourages them from thinking, testing out, seeing with fresh eyes.

Even the servant leader mantra of "servant first" cannot be issued as a decree, because *it is always a choice.*

It's interesting that the heroes of the Bible observed the laws, but not without challenging them. Healthy debate often strengthened their adherence and sometimes perfected the law itself. And when there was no rule to fit a situation, they relied upon Wisdom and Compassion: they stepped out and led the way, risks and all.

Organizations promulgate rules to standardize, produce conformity, and to control. Standardization and conformity are useful for processes and procedures, but they crush human creativity. Servant organizations need heroes who observe the laws, but also challenge them, who listen to the wisdom and compassion of the ages—and of their own hearts— and who step out and lead the way when there are no answers and no prototypes.

By ignoring the rules, Biblical heroes risked a lightning bolt from Heaven. By putting the rules in their proper place, all contemporary leaders risk is a bruised ego, a lost job, a missed bonus—and just maybe the chance to blaze a trail of genuine service. Not a bad trade–off...

Strategic Planning

Nowhere is the servant leader characteristic of foresight more evident. The entire *administructure* revolves around strategic planning. It is the kernel from which everything else grows. It shapes operational functions, human resource activities, and customer service. Strategic planning is the process of determining where an organization is going over the next few years, how it will get there, and how it will know if it got there.

Strategic planning is "informed stargazing". The leader uses the data at her disposal as well as her educated intuition, to gauge where the organization is and where it hopes to be. Strategic planning is aspirational. Since it is a multi–year venture, the leader cannot predict with accuracy what world events will affect the course of the organization's orbit. And so the plan must be flexible, agile, and able to course–correct. The leader is the navigator.

Strategic plans cannot be short–term and cannot reverse on a whim; permanent enough to provide a solid base for programs and services to build upon, yet pliant enough to adapt. Strategic plans give birth to a myriad of other plans: tactical plans, succession plans, financial plans, capital improvement plans, etc. Those plans are where strategic subtleties become tangible and visible.

One staff member described her company's strategic planning exercise. They spent weeks with an expensive consultant, but never even considered the connection to their mission and values. She was charged to turn the final report into a work of art: the finished product was a beautiful, but meaningless plan.

Traditional leaders make several typical mistakes in strategic planning. Here are a few and my responses to them:

Mistake:	*The culture of the organization is not addressed first.*
Response:	Culture eats strategy for lunch (Coffman, Sorenson, 2013).
Mistake:	*It is treated as an annual exercise instead of a living document.*
Response:	I have attended countless strategic planning retreats. Representative employees and supervisors are convened and groupthink occurs. Sometimes the product ends up being a good one, but even if it is, participants all know that enthusiasm for the plan will soon wane, the document will be "archived" with all the past strategic plans, and they can get on with business as usual.

Mistake:	*The strategic plan is not integrated with the Core Values.*
Response:	In servant organizations, core values are fleshed out in the strategic plan, and the plan translates the values into actions. Every day leaders are faced with making decisions and approving or disapproving the decisions of subordinate supervisors. That requires a direct line of sight from the core value > to the strategic plan > to the action.

It's easy to fantasize magnanimous plans during times of plenty, but much harder to turn them into consistent, realistic actions when times are rough.

I have seen some **illogical examples** that stand out in review, where core values and strategic plans are completely dissociated from actions taken:

CORE VALUE		STRATEGIC PLAN		SUBSEQUENT ACTION
Community Partnership	→	"avoid duplication of effort; reduce physical plant"	→	build a new mental health wing
Stewardship	→	"direct resources to programs with highest client need and best outcomes"	→	demand 10% budget cuts across the board
Become a Learning Organization	→	"grow more servant leaders"	→	in a pinch, training dollars are frozen
Be an Employer of Choice	→	"recruit and retain a diverse cadre of staff"	→	planned layoffs
Respect	→	"include clients as partners in decision–making"	→	"emergency" closure of a convenient branch office

Decisions about whether to build or lease space, provide food service or contract it out, invest in technology or invest in people, all arise from a strategic plan. The intentional servant leader understands that the plan must be insightful and integrated if it is to be the origin of future decisions, future spending, and future programs.

Setting Priorities

Some Quick Hints about priority setting:

- Priorities flow from the strategic plan
- Sort out the routine from the urgent (not everything is urgent!)
- Prioritize items that may resolve other items
- Delegate
- Get rid of distractions—an issue may be small, but will haunt you until you do it
- Group actions/items together where possible
- When in doubt, put people first
- When in doubt, put service first

Performance Expectations

Measuring the results of our work is essential, but traditional leaders attempt to measure everything. At one agency, leaders could count more than 350 performance goals for which they were responsible. In an attempt to order them, they were divided into categories of performance measures and performance monitors: measures were worth more than monitors when it came to annual evaluations and bonuses. When top leadership was asked to prioritize the measures the answer was, "They're all priorities."

In a futile struggle to regulate, many organizations spread their performance goals too broadly, thereby ensuring that many of them are never met. Instead of being targets of excellence, they simply become overwhelming. A servant organization has the opportunity to do better by concentrating efforts on the goals that really make a difference. As stated earlier, when the focus is on doing the right things rather than meeting numerical goals, *performance measures take care of themselves.*

Leaders should not be held responsible for what they cannot control. Despite the tenet of *respondeat superior*, and notwithstanding "the buck stops here", there are measures for which leaders have no personal ability or knowledge to achieve. They must rely on others with the expertise to meet those goals.

For example, a health care organization included patient lab values in their performance measures. If a patient's Hemoglobin A1C exceeded 6.0, or his cholesterol was above 200, or his blood pressure surpassed the 120/80 range, the performance measures were not met. These measures were finely–detailed, generic, and did not consider special factors such as age or health history.

Clearly these are desirable indicators based on professional medical criteria, and unmistakably the leader can urge the clinician to work toward those goals, but their realization is plainly beyond the leader's scope. Would it not be better to have as a goal the overall health and functioning of the patient? Would it not be more effective to encourage caregivers to develop realistic and attainable goals in partnership with the patient? Could we not then measure excellence one patient at a time? Is the patient—body, mind, and spirit—*served well?*

Of course aggregated data are an important part of measurement, allowing providers to watch trends in population health and potential hazards to quality and safety. Intentional servant leaders find those connections. Clinical indicators in themselves mean little and they don't exist in a vacuum. For that reason, some organizations have crafted dashboards that relate standards to practitioners' performance and patient-preferred outcomes.

Staying with the health care illustration for a moment, conflicting goals are another problem in the traditional environment. A facility has among its goals, "The patient is a partner in decision–making", and "All patients will receive flu immunization". So what happens if the patient refuses the flu shot? In this case, both measures cannot be met. They have been designed *not* to be met!

Such situations are confusing and frustrating to the staff held accountable. (Note: in the hints for priority–setting above, "When in doubt, people first", would be applicable here.)

Another area that impacts the efficacy of performance measurement is the practice of rating and ranking. One national service organization has more than 150 locations. Each branch is held to the same performance metrics.

Some differentiation appears when the branch is *rated* against the service standard, but very little when branches are *ranked* against each other: there is almost no statistically–significant difference. Headquarters, however, is obliged to complete a system–wide ranking, upon which momentous decisions are based, liked evaluations and bonuses, layoffs, and branch closures.

When numerics are the predominant goals, people do strange things to meet them, sometimes in conflict with core values. If 100 widgets need to be produced every month, production may be slowed so as not to overtake the goal. Dollars earned in Quarter 1 may be attributed to Quarter 2. Some customer complaints may not be recorded. Waiting times for service may be falsified. Expenses may be under–reported. Performance goals that are too numerous, confusing, impossible to attain, or in conflict with organizational values can become ethical dilemmas or ethical breaches.

Performance measurement is exceedingly complicated and the aim here is not to fathom its mathematical and statistical permutations. The role of the intentional servant leader is to create and communicate at a level higher than performance measures and metrics: at the level of *performance expectations*.

While the traditional leader engages in a paper chase, the servant leader builds an environment that *expects* excellence; empowers employees to deliver it; defines, measures, and rewards success from a global perspective.

We began this Section by describing the *administructure* as a framework; the skin and bones that hold together the functioning parts of the organization. *Administructure* is not pro–forma and it is not delimiting.

From mission/vision/values to performance expectations, it defines both the floor and the ceiling of the organizational *home*. Servant leaders provide dependable shelter for the complex and chaotic workings within. Intentional servant leaders ensure the safe, secure, and stable surroundings that release their workforce to serve.

WHAT MATTERS IS PEOPLE, NOT STRUCTURE. EVERYTHING ELSE IS MEANT TO FUNCTION AS A SUPPORT TO THAT PRIORITY.

PARKER PALMER

Managing Priorities

You have been out of town and returned to the office at 1:00 PM on Friday. You are faced with critical problems which need to be handled by close–of–business. Assign a priority number to each of the following tasks:

___Personnel has informed you that your senior supervisor, Ms. K, is looking for another job outside the company. You want to talk to her before she makes any decisions. *Time: 10 minutes*

___The Boss left word that he wants to see you in his office ASAP.

___You have several emails marked urgent. *Time: 10 minutes*

___Your telephone is ringing.

___A piece of equipment has broken down, halting all production in your department. You have to either fix it or find someone who can. *Time: 30 minutes*

___Someone is outside waiting to see you. *Time: 10 minutes*

___You receive a note to call a Los Angeles operator. Both your mother and Headquarters are located in LA. *Time: 10 minutes*

___Another supervisor (peer) has sent a message that he needs 10 minutes of your time, asap.

___The local media want to interview you for tonight's news. *10-30 min.*

___You missed lunch. You are very hungry, but it would take you 30 minutes to get something substantial to eat.

With your team, discuss your priority patterns. Were there any differences? Why might one be better than another? Would you change anything on your priority list after hearing your teammates' responses?

Contrast: Administructure in a Traditional vs Servant Leader Organization

Administructure in the TRADITIONAL Environment	Administructure in the SERVANT Environment
Mission	
• Annual exercise • Limited staff investment • Meant to meet corporate mandate • Filed away for future use	• Used as a basis for planning and decision–making • Why does this organization exist? • Permeates the organization: subunits personalize their mission as "fractals" of the original
Vision	
• Uses forecasting • Sometimes participative • May be inspirational, but often passive: an ambition • Focused at a macro (organization) level	• Always participative • Uses foresight • Based on prdictive plausibility • Intentional, motivational, and action–oriented: a behavior • Personalized to level of employee
Values	
• Often top–down • May achieve little buy–in: lip–service • Buzzwords may guide company's actions unless challenged or over-taken by events	• Usually participative • Well–understood meanings • Generally shared throughout organization • Made visible • Guide actions: a cornerstone, especially in times of crisis

Administrature in the TRADITIONAL Environment	Administrature in the SERVANT Environment
Rules	
• Goal is to meet licensing or regulatory requirements • Parental, micromanaging tone • Interested in the "letter" of the policy • Policies cover every eventuality because employees can't be trusted	• Goal is to ensure safety and quality • Treats staff as self–motivated adults • Policies are limited to the basics; employees trusted to meet the "spirit" of the policy • Rules are judicious, flexible and consistent with servant leader philosophy
Strategic Plan	
• Uses data • If course–correction necessary, it is deemed a leader failure • Culture not considered as precursor to strategic plan • Managed participation • Another annual exercise • Referred to when needed	• Uses data and intuition: "informed stargazing" • Must be agile and open to course–correction • Unhampered participation • Culture is addressed *first* • Integrated with core values • A living document • Direct line of sight: Core Values → Strategic Plan → Actions
Priorities	
• Tyranny of the urgent • Crisis management	• Flow from strategic plan • People first • Service first
Performance Expectations	
• Numerics are the goal • The more performance measures, the better • Conflicting goals • Rating and ranking based on goal achievement	• Performance is the goal • Too many measures defeat the purpose • Goals are in alignment • Rate to standards, avoid ranking • Create an environment where excellence is *expected* and rewarded

Make Your Own Kind of Music

Try This...

1. Add a few customers and other stakeholders to your mission or strategic planning retreat.

2. Keep the plan in front of people. Schedule quarterly updates on strategic benchmarks–what has/hasn't been accomplished? Are we on target? Ten minutes in a Town Hall meeting or on an electronic message board is sufficient.

3. Link your decisions and major actions to mission and values. Referencing them routinely in this way links them in everyone's minds. A great way to prevent them from being "archived".

4. Hold a "values fair" where departments/teams exhibit how they fulfill one or two of the Core Values in a creative way. This not only causes them to think concretely, but sparks ideas in other teams.

5. How many rules do you have on your books? Set a modest goal to reduce that number. Have departments suggest rules to eliminate that would streamline their work.

6. Do the same with performance expectations. Tabulate the number of measures currently in place. Set a goal for reduction of measures and let employees suggest which ones to jettison.

 Note: Contrary to common belief, staff will not select the rules/ performance measures they don't like or are hard to achieve. You may be surprised at the wisdom of their choices.

Operational Synchrosystems

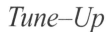

Tune–Up

Your service organization has received numerous complaints about computer-generated correspondence being sent to families of deceased contributors. This has now come to the attention of a Congressperson. Which answer best reflects servant leadership? *

1. You know you'll be pressured for a head to roll, so you begin disciplinary proceedings against the IT supervisor.

2. You discuss it with the supervisor and request a plan to correct the problem.

3. You call a team meeting to explore a process redesign.

4. You dispute the accuracy of the complaints.

"Operations" are the busywork of an organization; what is contained by the *administructure*. In the *symphony of service*, I see it as the horns, supplying a steady undercurrent of toots and oompahs that keep the orchestra on track; and every now and then a startling blare for emphasis or to reassert their presence.

"Systems" are the inner workings that underpin the effort, the functions that bubble up in our consciousness periodically, but are always just beneath the surface. Some of them are cool and sexy; others are more mechanistic, but they all exert an impact on service.

Operational functions move in systems—related parts working in synergy to create a product or fulfill a purpose. At their best, systems perform as an ensemble. Traditional organizations often devise well-oiled systems, but servant organizations strive to harmonize one system with another and, most importantly, to synchronize their systems with the principles or *charisms* of service.

That means that the tenets of servant leadership cannot be evident only in the outward amenities, but in the organization's internal mechanisms as well.

---

* ANSWER: 2 AND 3

Budget and Fiscal Systems

Accounting, billing, documentation. Counting widgets. The bottom line. Unless finance is your passion, it is often seen as a damper on creativity and an impediment to quality. Those in service or caring professions are reminded that if there's no margin, there's no mission—and that is certainly true. Sound financial management is an expression of stewardship.

Service professionals are constantly encouraged to understand the fiscal side of the house, but I don't often see fiscal folks being encouraged to understand the service side of the house. That is to the organization's detriment. There is no *back office* department that is exempt from servant leader ideology.

The customer service office may employ the right words and attitudes, but if the billing office uses language that is threatening or demeaning, the battle for that customer is lost. Quality of service in the customer's eyes is only as good as their last experience. Every department must sing from the same sheet of music.

In most organizations, budget is the driving force. I recall an episode where I approached a CEO to request a critical piece of equipment. The CEO turned to the Controller and asked if the funds were available. When the Controller responded that they were not, the CEO gave me an apologetic shrug. A few years later at another organization a similar situation arose. The CEO put the question to the VP for Finance, who stated that there was no money in the budget for this equipment. But instead of yielding, this CEO prompted, "Then how can we make the funds available?"

Traditional leaders are budget–driven. Servant leaders are service–driven. That does not mean that traditional leaders don't see the value of service, or that servant leaders don't understand the imperative of budget. But they make decisions differently based on their priorities.

In a servant organization, budget flows from the mission and strategic plan. Budget facilitates the mission and strategic plan. Finance systems are in synchrony with the mission and strategic plan. Fiscal personnel are clear on their roles as service providers—even in the back office—and how they partner with other staff to provide a total service experience.

Information and Data Systems

Information Technology and data systems are much "cooler" than budget. Oh, the possibilities!

Modern IT can collect, massage, manipulate, and translate fragments of information into statistical intelligence. It can compare, contrast, aggregate, and interpret data. It can be the height of big picture thinking or keep us mired in minutiae. It can supersede human judgement, confirm or deny human experience, and override human intuition. Some traditional leaders use IT to replace those human factors; servant leaders use IT to supplement and enhance those human factors.

The sophistication of the IT landscape cannot be refuted and no contemporary organization can compete without the most advanced technology. The opportunities lie in how we use it.

A proprietary health care organization spent millions of IT dollars on an application to maximize insurance collections, but put a program to catch harmful drug interactions on hold. A national for–profit chain concentrated its IT budget on complex staffing formulas that put quality at risk. One exemplary organization kept their IT business expenditures moderate so they could also invest in quality and safety systems.

How do your IT and data programs support your mission? How does your IT budget synchronize with your strategic plan? What do you measure?

One of the primary functions of IT is to measure: it measures process, performance, and results. Process measures lead to practice improvements. Performance measurement increases productivity and excellence. Outcome measures indicate our effectiveness in meeting organizational goals and values.

Aside from the obvious nexus to *administructure,* servant leaders can differentiate themselves in how and what is measured, how the data is used, and what comprises "results".

We are a results–oriented society. For reasons of stability, reputation, ethics, funding, and stewardship, *results matter.* The results that are measured in traditional organizations, however, are often one–dimensional or at least of limited dimensionality. They mainly collect results around statistical data and numerics. All results cannot be quantified, so they need to be juxtaposed with qualitative information and weighted for variables.

Do you measure the impact of workplace violence on staff retention? The effect of civility on worker's compensation claims? The significance of supervisor modeling on employee development? The efficacy of decisions that arise from consensus? The influence of psychological safety on innovation? Do you correlate how staff are treated with how customers are treated? How corporate community service projects increase service sensitivity inside the company? How moral authority generates more engagement than positional authority?

Servant leaders know that the best information comes from the totality of the data. They search for ways to quantify the unquantifiable and pin down the subjective. They *matrix* internal and external metrics, observation, and feedback into dashboards and balanced scorecards that broaden their perspective and inform their assessment. In so doing, they find new relationships and measurement connections that continue to refine their insight into the organization.

Quality Systems

Early in my career the catchphrase was quality compliance; later it became quality assurance; then quality improvement; and now that has been amended to continuous quality improvement. We have learned over the years that quality is more than meeting regulations: it is an ongoing process of raising the bar.

Quality is a nebulous subject—"We know quality when we see it"—but to avert unintended consequences, it needs to be defined, communicated, measured, and rewarded. Many organizations have a Quality Department of one name or another, but the best organizations have adopted quality systems. Quality is not the function of one person or one office: quality is a part of every employee's job description.

So what is different about quality in a servant leader environment?

- The Quality function itself: is it sufficiently staffed? Does it report to executive leadership? The Quality Office has the influence needed to maintain quality at the head of the agenda.

- It's not just what the organization does, but how it does it: the right actions, the right way, for the right reasons.

- It is heedful of the impact of quality on the consumer, the staff, and all stakeholders. Does it instill confidence? Motivate? Improve life function or capacity? Enhance reputation? Bestow a benefit? Quality is not viewed as a drain or a chore, but a happy challenge.

- Quality is integrated throughout the company and all staff comprehend what it means in their department. They can visualize and actualize quality.

- Leaders model quality in their work, their integrity, and their ethics.

- Individuals and teams methodically evaluate their quality: what can we do better?

- Quality metrics are publically displayed for personnel and customers

- Quality happens every day. It's not just a game of catch–up when an inspection is scheduled

Traditional leaders are most interested in respectable scores on their quality report card. Servant leaders take note of the figures, seeing them as opportunities for improvement, but are more concerned with substance than with scores. Intentional servant leaders are absorbed in creating a *quality culture* where employees take pride in surpassing standards and are rewarded for reaching new pinnacles of excellence—not because they are compelled to, but because they choose to. In a servant organization, quality is a path of perfection without the stigma of not being good enough.

Systems Improvement

All things are connected. That is the basic hypothesis of systems thinking. Servant leaders seek to understand as deeply as possible the interconnectedness of relationships within the larger system—between people, processes, structures, and beliefs.

> ONE IS AT ONCE, IN EVERY MOMENT OF TIME, HISTORIAN, CONTEMPORARY ANALYST, AND PROPHET—NOT THREE SEPARATE ROLES. THIS IS WHAT THE PRACTICING LEADER IS, EVERY DAY OF HIS LIFE.
>
> **ROBERT K. GREENLEAF**

We are predisposed to live in the weeds. The pressures of the workday and the *crisis du jour* keep many leaders earth–bound. From that vantage point, we see only what is in our immediate vicinity. It's hard to tell what's beyond that proximate space—how it might affect us and how it might influence our work—when we're slogging through the mud.

Locate your home on a Google map. As you zoom out, you begin to see the whole area, a nearby park, a small lake, the mall, etc. They no longer seem like disparate features, but part of a larger scheme. There's a short–cut you hadn't spotted before and a new neighborhood a few streets over. There's more green space than you were aware of and bicycle trails meandering through the community. Instead of trees, you see an ecosystem; where you saw roads, you now recognize a transportation system.

Or think about being in an airplane. At 30,000 feet you are able to pick out patterns and relationships you hadn't noticed at ground level. Flying at 30,000 feet or zooming out puts things in perspective. Servant leaders who zoom out at work can discern the flow of the organization, find and redistribute resources, share best practices, identify policy implications, detect where people and programs overlap, and where there are gaps. They distinguish linkages—systems—where they never perceived them before. And once perceived, they can be synchronized like intermeshing gears.

Systems thinkers are comfortable with complexity. I remember interviewing a candidate for a job in a newly restructured organization. This was a major shift, moving from a tightly centralized to a decentralized model. The new organization was to be considered a laboratory of innovation, so the future was fuzzy and there were many unanswered questions.

Ms. S. applied for a mid–level leadership post which she would be able to design herself. Most people would have jumped at the chance to build their own job, but Ms. S. had great difficulty. She was distressed that I could not fill in the blanks; uneasy at the open–ended job description; she wanted information I simply did not have and direction I could not yet give.

Despite this, I hired Ms. S., and it was a mistake. While she was highly skilled, she never adjusted to the flexibility and independence of her role, preferring the security of clear parameters. Ms. S. continued to work there until her retirement, but was never happy in the position.

Complexity comes with the territory. Traditional leaders often perpetuate complexity to consolidate their power. Servant leaders can not only handle complexity, they also take every opportunity to help simplify systems so they are less likely to break down or result in "glitches". There is great intentionality in Systems Redesign. Systems redesign programs can be nationally certified or home–grown versions. Regardless of whether we use formal redesign programs, we are always redesigning our processes.

Systems redesign is a philosophy that engages everyone in improving the work. Employee errors are frequently the result of design flaws that are hardwired into systems. If an automobile is designed to run at a maximum speed of 70 miles per hour, flooring the gas pedal will not make it move faster. If a computer is programmed to use only one type of software, there's no way you can engineer it to use another type of software.

The servant leader's task is to foster a redesign mindset throughout the organization. This often requires a change in the way we think about our work and who should be involved. The people who use the system know best how to redesign the system. That means interdisciplinary participation in redesign projects—anyone who touches or is touched by the process, commonly even including the customer. The function of the team is to redesign the process or system from the bottom up, removing any steps that don't add value and incorporating anything that is value–added *from the customer's perspective.*

Figure 5 shows the benefits of systems redesign from the viewpoint of the customer, the employee, and the organization:

Systems Redesign: What's in it for me?

Customer	Employee	Organization
• Convenience	• Quality product	• Collaboration
• Respect	• Safety	• Innovation
• Streamlined process	• Participation	• Cost savings
• Quality	• Streamlines the work	• Engaged employees
• Participation	• Satisfied customers	• Communication
• Partnership	• Predictability	• Optimizes team
	• Efficiency	• Catalyst for other changes

Figure 5

At a sports arena, staff were worried about the location of the defibrillator, in an office far from the playing field. In an emergency someone would have to run across the stadium to obtain the equipment. A team met to discuss the problem—a middle manager, the equipment director, the paramedic, a coach, and a player. They devised a proposal to purchase several additional defibrillators and locate them at strategic spots throughout the venue, and they pitched it to executive leadership. Not only was the proposal accepted, it demonstrated to the team the capacity of systems redesign.

There is too much to be gained in systems redesign to ignore: it is worth the effort. When staff begin to tune in to systems, they become conscious of design flaws everywhere: airport check–in and grocery store check–out; insurance billing systems and online complaint procedures; rigid official protocols and bureaucratic red tape.

Intentional servant leaders turn that scrutiny to the work environment where everyone knows what could be done better and how it could be done more efficiently—*but were never asked*; and then empower employees to *be the change they want to see.*

Managing Change

Even the gratifying, participative change of systems redesign is still *change*. Change is often misunderstood. Some common **misperceptions** that leaders hold about change (and my **responses**) include:

1. *"No one welcomes change, so I'll have to drag them kicking and screaming into the next company evolution."*

    Most people will embrace change if they:
    a.) participate in the change
    b.) understand why change is necessary, and
    c.) know how it will affect them. "What's in it for me?" is not a selfish question: it's an honest one.

2. *"Crisis is a powerful impetus for change."*

    90% of people do not change their behavior even when doing so will prolong their lives. The "burning platform" that many traditional leaders exploit to trigger change is a manipulative strategy and perhaps even an abuse of power.

3. *"Change is motivated by fear."*

> Compelling positive visions of the future are a much stronger stimulus for change.

> PEOPLE CANNOT MANAGE CHANGE WHEN EVERYTHING IS CHANGING. FIND SOMETHING THAT ISN'T CHANGING.
>
> **KIM S. CAMERON**

Have you ever seen the YouTube video "Swedish Stairs"? If not, check it out. The local government wanted to encourage subway travelers to take the stairs rather than the escalator up to street level. Healthy or not, it was a behavior change that just didn't get traction, until they made it fun.

The stairs were painted ebony and ivory to simulate a piano keyboard, and each step was engineered to sound the corresponding note. You can watch as people test the steps—gingerly at first, then more boldly, walking up and down and back and forth to play tunes on the stairway. Behaviors changed here because change was not coerced, but made enjoyable. The city gained the behavioral change it sought without having to preach a word.

Research tells us that change is more likely to occur if:

✓ Psychological safety is high

✓ Motivation for change is high

✓ The reason for change is persuasive

✓ The workplace culture is supportive of change

✓ Resistance is managed

Managing resistance equals managing change. Experts have found that there is a natural arc to change. It starts out flat (people are listening to/absorbing the prospective change). As they do, resistance actually increases (the curve drops below the base level). This is where leaders who are unaware of the natural progression of change panic and begin to take irrational actions to force the change. By assertively nudging the change along, however, it develops momentum and the arc curves upward toward acceptance and even enthusiasm for the change.

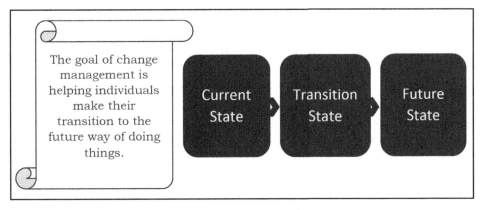

The goal of change management is helping individuals make their transition to the future way of doing things.

Current State ▸ Transition State ▸ Future State

Figure 6

On a number of occasions I was called in to assist large institutions that were scheduled to move into brand new facilities. Without exception, leadership felt they were managing the change responsibly and could not figure out why employees weren't cooperating.

My team spent countless hours interviewing supervisors and front–line staff, asking whether they understood and supported the change, what was working well and what wasn't, and what they thought management could do differently to ease the change.

Invariably we learned that despite management's attempts at communication, they were never enough. People needed regular updates on the progress of the change, and in multiple formats—written, verbal, and electronic. They needed to hear a consistent message throughout the leadership ranks (immediate and mid–level supervisors were often the least well informed).

By and large, staff wanted to support the change, but felt peripheral to the effort. They had ideas about streamlining the change and recognized potential problems, but weren't listened to.

Leadership took note of our findings, but in some instances, it was too late to make adjustments. For example, an expensive piece of equipment that couldn't be installed in the new workspace and a work process that would be fragmented by the new plant design ended up being sunk costs. Employees had been aware of these snags, but had no forum to voice their cautions. One person said of leadership, "If they don't have the courtesy to ask, they can just learn the hard way."

We did find plenty of "low–hanging fruit", junctures for management to get it right, even at a late point in the transition. In some cases, staff were simply worried about having boxes to pack up their belongings or how to contend with the new security system.

Giving employees a chance to personalize the change was invaluable—merely picking out a paint color, arranging their own office furniture, or bringing in a favorite picture sparked a sense of engagement in the change.

We identified issues with the parking garage, the bus routes, and emergency processes that had been overlooked, and as employees saw the impact of their suggestions, leadership found their change curve trending upward. When the facility moves were completed, open houses were held for staff, families, and customers, helping to sustain the trajectory of the change.

I have encountered some traditional leaders who are not really interested in the effect of change on those who will have to live with it. In their arrogance and autocratic style, it simply doesn't register.

But I believe that most leaders want to soften the discomforts of change and don't always know how. Intentional servant leaders plan the course of change, collecting input and ideas from the outset and communicating *ad nauseum* to keep all stakeholders in the loop. Along the way, they not only mitigate resistance, they cultivate champions.

When we don't manage change effectively, we can expect to experience (Prosci, 2012):

- Lower productivity
- Passive and active resistance
- Turnover of valued employees
- Arguments about the need for change
- Increased use of sick time
- Changes not fully implemented or sabotaged
- People finding work–arounds or reverting to the old way of doing things
- People disengaged
- The change failing altogether
- Divides created between "us" and "them"

Servant leaders facilitate change. They enlist everyone in the change; are open to feedback, listen, and reflect. They institute change for the right reasons and execute it in the right way. Because the change is not ego–based, servant leaders stay open to tweaking along the way. They share the credit when change goes well, and share concern, but not blame, when it doesn't. And because change doesn't happen in a void, leaders foresee and finesse the cultural implications of change.

Managing change is intentional. In learning to manage even the everyday or incremental changes, the intentional servant leader nurtures an environment that prepares staff for perpetual and transformational change. Change is not a light switch: it's an ongoing process.

> REVOLUTIONARY IDEAS DO NOT CHANGE INSTITUTIONS. PEOPLE CHANGE THEM, BY TAKING THE RISKS TO SERVE AND LEAD, AND BY THE SUSTAINED PAINSTAKING CARE THAT INSTITUTION–BUILDING REQUIRES.
>
> **ROBERT K. GREENLEAF**

Managing Change

By yourself or with a partner, recall 5 major changes you have experienced in your lifetime. Draw a timeline of your life and mark each change with an X at the appropriate place on the timeline. Select one change and share it with your partner, answering the questions:

- What made the change difficult?

- What was your key to success in dealing with the change?

- How did you feel before, during, and after the change?

- How did other changes going on around you affect your ability to deal with this one?

Some additional thoughts to explore:

- Did this change have an impact on you at work?

- What did you learn about the compounding effect of changes that are close to each other?

- What helped you navigate those changes?

- How can you learn to successfully cope with future changes from the lessons learned around past changes?

Analyzing your personal patterns of change and hearing how others have weathered change can strengthen your own mechanisms for change and resilience, sensitize you to the resistance of staff, and clarify the arc of change in your organization.

Ten Tips for a Trouble-Free Transition

Transitions are a fact of life. We transition from childhood to adulthood, military to Veteran, single to married and perhaps to parenthood, employment to retirement, and life to death. We move to a new home, start school, change jobs, celebrate a promotion, and weather the loss of a loved one.

Transitions are always difficult; bittersweet. There is always a *coming from* and a *going to*; a giving up of one existence and embracing another. Henry Van Dyke says it brilliantly in his poem, "Gone From My Sight", where he describes watching a ship disappearing into the horizon.

> AND JUST AT THE MOMENT WHEN SOMEONE SAYS, "THERE, SHE IS GONE," THERE ARE OTHER EYES WATCHING HER COMING, AND OTHER VOICES READY TO TAKE UP THE GLAD SHOUT, "HERE SHE COMES!"
>
> **HENRY VAN DYKE**

Transition is about people. Seasoned leaders retire and new leaders take their place, with the concomitant handoffs of responsibility, accommodation of learning curves, and establishment of trust. Transition is also about ideas—new work models; changes in policies, priorities, directions, and goals; and in reorganizing and restructuring.

Transition is the interstitial space between a known and an unknown state. Transition is hard because it leaves us suspended briefly in the *not knowing*. But it can also be a time of possibility or unfolding, when we stop clutching at what has been and become curious about what will—what can—be.

Sometimes we are responsible for leading change. At other times it's our job to accept and support the change. Whether you are adjusting to a new boss or a new IT system, adapting to a process redesign, or acclimating to an unfamiliar team or environment, there are some things you can do to make the transition easier and more successful:

1. **Communication**
   Be transparent: why is this change necessary? What do we hope to accomplish? What will it take and what is expected? What outcomes are we looking for? Be specific about what we're transitioning *to*; how it will look. Understand that all change is not welcome. If you are asked to support a change you believe is the wrong move or that will have unintended consequences, be honest with staff. "This idea will never work, but they're making us do it," is not helpful. Try instead, "I think we all have some reservations about this new approach, but let's talk about how we can make it work for our customers."

2. **Find the hook or "WIIFM" (What's in it for me)**
   We are all motivated by different things. An academic facility announced that it was planning a hiring freeze. The move motivated fiscal staff, but did not get teachers on board. Educators needed to hear that the freeze was expected to stabilize quality, provide opportunities for overtime, and decrease turnover. Help people find a reason to support the change.

3. **Create clarity and continuity**
   Every employee should be able to explain the reason and the plan for change. Walk around and ask—it's a good way to gauge understanding and correct misconceptions. Change is not an on/off switch and transition doesn't happen overnight. Convey a reasonable timeline and give regular reports on milestones. Talk about them in meetings, post them on message boards, and write about them in newsletters and emails. Dispel the notion that this is just another "flavor of the month". Show how the change will improve organizational health and culture, and link it to other established priorities and initiatives. For example, "Besides saving money, our new process will pay dividends in customer service and reinforce the effectiveness of our team."

4. **Listen first; invite feedback; grow investment**

    Supervisor A began a new job by telling staff on day one what he planned to accomplish in the first year. Supervisor B began by meeting with staff, listening to their concerns, and observing their processes. Supervisor A might have gotten off to a quicker start, but supervisor B is likely to have achieved the same or better results, made fewer mistakes or blunders, and earned the confidence and trust of staff.

    Creating an environment that encourages honest feedback can save countless missteps during transition. When a new informatics center was built, staff complained that the expensive computer equipment ordered would not physically fit into the new construction. Managers eventually sought input about the problem, but too late to avoid costly (and embarrassing) re–work. We can rarely wait until all the data are in to make decisions, but taking some time up–front to listen builds investment and averts error. Transitional blueprints must include "space" for inclusive dialog and interaction.

5. **Identify cheerleaders and champions**

    In any transition, there are early adopters. Some of them will be in leadership roles, but many will be informal leaders who, without benefit of position, enjoy the respect of their colleagues. People listen better to those who share common language and concerns. Doctors listen better to other doctors, accountants to other accountants, data techs to other data techs, union members to other union members. Find your champions from within the ranks. They are servant leaders in the best sense.

6. **Align the message**

    There are many layers in most organizations; many tiers of staff to reach. It may seem like you're communicating painstakingly, but employees at the front–line still don't seem to grasp it. You've given suggestions to the CEO about how to make the transition smoother, but have had no response. You're feeling ineffective both up and down the hierarchy. Like an hourglass, organizations tend to constrict in the middle. Supervisors are the gatekeepers of intelligence; the eyes and ears of the organization. Empower them to cut the red tape and shake loose the obstructions.

7. **Train and retrain: accommodate learning**
   Transitions often demand new skills and knowledge. Most
   companies offer plenty of training, but cannot always ensure
   that learning has taken place. Be sure to employ varied modal-
   ities—e.g. on–line and in–person; study and practice. Skill–
   building is not a one–time event. It needs to be revisited and
   reinforced regularly. Assuming everyone gets it can be a fatal
   error in judgement.

8. **Do it right, don't just beat the deadline**
   Delivering a product on time is important to credibility and
   accountability. A number of years ago, when a pharmaceutical
   company announced it would be bar–coding its medications,
   the idea was considered a cutting edge practice. A date was
   publicized for all its outlets to be up–and–running. The problem was that the equipment necessary to bar–code the medications would not be available to all stores by the starting date.

   Despite this, the executives did not reschedule implementation: it had been too well advertised. The upshot was that
   pharmacy employees were forced to create temporary "work–
   arounds", impairing the very safety the new system was meant
   to ensure. Delivering a sub–standard product to beat a deadline defeats the purpose.

9. **Be willing to fine–tune**
   A new leader inherited a capital improvement project that
   had been in progress for ten years. The original plans were no
   longer functional because of technical advances and customer
   expectations. When the leader suggested to the Board that the
   project be updated, she was told that it was too far along, it
   would cause public embarrassment, and it could be retro–fit-
   ted after the fact. There are many reasons we don't course–correct, but when new information comes along we need to "Stop
   the line!" Tweaking, fine–tuning, or course–correction is not a
   leadership failure: it's an ethical and accountable response.

10. **Celebrate**
    Surviving transition is victory! Everyone has worked hard to
    bring the change to fruition and your efforts have crystallized.
    You may also have reaped "secondary gains"—unexpected

outcomes—for example in engagement, psychological safety, or teamwork. Recognition and acknowledgement reinforce future change efforts. Don't wait until the final sign–off; celebrate milestones met along the way. *In servant leader organizations, celebration is an attitude, not an event.*

It helps when transition is anchored in a *constant*, for instance in an organizational mission or commitment. That *constant* provides an origin and a destination, a vision and a fulfillment, a purpose and a practice, an ambition and an achievement. In each of those counterparts exists a transition that is ripe with promise. And in each is a choice to serve; to serve better.

Whatever transition you are experiencing, let it be an opportunity to serve; to serve better.

Communication

We have and will continue to talk about communication in every section of this book because it is ubiquitous. I have highlighted it here since in the tedium of operational functions, it is easy to neglect.

If systems are the gears of an organization, communication is the lubricant that keeps them running smoothly. Communication sometimes seems so complicated as to be overwhelming. It can be botched and bungled in so many ways. At other times it is treated as a cakewalk, with little forethought and minimal effort. Leaders ping–pong between being overly–stressed about communication and being careless about it.

Simply, *the purpose of communication is to establish connection.* If you have ever had surgery, you know that an IV drip is typically inserted preoperatively. The IV might contain no medication and be infused at a barely perceptible rate. Its only purpose may be to *keep a line open.* Communication keeps the lines open. The leader may not need that open line today or tomorrow, but maintaining its viability is critical.

When it comes to communication, more is better. I don't believe it is possible to over–communicate, although it is not always necessary to be verbal. Sometimes a nod or a glance says everything. It's also more important to be honest than conclusive—no need to wait until all the "i's" are dotted before communicating.

I like to *speak in draft.* "I'm not certain where I'll end up on this decision, but here's what I've been thinking…" This approach has been particularly helpful with stakeholder groups and labor unions who are contractually guaranteed pre–decisional input. It's a practical tool to indicate intent, test reactions, elicit advice, and develop support.

If you are like me, you spend inordinate amounts of time crafting your message. Whether I am writing a paper, presenting a lecture, dashing off an email, or speaking at a town hall meeting, I struggle with the preparation, the clarification, and the wordsmithing.

I often get that right, but what about the times when communication is extemporaneous? Being prepared to communicate cogently and spontaneously is an art. I believe it comes from being immersed in servant leader charisms such as humility, integrity, and moral authority. Without the exaggerated pride of self–centered leadership, meaningful communication flows from the leader's heart in ways that genuinely connect.

Trickier yet is communication that takes place outside the realm of speech. I may have nailed the words, but what am I conveying through my body language, gestures, and tone? I have been caught eye–rolling when I wasn't even aware I was doing it!

Most challenging of all, are my words borne out in my actions? Do my decisions reflect my message? Behaviors are means of communicating. Think about what you communicate when you (Hess, 2013):

- Treat people with dignity
- Remain in the moment, not multitasking
- Refrain from interrupting others
- Listen intensely
- Smile, say please, and thank you
- Acknowledge the contributions of others
- Admit mistakes or apologize
- Don't have to be the smartest person on the room
- Spend time on the front lines with employees and customers

The Transactional Analysis model is useful in considering the impact of tone and non–verbals on communication. We communicate from one of three ego states: **parent (P), adult (A),** or **child (C)**. In the workplace, that can play out in ways that shape the relationship. Which of us has not been scolded by a supervisor at some point in our career? You arrive at work a few minutes late or make a mistake and the rebuke begins. You can picture the wagging finger or hands on hips; you can hear the brash and cutting words; you catch yourself making excuses; and you feel … like a child! That supervisor approached you from the ego state of parent, and you responded from the ego state of child.

Transactional Analysis Model
Ego States *(Parent, Adult, Child)*

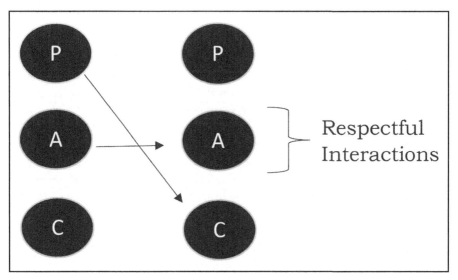

Figure 7

Respectful interactions arise from adult ego states, where we appeal to each other's maturity and relate from a level playing field. "Alex, you've been late for work a few times this week and I'm concerned about the effect on your performance. Is there something I can do to help? Let's talk about getting you back on track." The supervisor sets a respectful tone and so you respond, "Thanks. I'm working out a personal scheduling issue, but I think I have it resolved. I'll really make the effort to be more punctual." Adult to adult communication is courteous, caring, and productive.

Respectful interactions are as much about listening as speaking. Deep listening creates a shared space where profound understanding can occur. "One of the most common laments of our time is that no one really sees me, hears me, or understands me" (Palmer, 2004).

Listening connects and listening heals. It hears what is being said and what is not. The servant listener is an auditory satellite dish, roaming in all directions to pick up the signals. This is especially important when a power differential exists between participants. Unless the leader is very skilled and the environment is very safe, employees can retreat into silence or violence.

EVEN THE FRANKEST AND BRAVEST OF SUBORDINATES DO NOT TALK
WITH THEIR BOSS THE SAME WAY THEY TALK WITH COLLEAGUES.

ROBERT K. GREENLEAF

Take for example a CEO who calls a meeting to announce a new policy. When she asks for feedback, no one responds and she interprets the silence as assent. She doesn't hear the hallway conversations after the fact, where people are expressing vehement disagreement.

Servant leaders are judicious with their words, understanding that words are potent. They are also economical with their words. In one large group of peer leaders, several people habitually responded to every issue, and every response to every issue. There was hardly a statement made that didn't provoke a comment from these members. One or two others in the group rarely spoke up, but when they did, people listened.

Leaders take for granted that they communicate clearly and audiences grasp their meaning, but that is often not the case. Colleagues, particularly employees, may not feel comfortable asking questions so they make and act upon assumptions. There are as many interpretations of a leader's comments as there are people in the organization. Everyone filters the leader's communication through their own frame of reference.

To prevent misunderstandings that can result in serious errors or oversights, the servant leader anticipates confusion, spells out the message succinctly, and double–checks that it is accurately received.

With honest feedback, leaders become more attuned to employees' need for precision, relevance, and compassion in their communication style, and they are more likely to achieve the desired result.

Servant leaders communicate as coaches, not critics; they are generous mentors. They give continual feedback, reinforcing favorable behaviors and gently correcting less favorable ones. Employees of a servant leader never have to guess where they stand. There are no surprises. Constructive feedback is a gift and loving correction is a kindness. Servant leaders seek the success of their employees because by doing so, they ensure their own success.

"Your attitude is showing." Even when leaders do not intend to, they are communicating something.

To Centralize or Decentralize

All of the systems we've discussed in this section have to be situated in a configuration. Whether organizations are hierarchical, matrixed, autonomous, vertical, or horizontal in structure, the fundamental choice is between centralizing or decentralizing the power. That decision is arrived at by weighing several factors (Chapman, 1975):

> ➤ The kind of work your department does: creative people may need and be able to handle more freedom than production workers

> ➤ The individuals in your department: employees may react differently to the same climate

> ➤ The physical environment: it's risky to have a permissive climate around dangerous machinery or hazardous materials

> ➤ The kind of latitude you are given by your boss: a supervisor working under an autocratic manager might have a conflict if she allows a permissive atmosphere in her department

> ➤ The kind of oversight your organization is subjected to: government agencies and contracted functions often demand stricter control

While centralization is almost always an accumulation of power at the top, decentralization is "not so much handing over the steering as letting up on the brakes" (Edmondson, 2014).

The decision is generally made at the height of the hierarchy, but can vary as it works its way through the organization. Considering the factors above, some areas of an organization can function better with tight reins, some with looser control, and others in leaderless groups, regardless of the overall mood of the power structure.

It also reacts as a pendulum, moving from one extreme to another in response to internal and external events. I mentioned earlier an organization that was restructured to give more autonomy closer to the locus of service. It had previously been a tightly-managed, centralized organization. The new CEO wanted to make the 150 field facilities independent "workshops" of transformation. He decentralized much of headquarters' power to regional managers to whom the field locations reported. To the national headquarters group, this seemed like a massive wave of decentralization, but to the managers of the field facilities, it was still not enough. It all depends on where you sit.

The more decentralized approach worked well for a while, but as issues arose or failures occurred, headquarters gradually recaptured bits of the power until one day the pendulum had completely swung back. Recentralization did not take place because it was a superior model, but as an effort to reassert visible authority.

> THERE IS IMMENSE POWER WHEN A GROUP OF PEOPLE WITH SIMILAR INTERESTS GETS TOGETHER TO WORK TOWARD THE SAME GOALS.
>
> **IDOWU KOYENIKAN**

I have witnessed companies slide back and forth on the scale of centralization in hopes of finding the perfect balance, but in reality that is a fluctuating dynamic. The reason for the choice, however, should not be based on public opinion, political correctness, or personal power. It should always hinge on service: which model serves consumers most effectively, which uplifts employees, which one "stewards" the organization's resources, and which best serves the community.

Power vs Service

Offices that deal with regulation, policy, and administration are often perceived as bureaucratic, rule–bound, and insensitive to the customer. Servant leaders use power as a shared commodity. They exercise power on behalf of, not over, others.

List words in each column that describe characteristics of the model as your customers might see them. Do these describe your behaviors? Does this prompt you to make any changes in your power style? Does it help you find the "perfect balance" on the centralization continuum?

Power Model   **Service Model**

_____   _____

_____   _____

_____   _____

_____   _____

Contrast: Operational Synchrosystems in a Traditional vs Servant Organization

Operational Synchrosystems in the TRADITIONAL Organization	Operational Synchrosystems in the SERVANT Organization
Budget and Fiscal Systems	
• Organization is budget–focused • Decisions are based on funding • Budget drives strategic plan • Back office staff divorced from the service side of the house	• Organization is service–focused • Decisions are based on mission and values • Mission and strategic plan drive budget • Everyone is a "care giver"
Information and Data Systems	
• IT supercedes human factors • IT decisions follow the trendy technology • Data is statistical and numerical	• IT supplements human factors • IT decisions follow the mission • Data is qualitative, quantitative, weighted, and matrixed
Quality Systems	
• A function of compliance • Organization plays catch–up before a survey or inspection • Has a localized quality department • Quality is the responsibility of the Quality Manager • Quality metrics are considered protected information	• Quality is an ongoing process • Organization builds quality systems • Quality function reports to the C–Suite • Quality is integrated throughout the organization • Teams regularly evaluate the quality of their work • Quality metrics are publicly displayed

Operational Synchrosystems in the TRADITIONAL Organization	Operational Synchrosystems in the SERVANT Organization
Systems Improvement	
• Leaders are bound by everyday pressures or the crisis du jour • Systems/processes redesigned from the top • Systems/processes redesigned only when necessary • When something goes wrong, it must be human error (witch hunts)	• Leader regularly "zooms out" to see the big picture • Invites multi–disciplinary and customer participation in redesign projects • When something goes wrong, looks for systems errors (glitch hunts)
Managing Change	
• Change is centralized to avoid dissent • Communication is limited; change is coerced • Comfortable with complexity; complexity consolidates leader's power • Creates a "burning platform" to motivate change • Suppresses resistance • Not really interested in staff reaction to change • Course–correction is admission of leader error	• Invites wide participation in the change • Communicates liberally • Comfortable with complexity, but simplifies systems for better results • Change is managed • Creates a positive vision to motivate change • Mitigates resistance and develops champions • Course–corrects when new information comes along

Operational Synchrosystems in the TRADITIONAL Organization	Operational Synchrosystems in the SERVANT Organization
Communication	
• Communicates with words	• Communicates with behaviors
• Relates from parent ego state	• Relates from adult ego state
• When asked for input, employees can retreat into silence or violence	• Leader is skilled and environment is safe for employees to give honest feedback
• Communicates as critic	• Communicates as coach
	• Sensitive to non–verbal cues
Centralize/Decentralize	
• Accumulation of power at the top	• Not so much handing over the steering as letting up on the brakes
• Swings like a pendulum in response to events	• Model variable according to the needs of each department
• Choice based on public opinion and optics of power	• Choice based on which model serves more effectively

Make Your Own Kind of Music

Try This...

1. Decentralize budget responsibility closest to the customer. This teaches middle managers to balance funding and service, making them customer advocates. Allow them to negotiate their budget needs with those of other departments, so budget becomes a shared financial plan.

2. Issue a call for IT proposals. Proposals should include costs, return on investment, and system requirements. All proposals are linked to the applicable mission, value, or strategy. Compile the suggestions and ask staff to rank them. Use this information to develop an IT plan.

3. Quality is a nebulous subject—"We know quality when we see it". In a large group or town hall meeting, ask people to describe how they "see" quality in their work area, on their team, and in their own practice. This helps staff to visualize excellence, a precursor to actualizing it. Speaking this aloud solidifies their commitment.

4. Authorize a two day "time out" for all managers to select and complete a process redesign project in their area of responsibility. Pair each manager with a systems redesign expert to guide them through the tools and procedures. Leaders should not delegate this activity down the line, but actively engage in it themselves. To embed systems redesign into the culture, repeat quarterly, introducing more staff into the exercise.

5. Select a few employees from different departments and hierarchical levels to evaluate your communication skill. After issuing a written memo or verbal announcement, ask them to summarize the three most important points of your message. What did they hear you say? How do they understand it to affect their work? How did your presentation cause them to feel? Do this exercise regularly, rotating your evaluators.

Tune–Up   You have an ethical problem with the latest policy directive. Which is the best servant leader response? *

1. Follow the policy anyway so as not to jeopardize your performance rating and promotion potential
2. Instruct your staff to follow the policy loosely, but document their resistance to it
3. Act in accordance with the organization's Core Values
4. Have an honest conversation with your boss and subordinates

IN THE SYMPHONY OF SERVICE, CULTURE IS THE HARP. IT weaves its ethereal notes through the sounds of the other instruments. The presence of a harp raises the vibrations of the music and the consciousness of the orchestra.

Planet Earth is suspended in space and surrounded by forces of energy that influence life on the globe. It is enveloped by fields of gravity and atmospheric layers—troposphere, stratosphere, ionosphere—that protect us from harmful elements and keep us grounded. We seldom think about those fields or forces, but their effects are inescapable.

I once heard someone explain an atom as a collection of tiny particles existing in vast amounts of empty space—much the same as we describe our universe, but in microscopic relief. That is how I picture an organization—a body of related functions suspended in an *ethosphere*. The ethosphere is a field or a force that encompasses and enfolds the people and the work and, although we are only rarely aware of it, its effects are inescapable.

The ethosphere of an organization is its culture, beliefs, customs, norms, and values. Culture is a container for both the philosophy and the practice of work. It is identified in the subtle *feeling* of a place and in the

---

*   ANSWER: 3 AND 4

mundane details of daily work life. Culture is not a quality we can reach out and touch, but we gather clues about the culture by observing how employees and customers are treated, what behaviors are rewarded and which are not tolerated, how leaders deal with crisis, and the degree of openness and engagement of staff. Culture is the animating spirit of the workplace.

Culture leaves an almost palpable impression. Sometimes it meshes with the official "culture statement", but often it does not. The thing about culture is that everyone knows what it is and reacts accordingly. You sense the pulse of a place just by walking through the entrance. Some stores are welcoming and others are aloof; some clinics are professional and others are paternalistic; some businesses are inviting and others forbidding. It doesn't take long to pick up the cues. *Corporate culture defines the corporate character.*

Being employed in an organization is to be immersed in its culture. In a fearful culture, staff are in CYA (cover your assets!) mode. In a rigid culture, rules trump compassion. In a culture of accountability, we learn to trust. In a servant culture, employees flourish.

FAILURE TO CHANGE THE CULTURE DOOMS OTHER ORGANIZATIONAL CHANGE.

KIM CAMERON

Once the organizational structure and framework have been established, culture is Job One. The leader sets the culture in motion and reinforces it (or not) via every message, every decision, every action, and every interaction. You can't fake culture. Culture precedes strategic planning, budgeting—even service—because it is the axiomatic bedrock. Culture inundates, inoculates, and pollinates. A virtuous culture needs to be groomed and guarded. Service and good works soon perish in an unnourished or undernourished culture.

Intentional servant leaders achieve the ideal culture and they *enculturate* the ideals by ensuring a healthy organizational environment. Healthy organizations are where employees choose to work, consumers choose to receive service, shoppers choose to spend their money, students choose to learn, families choose to entrust their loved ones, managers choose to build a career, professionals choose to elevate their craft, merchants choose to do business, leaders choose to serve, and communities choose to support. "Choice" is clearly a hallmark of a healthy organization.

How Does the Leader Build Culture?

→ Start with mission, vision, and values. Achieve shared understanding and buy–in.

→ Construct policies, rules, plans, and budgets that reflect mission and values.

→ Consistently actualize core values. Everything the leader does and says affirms or denies his/her commitment to them.

→ Reward behaviors you want to replicate. Value–driven behavior spreads like a virus.

→ Deal with problem behaviors expeditiously. Don't wait for them to go away or infect the whole environment. One bad apple…

→ Create "fields" of service, ethics, respect, trust, and innovation that guide employee formation and motivation.

→ Leaders are the primary messengers of culture. Talk about it, keep it on the front–burner, and make it a customary part of conversation.

→ Link and label: link decisions, programs, results, etc. to the culture; label actions and outcomes that reflect the culture. Teach people to recognize the connections in order to foster commitment.

→ Clarify and communicate. Make certain your message is not misinterpreted.

→ Leaders are the primary models of culture. Watch your non–verbals. Align words and actions. Caution: this can be a key dynamic or a calamitous derailer.

→ Celebrate cultural success stories.

→ Go back to the top of the list: you're never finished. Remember to sustain your efforts.

Healthy work environments demonstrate "organizational ecology": the equilibrium between handling immediate tasks and concerns, and establishing systems that strengthen the organization over time.

Healthy organizations are agile in managing incremental change and astonishing in leading revolutionary change. Often their blueprint for success includes a leadership/cultural model that is *obsessed* with service and maximizes the contributions of all personnel. That kind of foundation *serves* the employee, *serves* the customer, and *serves* the organization. This is the essence of servant leadership.

Healthy organizations are not happenstance. They require a philosophical grounding, purposeful planning, deliberate action, collaborative communication, reinforcing behaviors, and a dynamic feedback loop. The outcome is continuous enhancement of all their "dashboard" indicators.

Figure 8

Healthy organizations—organizations of *choice*—must be *grounded on attention* and *founded on intention.* Attention (awareness) is rooted in intention (beliefs and attitudes). What we think and what we believe drive our behaviors. *Intention* is at once the source and the success of a healthy organization, affirming both the mandate and the magnitude of *intentional* leadership.

Healthy organizations and cultures have many characteristics in common, among which are teamwork, psychological safety, diversity, and ethics.

Teams

"Teaming" is not just an activity; it is a culture. Team cultures meld other qualities like diversity, psychological safety, and interdependence into a servant organization.

The contemporary work world is intricate and complex. The pace is phenomenal and the expectations are formidable. Organizations form groups to meet the demands of the job.

All collections of people are not teams. Merely sitting in the same office or sharing the same supervisor does not make us a team. Some assignments predispose to different arrangements: workgroups, task forces, details, committees, panels, etc.; all have their place, but teams exhibit special features that enhance their value to the organization (Katzenbach & Smith, 1993).

Workgroup	Team
• Strong, clearly-focused leader	• Shared leadership roles
• Individual accountability	• Individual and mutual accountability
• Group's main purpose is the same as the broader organizational mission	• Specific team purpose that the team itself delivers
• Individual work products	• Collective work products
• Runs efficient meetings	• Encourages open-ended discussion and active problem-solving meetings
• Measures effectiveness indirectly by its influence on others	• Measures performance directly by assessing collective work products
• Discusses, decides, and delegates	• Discusses, decides, and does real work together

Figure 9

Teams are microsystems that can experience all the delights and drawbacks of the larger organization. At their best, teams lighten the load, improve the outcomes, and strengthen the work community. At their worst, teams blunt individuality, develop dysfunctional "family" dynamics, and distribute tasks disproportionately.

In order to reap the benefits and avert the downsides, leaders aim to produce high–performing teams. The National Center for Organization

Development of the Veterans Health Administration has crafted a model called the Team Ladder. I borrow freely from this concept because it is a superior model. Barnes and White (2011) offer a masterful explanation, but let me give you the highlights.

Engaged, Effective Teams

Cohesiveness

Assessment & Responsiveness

Psychological Safety

Communication

Respect

Role Clarity

Civility

Purpose & Methods

Relationships   Functions

Figure 10

High–performing teams are simultaneously engaged and effective. Their success depends on meeting two key challenges: 1.) team relationships—how they approach one another and 2.) team functions—how they approach their tasks.

The relationship side of the ladder starts with the basics of civility (ground rules for interaction), moves on to respect and psychological safety (trust and openness among team members), which promotes cohesiveness (a climate that ensures the team's purpose and outweighs any personal agendas; mutual support).

The function side of the ladder must be scaled at the same time, i.e. step one on the relationship side is equivalent to step one on the function side. It's no good to be engaged, but not effective or vice versa. The first rung here addresses the team's rationale for existing and how it will accomplish its goals. Then on to role clarity, each team member knowing what the other is expected to do and how they interplay. Communication tackles how information will flow, and assessment and responsiveness calls for regular review of the team's processes, and how they will continuously improve.

The Ladder is helpful to the intentional servant leader as a road map. Before the leader can embark on that road, however, she needs to consider the vehicle. Who should be on the team? Is it merely a chance collaboration?

One CEO uses results from personality type assessments to form well–balanced teams, members with harmonizing talents and temperaments. Another organization applies what they term a "lattice" approach, matching the people with the project and reconfiguring teams as the project requirements change. Whatever the method, servant leaders design teams deliberately, to the benefit of the company and the individual team members.

At the top of the Ladder lies another opportunity: reward and recognition. The intentional servant leader awards teams that meet or exceed their goals. I found an organization that defines goals as completed work products (as specified in the strategic plan) **plus** achieving and sustaining the stages of engaged and effective teams. Measures are negotiated with team members so they understand them and "own" them. The team award is monetary and amounts are pre–determined according to levels of success. The team succeeds or fails as one.

Teams bring complementary skills, expertise, and viewpoints. Working in teams has a *potentiating* effect. Productive and satisfying teams have a chemistry. Their members play off one another. I build on your idea and you add to my handiwork. Our accomplishment is greater than the sum of its parts. Converging on a common function and a meaningful purpose, we simply do better together.

<u>Cohesiveness</u>

Teams regularly engage in exercises that take them out of the job pressures for a few minutes to attend to the strength of their relationships. Many 10-15 minute activities are available to help group members get to know each other better and find surprising commonalities.

First Job is a light and enjoyable exercise.

Ask each team member to write down their first job on a piece of paper. They should be specific about whether they liked or disliked the job and why. The team leader collects and shuffles the papers, then reads them aloud one by one, allowing the group to guess which team member wrote which response. When the round is over, the following questions could stimulate discussion:

- How did you guess who had which job (you might find age/gender stereotypes here, another topic for discussion)

- What similarities did you discover? (Most groups find unexpected similarities, such as all first jobs were menial, including the supervisor's.)

- What did you learn about your differences?

- Did your first job set you on a path to your present career?

- Does the exercise give you new insights about your team members?

- Does it create cohesiveness?

Serving is a Team Sport

THERE IS A YOUTUBE VIDEO I'VE USED OFTEN WHEN TEACHING ABOUTCARINGFOREACHOTHER.IN2003,DURINGABASKETBALLGAMEBETWEEN THETRAILBLAZERSANDTHEDALLASMAVERICKS,COACHMAURICECHEEKS AIDED13-YEAR-OLDNATALIEGILBERTINSINGINGTHENATIONALANTHEM.AFTER GILBERTFORGOTTHEWORDS,"ATTHETWILIGHT'SLASTGLEAMING",CHEEKSRUSHED OVERTOHELPHERANDTHEYFINISHEDITTOGETHER,ASTHEENTIREROSEGARDEN ARENACROWDSANGWITHTHEM.CHEEKSANDGILBERTRECEIVEDASTANDING OVATION AFTER THE SONG WAS OVER.

Cheeks could have left Gilbert hanging—could have stared at his shoes and waited for the debacle to be over. Cheeks was famous; Gilbert was a kid. He walked over to her, put his hand on her shoulder, prompted her, and then shared the burden with her. He turned potential failure into victory for the entire stadium. It occurred to me that Cheeks' definition of TEAM was not just his players and staff; in that moment he made Gilbert and the fans part of the team as well.

Being part of a team at work is serious and satisfying, and to achieve the best outcomes, we need to take joy in the triumphs and avoid the traps.

Team Triumphs

- *Communication.* Some teams are so attuned that they finish each other's sentences or intuit the next move. They develop non–verbal signals and become so perceptive in picking up subtle cues that they know what their colleagues need before they ask.

- *Group identity and role clarity.* A shared purpose can be powerful. Teams that are in sync spend less time in rework. They build trust, security, and solve problems together. They are more likely to learn, grow, and attain excellence, and less likely to get swamped in hierarchy. Multidisciplinary teams appreciate both their complementarity and individuality.

- *Pride and accomplishment.* It just feels good to do a job well. Reward and recognition are the icing on the cake.

Team Traps

- *Competitiveness.* While competition can provide a spark, it automatically separates us from the other teams. If compensation, recognition, status, etc. are dependent on how our team ranks, what's the incentive to collaborate? If there is only one #1 spot, to what lengths will my team go to achieve it? Is being #1 the goal, or is it exceeding expectations and doing the right thing?

- *Exclusion.* Sometimes the cohesiveness of a team rests on keeping others out. Teams need to be constructed with "semi–permeable membranes" that allow an ebb and flow of members and ideas. Staff will come and go; experts/specialists will periodically be tapped; customers and clients will want to be involved. If the team can't inhale and exhale, it's no longer a living organism. Add a dissenter to the mix—someone who will shake things up, toss in "what ifs", and help keep things fresh.

Effective teams are microsystems that form productive bonds from within. They also understand their position as part of an integrated macrosystem: reaching out, inviting in, and providing a welcoming, supportive environment.

I recently read about a health care organization that was plagued with the hospital–acquired infection *Clostridium difficile (C. Diff)*. While some research showed that *C. Diff* was caused by overdoses of antibiotics, this medical center was concerned about environmental factors. Were patient rooms properly cleaned? How about instruments and equipment? Was strict hand–washing being observed?

They gathered the team together to search for answers. The usual culprits were there—physicians, nurses, and administrators—to which they added housekeeping staff, sterile supply technicians, and even a patient. The results were astounding. Due to the input of the non–traditional team members, they almost wiped out environmentally–caused *C. Diff* altogether.

Who is on your team? Who are you excluding, because of rank, or status, or simple inattention? What viewpoint is missing? Team is more than a collection of bodies: it is a consciousness.

THERE ARE NO PASSENGERS ON SPACESHIP EARTH. WE ARE ALL CREW.

MARSHALL MCLUHAN

Psychological Safety

Psychological safety has been portrayed as the "canary in the coal mine". Good leaders nurture it and monitor it. They pay attention to the singing in the background because if the song ceases, it is already too late.

The poles of psych safety are _crisis_ and _institutional silence_. Psych safety is defined as an environment in which employees and clients have confidence to ask questions and bring up thorny issues _without fear of reprisal._ For personnel, reprisal might include public chastisement, loss of opportunity, or termination. For clients and customers, it may mean gaps in service, unsafe care, being ignored, discounted, or banned from service.

> PSYCHOLOGICAL SAFETY IS THE PATHWAY OF ACCOUNTABILITY.

Employees in a pyschologically safe workplace are empowered to "Stop the line!"; to call time–out when an error is about to be made or when a problem is imminent. This is a solemn compact of trust. Employees have to report errors for organizations to recognize and respond to them. They need to feel safe to take the interpersonal risk that reporting an error requires. _Constructive accountability_ blossoms in a psychologically safe environment where employees at all levels are willing to speak difficult truths, question authority, and admit mistakes.

We learn what we live. If we learn to mistrust leadership through personal experience or observation of the experience of others, we retreat into our shell. When we see messengers "shot" and colleagues ridiculed, we don't discuss what should be discussed and we don't report what needs to be reported.

> WHEN OUR IMPULSE TO TELL THE TRUTH IS THWARTED
> BY THREATS OF PUNISHMENT, IT IS BECAUSE WE
> VALUE SECURITY OVER BEING TRUTHFUL.
>
> **PARKER PALMER**

Research shows that psychological safety is an important ingredient for employees' willingness to voice important concerns. Barriers to reporting involve fear of repercussion, self–incrimination, organizational bureaucracy, excessive punishment, a close relationship to the violator, the belief that no action will be taken, and a desire to "keep the peace". This is crisis in the making.

For servant leaders, crisis prevention alone is ample reason to support a psychologically safe environment, but there are data to corroborate other gains as well (VHANCOD, 2011):

- Better customer satisfaction
- Fewer serious errors
- Greater accountability
- Collaborative problem–solving
- Increased civility and respect
- Improved quality
- Enhanced learning and innovation
- Preemptive systems corrections
- Higher estimation of supervisor

Traditional leaders are typically impatient with appeals for psychological safety, seeing it as trivial or irrelevant. Servant leaders appreciate the practical rationale for psychological safety, but prize even more its benefits in transparency of communication and empowerment of the workforce.

How People Feel in a... *(Shain, 2010)*

Psychologically Safe Workplace	Psychologically Unsafe Workplace
Energized	Demoralized
Engaged	Disengaged
Enthusiastic	Depressed
Calm	Anxious
Creative	Resentful
Helpful	Unhelpful
More likely to care	Less likely to care

Figure 11

Practice Period

Psychological Safety Contract

If you were to create a "contract" with your supervisor to ensure a psychologically safe work environment, what would you want your supervisor to agree to?

What would you be willing to agree to?

The terms of the agreement are not as important as engaging in dialog about psych safety. Schedule time for interactive discussion with:

a.) your direct supervisor, and

b.) those whom you supervise

How Does the Leader Ensure Psychological Safety?

✓ State your objective: "This is a workplace that values honest communication".

✓ Highlight your expectation: "You should expect truth–telling from me, and I will expect it from you." Hold each other accountable.

✓ Promise a safe environment for: respectful disagreement, saying "no", reporting systems errors and near–misses, admitting mistakes, prudent risk–taking, truth–telling, giving feedback, challenging unsafe or unethical behavior, etc. Make it a *covenant*.

✓ Ensure that managers throughout the organization honor your promise as well.

✓ Reward truth–telling. Both privately and publically, make your commitment to a safe environment visible.

✓ Regularly assess how your covenant is being kept:

  ➤ How do employees see me reacting to bad news?

  ➤ Are employees comfortable expressing ideas, even when they're in the minority?

  ➤ Would they report a serious error, even if no one else knew?

  ➤ What in our workplace might cause employees to feel reticent about owning up?

  ➤ Would my employees risk telling me "the emperor has no clothes"?

  ➤ Are they secure enough to engage in constructive conflict with their teams?

  ➤ What can I do to improve the perception of psych safety?

✓ Measure and publicize positive outcomes of a psychologically safe environment: improvements in accidents and worker's compensation claims, EEO complaints and union grievances, attrition and sick leave, employee satisfaction data, team performance, etc.

Diversity and Inclusion

Diversity takes an organization broader; inclusion takes it deeper. Traditional leaders understand the legal requirements. They follow them to the letter when they must and skirt them when they can. They look at Equal Opportunity as a trap: "I can't hire the people I want to hire and I can't fire the people I need to fire." They survive the system by avoiding problems and watching their backs.

Servant leaders perceive Equal Opportunity as a tool to develop a workforce representative of their clientele and community. They do not select candidates out of fear or coercion, but because they are the best suited for the job. They do not hesitate to discipline or terminate if performance or behavioral standards are not met. They recognize that some employee classes are granted special protections, but they take the right actions for the right reasons.

Intentional servant leaders go a step further and set about actively creating diversity in their ranks. They do not hire candidates because they are in a protected class, but are delighted when a protected class applicant is the top choice. They enthusiastically search for diverse candidates and develop them in–house to ensure a pool of high–potential employees for future positions of responsibility.

Protected class status is just the beginning for an organization that is truly diverse. Staff may be introverts or extroverts, poor or privileged, professional or blue collar, thrive on data or relationships, and hail from New York City or Kansas City. All of these contrasts add spice to the environment and richness to the work.

Servant leaders rejoice in the capacity these differences bring. They use that capacity to inspire excellence by bringing all points of view to the table.

Exclusion and Homogeneity

The case has been made for diversity and inclusion. The benefits are well–documented. Yet in a society dominated by politically–correct thinking, the pendulum may have swung to a precarious extreme. We have become a citizenry that does not tolerate dissent.

Diversity works because it generates variation in thought, attitude, and creative ideas. That variation arises from differences in background, culture, demographics, and lifestyle. *Inclusion* works because it allows the variation to be heard. It gives voice to the individual and power to the group.

For years I opposed gender–specific associations. I disapproved of all–male clubs and applauded men in predominantly female professions. Then one day I joined a women's fitness center. I struggled with the exclusivity of it, but soon realized that I felt more comfortable and less self–conscious in that setting. The truth is, I probably would never have signed on to a coed gym.

Studies done on academic performance in single–sex schools (Eisenkopf, et al, 2013; Novotney, 2011) indicate advantages in scholarship and self–confidence in gender–specific education. Some studies, although mixed, indicate a patient's preference for a physician of the same gender. I opt for a female doctor, and an older one at that, when I have the choice.

So is predilection for what is familiar actually exclusion? Maybe not. On one hand, it's important to stretch our consciousness and our comfort zone. On the other hand, we all should be able to make informed and enlightened choices. True inclusion is offering those choices and not barring the door to those who make different choices than we do.

Diversity is a plus in any organization. Understanding other philosophies, cultures, ethnicities, religions, and generations makes it less likely that we will engage in overt or unconscious bias. The multiplicity of insights improves decisions and strengthen teams. We simply do better work from a comprehensive frame of reference.

I worry, however, that in an atmosphere of blistering political correctness, we are actually losing the diversity of thought that efforts over the past decades have fought to win. Just writing this piece feels risky. More and more, we are being encouraged to share the same judgements, subscribe to the same ideologies, and support the same concepts. Less and less are unpopular opinions, unfavored viewpoints, and contradictory positions accepted in public discourse. Disagreement is a civil liberty; sarcasm, derision, ostracism, and contempt are not and, in fact, mock the very liberty we claim.

Where is the diversity in homogeneous thinking? In capitulating to "thought police"? In silencing competing values? In putting down or writing off perspectives not our own? Bullies can be found on any side of the political divide.

Uniformity—homogeneity—is monotonous and stagnant; it inhibits growth. Tolerance is the very least we should strive for. Better yet, let's work toward patience, acceptance, and charity.

A melting pot is of little value if we lose our uniqueness. I cherish our differences—what makes you, you and what makes me, me. In the workplace, diversity is celebrating our commonality and capitalizing on our individuality. We are each remarkable in our own right.

> STRENGTH LIES IN OUR DIFFERENCES, NOT IN OUR SIMILARITIES.
>
> **– STEPHEN COVEY**

Ethics

Around the time of this writing, several high–ranking government officials have come under scrutiny for ethics violations: accepting contributions from lobbyists, traveling on the taxpayer's dime, upgrading airline and hotel accommodations, etc. These are violations of the public trust, but they are not violations of ethics. Governmental ethics are more about rules—rules that have been established for good reason; policies that have been written to protect both the voters and the officials. In those positions one is easily tempted to eke out additional benefits here and there, bend the truth a bit, or get sloppy. Officials are mandated to avoid wrongdoing and even the appearance of wrongdoing. But as necessary as these rules and regulations are, they are not ethics.

ETHICS OFTEN BECOMES JUST AN EXTERNAL CODE OF CONDUCT THAT WE CAN PUT ON OR TAKE OFF DEPENDENT ON THE RULES OF THE PLACE WE'RE WORKING, DIVORCED FROM OUR VALUES & BELIEFS.

It was stated earlier that ethics is doing the right thing when no one else knows. That implies that the most stringent ethical monitor is ourself. Leaders are faced with genuine ethical issues all the time. Traditional leaders may limit their ethical purview to end–of–life decisions or codes of professional conduct. Servant leaders consider ethics more broadly.

Some problems are violations of both ethics and the law. In my practice that could include falsification of timecards, inappropriate relationships with vendors, or diversion of drugs. Those rise to a high level of concern, however in the scheme of things, they are easier to handle because there are formal legal and personnel processes that take the guesswork out of them.

Other ethical problems pose more of a quandary. Some deal with systems and processes where a policy, process, or performance measure is inherently unethical:

- Flu shots are made compulsory for all clients and staff (violates ethical principle of _autonomy, self–determination_)

- Departments that historically have received a greater percentage of budget will continue to receive an inordinate share (violates principle of _justice_)

- A contract with a long–term supplier is broken when another supplier undercuts them (violates principle of _fidelity_)

- A system has a design flaw that forces employees to take risky shortcuts (violates principle of *do no harm*)
- "Spinning" an incident or information to look better than it really is (violates principle of *beneficence*)

Leaders also contend with ethical problems related to environment and culture, occuring when expectations are not clear or when they are misinterpreted. This often has to do with the "messaging" of the leader, where the listener takes away a different message than what the leader intended.

What the leader says is:	"Do whatever it takes."
What the listener hears is:	"Manipulate the data so we meet the performance goal. Don't let me down!"
What the leader says is:	"I don't want to hear it."
What the listener hears is:	"If I know about this problem I'll have to do something about it. Just don't tell me."
What the leader says is:	"Read between the lines."
What the listener hears is:	"I'm not going to ask that you ignore that directive, but I hope you do."

Ethical issues involving systems and culture are particularly challenging because they stem from perception and personal interpretation. If the corporate values and ethical standards are not clear, if there are not honest conversations about ethics when situations present themselves, if employees don't feel psychologically safe, unexpected ethical snags will crop up and carry with them unintended consequences.

Intentional servant leaders anticipate the difficulties inherent in human organizations and ambiguous circumstances. They put counter-measures in place to minimize the possibility:

✓ Avoid misinterpretation by asking staff: "Clarify what you hear me saying".

✓ Communicate transparently

✓ Explain the values underlying a decision or action

✓ Label the ethical implications of an action or situation

✓ Be consistent; don't make people guess

✓ Recognize barriers to ethics and redesign questionable processes

- ✓ Observe what employees are doing; how they are meeting policy or fulfilling your direction
- ✓ Reinforce and reward ethical behaviors
- ✓ Teach basics of ethics to all levels of staff
- ✓ Model ethical behavior *always.*

Intentional servant leaders also consider the realm of administrative ethics. Resource allocation, personnel decisions, policy ramifications, restructuring determinations, etc. all have serious ethical dimensions. These are the administrative functions that seem perfunctory, but affect employees, customers, families, and business associates in stunning ways. The ethics of that impact cannot be overlooked.

Some organizations develop strong practices to ensure that ethics sensitivity is woven into the work. One facility assigned an "ethics advisor" to budget and policy committees to alert them to potential ethical concerns and build resolution into the decisions up–front.

An interesting new slant on this is the hiring of Ethical Sourcing (ES) officers to ensure companies buy goods and services according to the standards set by shareholders, customers, and employees. ES officers would, for example, review every contract and purchase agreement for consistency with the company's ethical goals.

True ethical dilemmas—where there is no right or wrong answer, or where there could be more than one right answer—require rational thought. One CEO built a Framework for Ethical Decision–Making (Belton, 2017), an algorithm to guide decision–makers through a coherent course of judgment.

Yet another leader set up an ethics "hotline" that allowed staff to anonymously report ethical concerns or ask help with ethical uncertainties in their work. Ethics Committes evaluated the calls for trends as well as assisting in ameliorating single issues.

And impressively, a system of health care facilities instituted an "Extreme Honesty" policy which obliges employees to disclose regrettable errors. This might be witnessed in a surgeon telling a family that a medical misadventure has taken place (the wrong leg amputated or a preventable death.) Or it could be seen in a mass mailing to patients who had undergone a procedure with improperly sterilized equipment, alerting them to the potential of infection. Despite the unlikelihood of illness and the media drubbings they have endured, this organization persists in their ethical response because "it is the right thing to do".

Ethics is an essential characteristic of a culture of service. It is a commitment to honesty and moral integrity—even when it hurts; even when no one is watching.

MAIN STREET Culture Map

Every facility has a perceptible personality or culture as in the "downtown" street below. Try to pick up cultural clues at the businesses you patronize.

		MAIN STREET USA		
Optometrist exchanges your eyeglasses until you are satisfied	Culture of excellence		Culture of accountability	Teller re-counts deposit & re-checks your transaction
Nurse negotiates a plan of care with you	Culture of respect, partnership		Culture of service	Waitress happily makes substitutions
Cashier follows you to car to give you correct change	Ethical culture		Bureaucratic culture	Long lines, strict rules
Clerk does what it takes to make the sale	Culture of engagement		Culture of accessibility	Salesperson helps customer with special order
You are introduced to the cadre of staff who will repair your car	Team culture		We/They culture	Stylist complains about management policies while cutting your hair

Is Servant Leadership Countercultural?

As a CEO in a major health care system, I often asked managers, "Would you describe yourself as a good corporate leader or as a good servant leader?" That always stimulated spirited discussion on both sides of the question. And I was always gratified when someone would respond, "What's the difference?" The obvious answer is that *there should be no difference.*

The truth is, there are organizations that bill themselves as servant leader institutions and are anything but. There are too many corners of leadership where command and control management still exists. Culture is the personality of an organization. It is pervasive. It is the way things are *really* done. Culture is reflected in decisions, actions, and attitudes throughout the organization, and leaders are responsible for setting the culture. What behaviors do you reward? Do your metrics measure evidence of serving and caring, patience and growth, humility, and team accomplishment?

Servant leadership is countercultural because it validates leaders who are inclusive, generously offering seats at the decision-making table. It is countercultural in listening, sharing credit, addressing others' highest priority needs, upending the hierarchy—in being *servant-first.*

Servant leadership is countercultural in the best sense. Given the cultural shortcomings of traditional enterprises, a counterculture of servant leadership would do well to become the "new normal".

Setting and Sustaining the Culture

Changing culture requires changing how people think about the organization and comport themselves in it. It necessitates designing new strategies, structure, and processes, but modifying behaviors, attitudes, and performance is infinitely harder. Yet change is rooted in behavior.

Edgar Schein asserts that no matter what other systems the organization puts in place, the primary mechanisms of culture change are the leader's actions (Schein, 1992). Further, to continually reinforce the importance of servant leadership and to institutionalize it within the culture, organizations must evaluate managers on aspects of servant leadership in performance reviews, rewarding and promoting those who are the best examples of the servant leader (Claar, et al, 2014).

Leaders, and especially senior executives, should be asked to demonstrate how they model and support servant leadership throughout the hierarchy. The most obvious step an organization can take to establish a culture of servant leadership is to hire people who already have the desire to serve others, by adapting the interview process to sift and select for servant leader qualities (McCarren et al, 2016).

Maybe your organization's culture is already headed in that direction, so changing your culture is not as much an issue as sustaining it. Traditional leaders are impatient to measure change and often give up prematurely if the metrics don't demonstrate quick results. Servant leaders allow time for culture to take hold and grow, to develop organically. They are *intentional* about cultivating servant leadership for the long haul, initiating a persistent stream rather than a crushing surge.

To maintain the momentum, servant leaders plan regular events that reinforce the principles and ripen the practices. Time for support and reflection—both self and team—is scheduled into the work day. Accommodation for leader and supervisor turnover is factored in for smooth transitions.

Intentional leaders methodically communicate and model the behaviors they want employees to adopt, understanding that *every* staff member must personalize them to their own scope of work.

The concept of quantum emergence affirms the impact of every organizational member. Envision a school of fish that swims as one body. They turn and dive and move in unison. They appear to be synchronous, connected in some intuitive way. I often say that culture change must be top–down, bottom–up, and side–to–side. In organizations where leaders set the cultural tenor or where leaders float in a cultural void, emergence can take over, rendering staff interdependent on each other instead of dependent on one person at the summit.

Emergence demonstrates that we're all leaders, all the time. What a novel concept! Only then does the environment become a culture of servant leadership. Only then does it become a servant institution.

Culture **Snap**shot

Below is a snapshot of cultural profiles adapted from Cameron and Quinn's Competing Values Framework. It highlights four culture types, their charateristics and values, best behaviors, and worst behaviors.

Which profile describes your current organization? Which profile describes where you would like your organization to be? Servant leadership can be found in each profile.

	Collaborate	Create	Control	Compete
	Group Culture	Entrepreneurial Culture	Bureaucratic Culture	Rational Culture
Values:	• Teams • Relationships • Civility • Consensus	• Innovation • Reasonable risk–taking • Adhocracy • Independence/team	• Hierarchy • Structure • Standards • Consistency • Process	• Reliability • Performance • Measurement/ • data • Competition • Market forces
Best:	• Fairness • Justice • Information flow • Participation	• High trust • Psychological safety • Continuous improvement • Opportunity • Reward	• Reliable • Supportive • Systems-thinking	• Customer–driven • Advocacy • Accountability • Results–oriented • Stewardship
Worst:	• Closed • Protective • Clannish • Defensive	• Lone Rangers • No tradition • Lack of continuity • Too much risk	• Low trust • Work–arounds • Rule–bound • Slow • Red tape • Limited information • Work in "silos"	• Trust but verify • Win at any cost • Spin the message • Data–myopic

Figure 12

Contrast: Culture in a Traditional vs Servant Organization

Culture in the TRADITIONAL Organization	Culture in the SERVANT Organization
Build and Sustain the Culture	
• Culture is fluff • Organizational health is fluff	• Culture is Job One • Culture is the animating force • Leaders build the culture • Culture eats strategy for lunch • Culture encompasses mission/vision/values • Healthy organizations support culture • Healthy organizations are obsessed with service • Leaders create a plan to sustain the culture
Teams	
• Workgroups are not teams • Groups form by happenstance • Employees rewarded individually • Group effectiveness ignored in favor of work products • Cohesiveness left to chance	• Encourages high–performing teams • Purposeful • Deliberately constructed • Attends to both relationships and tasks • Team rewards: measures work products + team effectiveness • Regular efforts at cohesiveness

Culture in the TRADITIONAL Organization	Culture in the SERVANT Organization
Psychological Safety	
• Climate of institutional silence • Messengers "shot" • Crisis in the making • Employees disengaged and demoralized • Suppresses reporting of errors	• Employees are empowered to "stop the line" • Engenders constructive accountability • Safe environment for disagreement, admitting mistakes, truth–telling • Employees energized and engaged • Rewards reporting of errors
Diversity	
• Follows legal requirements when necessary • Avoid problems/ watch your back • Focuses on diversity of protected class employees	• A tool to develop workforce excellence • Takes the right actions for the right reasons • Seeks diverse candidates and grows a diverse succession pool • Broadens the definition of diversity to add richness to the work
Ethics	
• Ethics = regulations and external codes of conduct • Ethical issues often the result of unclear or misleading messages • Leader sees ethics as situational • Limited definition of ethical issues (end of life, etc.)	• Ethics are tied to values and beliefs • Leader is the primary model • Communicates clearly and institutes measures to prevent misinterpretation • Ethics involve critical decisions, administrative decisions, and preventive decisions

Make Your Own Kind of Music

Try This...

1. Research existing culture assessment tools or design your own. Cameron & Quinn's Competing Values Framework is an easy to use and adaptable model (Dignosing and Changing Organizational Culture, 2011). Find a baseline and re-evaluate periodically. Once you know where your organization is, determine where you want it to be and develop a plan to move toward your desired culture. **A critical step.**

2. Discover how your stakeholders view the organizational culture by listening. Schedule an "Administrator on the Hot Seat" Day in the major areas of your responsibility (facility, branch office, department, etc.). Camp out in a private space *on their turf* where people can have one–on–one time with you to talk about anything they choose: complaints, suggestions, concerns, compliments. Listen and let them know how you will follow up.

3. Or, make Culture Rounds in those same areas of responsibility. As you walk about, 1.) try to identify the "personality" of that area in a few words and 2.) look for evidence that reflects the culture of the larger organization (behaviors, documents/notices, work spaces, etc.). Share your observations with staff.

4. Encourage work areas to "brand" their culture. Groups list the characteristics and behaviors they agree to adopt that will identify or brand their office/unit/program as a servant leader workplace, and how that will play out in daily operations. Let them create a logo that represents their servant leader brand and share it with other groups.

5. Locate or design a Team Assessment. The Team Ladder is a great example. Use as an educational and review tool to emphasize the value of teams in a servant organization.

6. Build a library of team–building exercises (many are available online and in the public domain). Urge supervisors and managers to use activities regularly, as in scheduled staff meetings or at the start of a work day.

7. Identify a PC–Free Zone—a place, a time, and a person where people can ask sensitive questions without fear of being politically incorrect: what they always wanted to know, but were afraid to ask. This cultivates genuine curiosity about experiences and viewpoints of ages/races/gender outside the questioner's own frame of reference. Set ground rules that will screen out harmful or insincere queries, and select "owners" of this process who are open, tolerant, helpful, and effective communicators.

8. Establish a Psychological Safety Covenant with staff. Commit to ensuring a safe environment and state how you will accomplish that. In constructive dialog, ask colleagues and subordinates to commit to support a safe environment and define how they will do that. Each group should be as specific as possible. Agree to hold each other accountable, indicate how that will be implemented, and set a date to review effectiveness from both staff and leadership perspectives.

   Keep in mind that some degree of psychological safety is groundwork for this activity. If that does not exist or if trust has not been established, people will not go there with you. Communicate your intentions and begin the pre–work necessary to build that trust.

9. Assign an "ethics advisor" to significant boards, committees, and decision–making bodies. This person does not have to be an expert, but is familiar with ethical principles. The advisor is not meant to be an "inspector", but to *red–flag* decisions or policy discussions that have ethical overtones or may lead to ethical repercussions. The function of the ethics advisor is to raise awareness and refer to the group for consideration.

Humanagement

Tune–Up   *Trust in the workplace means that leaders:* *

1. Delegate duties they do not want to do themselves
2. Provide stretch assignments and growth opportunities
3. Avoid micromanaging
4. Maintain accountability
5. Are no longer responsible for the tasks they delegate

IN THE *SYMPHONY OF SERVICE*, HUMAN RESOURCES ARE THE CHOIR.

Adding a chorus to a symphony orchestra makes it personal. It softens the instrumental timbre and, very literally, gives it voice.

Humanagement is like that: it civilizes the instrumentation of business. It connects people to the administructure and blends them into the synchrosystems, transforming the work environment into a work culture.

Leaders often delegate this work to the Human Resources Department, but HR is more than a physical location and a cadre of Personnel experts. I am aware of organizations that value their HR departments, respect their counsel, and include them on the executive management team. I know others where HR is feared, used as the disciplinary arm and the disseminator of bad news. How an HR department is situated and regarded tells whether it performs merely a transactional function or is an advocate and facilitator of the organization's most precious assets.

HR transactions may be the responsibility of the experts, but HR principles are every leader's job. I coined the term *Humanagement* to characterize an attitude of caring and commitment to those whom leaders lead; those whom leaders serve.

Management is the directing or supervising of something; the hard skills.

Leadership is the art of getting things done through people; the soft skills.

Servant leaders must be adept at both. ***Humanagement*** melds the two. It sensitizes leaders to the human impact of hard choices and reminds us that the human side of decisions, actions, and interactions *comes first.*

DIVIDEDNESS IS A PROBLEM FOR EMPLOYEES WHEN SUPERVISORS HAVE PERSONNEL HANDBOOKS WHERE THEIR HEARTS SHOULD BE.

PARKER PALMER

The contrasts bear examination. In traditional organizations, employees are often seen as a means to an end, pragmatic and utilitarian. Nowhere is this spelled out in a mission statement, but it is patently self–evident. These are the companies that clamor for technology and robotics as substitutes for staff, who use reductions in force as a first resort for belt–tightening, or who drain front–line budgets to fatten the bottom line.

They are the leaders who treat workers as commodities, who hire part–timers to avoid paying benefits, whose rules and policies typically disadvantage the rank–and–file. These are the leaders who relegate the "people problems" to unempowered personnel offices and see relationships as a distraction to the *real work.* This may sound harsh, but whether such behavior is deliberate or inadvertent, insensitive or uninformed, callous or careless, the results are the same: a disheartened, detached, and exploited workforce.

Traditional managers have little distress about the impact of corporate decisions; they are adept at divorcing expediency from sentiment, absorbed by the need to perpetuate *the command and control* fiction. "Don't take it personally; it's just business," is a familiar mantra.

Servant leaders are *humanagers.* In my experience, these leaders have discovered that their business goals are not achieved in spite of human resources, but as a result of them. Subscribing to servant leadership or *humanagement* in no way lessens responsibility or excuses mediocrity. If anything, it heightens a sense of duty and stewardship. The *humanagers* I know supersede the expectations of society and the restrictions of their traditional counterparts by becoming a filter of goodness in an exacting workscape; a blessing, not a burden in their sphere of influence.

Humanagers are **intentional.** They understand the rules, and they understand how rules affect people. They are devoted to their mission and true to their staff. They motivate, meaning to arouse and compel, and they inspire, meaning to fill with spirit. You can't do those things from a *leader–first* position! You can't navigate this course without conviction, courage, and a strong internal compass!

The myth of command and control is founded on erroneous—and dangerous— premises:

- The leader must know everything
- If something goes wrong, it's the leader's fault
- Organizational culture does not permit failure

Servant leaders—*humanagers*—recognize that even with the best due diligence, *things happen*. Environments cannot be controlled; at best they can be managed. Complications cannot be eradicated, but they can be diminished. Employees can be ignored, misused, or coerced for a time, but eventually they will disengage, sabotage, or retire in place.

There's nothing impersonal about firing, freezing wages, abolishing jobs, shutting down a department, forcing overtime, etc. *Humanagers*—servant leaders—make the hard decisions, but they take the consequences of their actions *very* personally.

> LIFE IS ART, AND WORK IS THE CANVAS ON WHICH WE DISPLAY OUR SOULS.

Let's look at some of the most common functions of leadership and what they might look like in a servant organization.

How do Servant Leaders Hire Differently?

I have worked in institutions that hired any warm body that walked in the door. Some places are too remote, have a dicey reputation, or aren't competitive with other employers. Hiring is a process, not an act. Humanagers begin by setting the stage—creating an environment that entices the best applicants.

One organization is located in a rough neighborhood and pays a tad below scale, but there are multiple candidates for every opening.

What draws them? A customer service mentality that stresses excellence, regards employees as "partners", and authorizes them to make independent decisions to please patrons.

A well–known hospital turns away candidates without a track record in patient–centered care. Despite a below average salary range, being   accepted there is such a badge of distinction that contenders are happy just to be on the waiting list. Intentional servant leaders recognize their organization's special niche and highlight it. Make your place of work special. Everyone wants to be part of something special.

Interviewing is often perfunctory in traditional facilities. In some places (e.g. government), interview panels ask questions but do not answer them or respond to the candidate in any way. Interviewees leave the meeting with little idea how they were perceived. This effort to "neutralize" the experience and be uniform from one applicant to another numbs the impressions of the interviewers and does little to help differentiate the candidates.

Humanagers ensure interviews are fair and consistent, but they connect   with the applicants and make it comfortable for them to shine. They formulate interview questions that unearth examples of the organization's values: "Tell me about a time that you gave exceptional service to a client or colleague", or "Relate a story about a mistake you made and how you applied what you learned in another situation," or "Give an example of an ethical concern you had and how you dealt with it."

Servant leaders call upon the wisdom of others to help make the best decisions. Some organizations use multiple interview panels to garner the most comprehensive input. For executive positions, I always appointed a senior leader panel, a panel of managers from collaborating departments, a panel of customers and external stakeholders, and often a panel of subordinate level employees. In environments where that was not possible, I arranged for front–line staff to meet and casually assess candidates on a tour of the organization. Rather than demand firm choices from each panel (which may be divergent), I generally asked, "Who could you not live with?" This gave me enough leeway to choose while respecting their deliberations. The panels understood their role was advisory and that I would consider their feedback when reaching my decision.

Humanagers know that "warm bodies" don't solve staffing problems, they exacerbate them. They are judicious up–front in selecting people who share the organization's values. Skills can be taught. This is tough where hiring options are limited. I admit I once hired a man experienced as a boiler operator for a nurse aide position: he was not an intuitive choice, but a willing learner and service–minded, and he became a favorite of the patients.

Humanagers match the candidate with the job. I'll never forget the greeter who accumulated one complaint after another until the CEO finally had to do something. When he informed the greeter that she was not making the grade she responded, "I hate people! I never wanted this job; I wanted to work in the file room!" The CEO accommodated her—a win/win solution and a lesson learned.

Too often leaders try to fit square pegs into round holes. Employees are not interchangeable parts. Servant leaders who take the time and interest to match skills, personality traits, and career goals with position requirements are more likely to hire—and to retain—the stars. And finally, they do not keep the applicant on tenterhooks, waiting for a decision. They make the choice timely, allowing unsuccessful candidates to move on.

Humanagers couple facts with intuition. Servant leaders are not afraid to listen to their "gut". I have made some of the most spectacular hiring decisions of my career with an ear to my instincts.

One servant leader author recommends abolishing the conventional probationary period for new employees. I'm intrigued by this idea, although I have never worked in an organization where this was permitted. It is, however, a reasonable sequela of sound interviewing and selection.

A probationary period is technically a free pass for either party. The boss can terminate without notice, often without counseling or any attempt to salvage the employee. The new hire can quit without explanation. It's a kind of "trial marriage", with no real commitment and an easy out. If the employee has taken care in researching the job, he should be willing to jump in with both feet. If the leader is confident in the process and in her judgement, eliminating probation seems a gamble worth taking. In the vernacular, "go big or go home".

How do Servant Leaders "Onboard"?

In many organizations onboarding, or orientation, is mechanical. In fact, some wouldn't provide it at all if there were not professional or regulatory requirements to do so. Orientation is a matter of bringing new hires up to speed. They can be dull affairs. My orientation to one job was six weeks of reading policy manuals! "Onboarding" implies a welcome and a commitment—an acceptance to the team. Servant leaders receive new employees with hospitality.

They also afford an experience that is interactive, engaging, effective, and just–in–time. No sitting and listening to "talking heads" for hours on end. Orientees learn what policies will mean to them, how they can translate the mission and values to their particular work, and practice the skills they will need. A nursing home oriented staff to the effects of sensory deprivation or loss of bodily functions common to residents by letting new hires spend time blindfolded, restrained, or sitting in a wet chair. This brought instant understanding and empathy; it was effective and not easily forgotten.

Trainees do not have to absorb everything at once. As a matter of fact, alternating didactic sessions with actual time in the work area brings the training to life, makes them informed learners, and assimilates them more readily into the team. In a servant organization, orientation may occur in bursts, with new information presented when needed (just–in–time); and when it will make the most sense. Onboarding is not a one–time activity: it is tailored to the needs of the individual and reinforced periodically.

Humanagers take a personal role in onboarding. They are the service storytellers, the mission champions, and the values cheerleaders. They capture the hearts and imaginations of the newly hired and galvanize them to act as co–owners of the organization from Day One forward. Servant leaders do not micromanage the task of orientation, but comprehend completely how eloquent their presence in the process can be.

How Important is Retention to the HUMANAGER?

Retention is just common sense. Recruitment, interviewing, and selection can be a nightmare—a time–consuming and expensive one. Vacant positions wreak havoc on performance and morale. Employees *transitioning out* are not the most productive and already beginning to disinvest. Employees *transitioning in* struggle with a learning curve and admittance to the group culture.

People who feel accepted by the group, who are given rewarding and challenging work, and who have a satisfying relationship with their supervisor, tend to remain with the organization longer and contribute more fully.

At a rural hospital, recruitment of nurses was a perpetual trial, so retaining them was imperative. Leadership commissioned a survey to determine what elements weighed most heavily in staff decisions to remain. They were asked to rank twenty five retention factors in order of importance, #1 being the most important and #25 the least important. Responses were aggregated and correlated with the levels of Maslow's Hierarchy of Needs (Ganong, 1976). The findings sparked changes in employee programs, education and development, and administrative stability. Three years later, during which time recruitment spiked and attrition slowed, the survey was repeated. Allowing for some effect of turnover, the results (edited below) were startling.

Ranked Motivation Factors	Year A	Year B (resurvey)
High level care provided	14	2
Adequate RN staffing	9	4
Appropriate professional use of RNs	19	3
Appropriate use of ancillary staff	5	11
Recognition	17	8
Good administrative support	7	1
Professional relationships	22	5
Competitive salaries	1	13
Desirable hours/shifts	4	10
Benefit package	3	12
Safe and conducive working conditions	2	20

Figure 13

The primary motivating factors in Year A were clustered at Maslow levels I and II. As those basic needs were addressed and staff grew more confident in their environment, those outcomes changed dramatically, with levels III, IV and V emerging in importance in resurvey Year B (Belton, 1984). This information and the consciousness it ignited were invaluable for recruitment and retention well into the future.

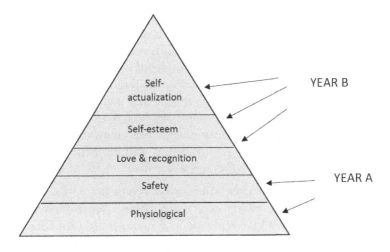

Figure 14

In my parents' day, jobs were kept for a lifetime. That is not the case today. Staff don't necessarily jump ship for better pay, and we know that when employees leave their company, they are often actually leaving their supervisors. Workers seek advancement and growth opportunities, meaningfulness in what they do, a sense of belonging, and a chance to be their highest selves. Servant leaders—*humanagers*—feed those dreams. Give people a reason to stay.

What is Different about the Way HUMANAGERS Motivate and Inspire?

Motivation in many organizations is one–size–fits–all: a uniform benefit package, a pre–determined career ladder, or a performance bonus plan. Those "motivators" might seem exciting at the start, but soon lose their cachet. Benefits are situational—you may not need child care and you have health insurance through your spouse. What looked like a steady promotional path might become an obstacle to quicker progression. The year you don't receive a bonus is a bigger deal than all the years you did.

People need different things from the workplace, and those needs are not static. A change in life circumstances can knock someone in

Maslow's level III back to level I in an instant. Traditional leaders make assumptions about what motivates their staff. Servant leaders ask.

In addition to one–on–one communication, servant leaders use satisfaction surveys to gauge collective opinion. There are a number of considerations here including:

- Proprietary or home–grown? Cost is one issue, statistical rigor is another. Be sure your survey measures what you want it to and that it can be cross–referenced in useful ways.
- How often? It's helpful to accustom staff to an annual schedule, but once a year might be too much. Give yourself enough time to make changes and give employees time to recognize them.
- Follow up. The biggest reason employees "blow off" surveys is because they don't see results. Asking staff for their opinions, then failing to act on them, is worse than not asking at all.

Humanagers have regular conversations with employees and colleagues to "take the organizational temperature". What do you enjoy most about the job? What keeps you up at night? If you could drop one task from your job description, what would it be? What talents do you have that are not being used in your work? Where do you want to be in five years? How is your work/family balance?

Servant leaders treat each person as an individual. Every employee who reports to you has a job goal, a work style, a communication preference, an ambition, a dread, a driving force, and a home situation that is unique to all others. I have supervised workers who are motivated by an upgrade, a learning opportunity, a stretch assignment, a compressed work schedule, a snazzy title, some extra attention, or a chance to innovate. *Humanagers* find out what motivates each person and they pursue ways to accommodate them.

No one suggests that leaders must satisfy all the needs of their employees, but *humanagers* are sensitive, observant, and generous in addressing the high priority needs of others. To be honest, this is not merely altruism, it is smart. People who feel personally motivated and uniquely inspired develop deep loyalty to the leader and deep commitment to the organization.

Practice Period

Factors That Motivate Me

Select the five factors that motivate you most.

_____ Physical working environment
_____ Opportunity to learn
_____ Recognition from management
_____ Recognition from colleagues
_____ Salary and fringe benefits
_____ Opportunity to do quality work
_____ Job security
_____ Harmonious relationships with co-workers
_____ Autonomy
_____ Being treated as an individual
_____ Job location

Do you see a pattern? Can you identify the commensurate level on Maslow's model?

Do Servant Leaders Promote Differently?

Not everybody wants to climb the ladder in the same way. Some people don't want to climb it at all. In traditional organizations, this is anathema; it connotes laziness and lack of initiative. Traditional companies soon sort out those who lack initiative.

But that may be a mischaracterization. I know professionals who want to move forward in their field of expertise, but have no interest in management roles. The brightest doctor doesn't always make the best administrator, and the most gifted accountant isn't necessarily a good supervisor, but there may be little choice.

Sadly, management is often the only route to advancement. I have worked with mid–level supervisors who acknowledge their limitations and do not want to "Peter Principle" in a bigger role. And there are front–line employees whose greatest satisfaction is working directly with clients and customers and have no desire to forfeit that.

People are the best judges of their own competence, what will make them happy, and where they can best serve. Systems that push employees into positions that reject their internal wisdom eventually suffer for it.

Servant leaders promote upwards, laterally, and in place. They develop, encourage, advocate, and urge employees to stretch their capacity and remain open to possibilities, but they respect that not everyone travels the same highway.

Humanagers create byways and scenic routes. They allow people to progress at their own pace, they provide lateral as well as upward mobility options, and they reward excellence in service in every tier of the hierarchy. They recognize the informal leaders, team leaders, and thought leaders.

Servant leaders help staff members to fulfill their promotion goals by alternative means: appointing them to a committee; making them the "point person" for a project; asking them to help with onsite training, or buddy up with a new employee, or organize an activity, etc.

Servant leaders take some pride in the originality of their promotional practices, with the objective of using each person's talents fully wherever they sit in the organization. Leadership, after all, is not a place, but a mindset.

How Do Servant Leaders Delegate?

They delegate courageously, responsibly, and accountably. Leaders who fail to delegate often do so because they fear losing control: "If I want something done right, I have to do it myself", or worse yet, "There's only one right way to do this."

Servant leaders do the pre–work. They make certain employees have the skills to accept the delegation; they do not delegate at random. Delegation is a form of mentorship and employees are assured of both the readiness and the support to succeed.

Paul was a mid–level bureaucrat with a veneer of defiance. He had been bypassed many times for promotion and was a sour apple in the workplace. I recognized in him more than that and delegated a major assignment which Paul rose to meet, gaining the respect of his colleagues and surprising even himself.

And there have been many others. I have taken great joy in delegating significant responsibilities to people I was positive could do the job, but who may not have been predictable choices.

Humanagers look for both momentous and modest opportunities to delegate. Once delegated, the servant leader refrains from micromanaging. She may be nervous about the outcome, but hides her anxiety. She may be tempted to intervene or take over, but stands back and resists. She may have critiques and pointers after the fact, but does not let the employee fail. Delegation is an expression of trust, communicating the leader's willingness to take the chance, confidence in the person's ability, and conviction that they will excel.

Through it all, servant leaders maintain accountability. A task can be delegated, but the obligation cannot. If the outcome does not make the grade, they cannot shift the blame. They alone are answerable for the final result, and for that reason, delegation is a courageous act. *Humanagers* accept this as a risk worth taking.

How do Servant Leaders Evaluate Differently?

Lots has already been said about evaluation in other sections of this book, so let's spotlight the key points. In a servant organization, where one stands is never a surprise. I have seen employees leave an annual appraisal session stunned at the results. Evaluation should be continual and explicit. One company required leaders to create "Progress Notes" for each staff member at least once per week. These 2x4 inch carbonized forms gave constant coaching comments and compliments to staff. They never had to guess how they rated and yearly evaluations simply confirmed what they already knew.

Another organization unfailingly evaluates personnel every six months, but does not discuss the appraisal with the employee. Since the whole purpose of evaluation is to acknowledge and improve performance, this practice is blatantly counterproductive. Evaluations must be shared. In servant organizations, the value of the appraisal is not the document, but the conversation.

The best conversations are dialogs. *Humanagers* give honest and constructive feedback to employees, but they are eager to know how they measure up as well. I will not forget the first time one of my supervisors ended a performance review with, "And how am I doing as your leader?" I have since become a real fan of 360 degree assessments. Evaluation should be reciprocal.

Humanagers use evaluation as a communication tool, a motivational tool, and a recognition tool. At the conclusion of the appraisal meeting, employees are clear about their strengths, areas for improvement, mutual expectations, and their value to the organization. Managers and staff view this feedback as a gift.

What is Different about the Way Servant Leaders Discipline?

Too many people in positions of authority use discipline for the wrong reasons. Bill uses it to reinforce his control; Leonard disciplines as payback for disagreement or disloyalty; Annie finds that disciplining one team member as an example will keep the rest in line. The only legitimate purpose of discipline is to improve performance or conduct. Anything else is retribution and misuse of power.

Anyone in a leadership role has had to make difficult decisions about problematic employees. The first question *humanagers* ask themselves when contemplating the use of discipline is, "Is my intent here punishment or correction?" Punishment looks like revenge. Correction looks like redemption.

Servant leaders take discipline very seriously. If done well, it can put a straying employee firmly back on course. If done poorly, it can do emotional harm, reinforce the negative behavior, and permanently damage the relationship. It may also set the employee on a path of progressive disciplinary action.

I'll never forget my middle school classmate who committed some unremembered offense for which the teacher rapped his knuckles with a ruler (yes, that was permitted back then!) The next day, the student repeated the offense and received another rapping. This seemed to set up a pattern: the boy stubbornly misbehaving and the teacher feeling compelled to repeat the punishment. This standoff went on for the remainder of the school year, each daring the other to break the cycle. It diminished the student, defeated the teacher, and demeaned the watching classroom.

I have known work relationships like that. The more an employee is called out for substandard behavior, the more entrenched he becomes. This is not correction. When managers wait too long to initiate correction, or when they are frustrated by lack of success, they may resort to a campaign of disciplinary actions.

Most organizations have policies of progressive discipline, rules that govern the step–wise sequence of reprimands and warnings. Only truly egregious transgressions can bypass this. And so, well–intentioned, but exasperated leaders—or those intent on reprisal—start down a road where the destination is all too clear and there are no off–ramps. *Humanagers* seek alternatives. They exhaust the course correction of progressive action before documenting the employee "out the door".

When discipline is necessary, the servant leader administers it with fairness and compassion, and he doesn't leave the charge hanging over the employee's head. Letting the person know how he can be reinstated in the leader's good graces underlines the optimism that the aberration is a temporary one.

> SERVANT LEADERS ARE CARING ENOUGH TO HOLD PEOPLE ACCOUNTABLE FOR THEIR CONDUCT, AND THEY ARE STRONG ENOUGH TO SHOW THEM MERCY.

Can I be a Servant Leader and Fire Employees?

Some people think of "servant leadership" and "termination" as an oxymoron. But it is often the management functions *in extremis* that differentiate the *humanager*. Servant leaders are not afraid to fire, but they do it with grace, with compassion, and for the right reasons.

We have all witnessed terminations for the wrong reasons: scapegoating, revenge, jealousy, greed, etc. Then what are the right reasons?

As we learned in the previous section, conduct that is illegal, flagrant, unsafe, or unremitted, or performance that continues below standards.

Servant leaders take swift action to remove legal or safety liabilities, they attempt to mitigate unchanged or unacknowledged behaviors, and they make every effort to shore up unacceptable performance. They go to this extent not because they are idealists, but because they are pragmatists: it's the most rational course for the organization.

A leader in one social service agency does some extra soul–searching before deciding to fire: "Have I given this person ample support? Was it a good job fit in the first place? Has the system in any way set up this person to fail?" She does not do this out of guilt or reluctance, but to ensure she does not repeat errors with other employees. Servant leaders face up to their part in an unsuccessful outcome.

I have known leaders who carry out terminations with grace and compassion; who leave the employee their dignity. After giving a worker repeated chances, Sue went the extra mile to find another position for a team member who was trying his best, but simply could not meet expectations. She secured a more appropriate spot in another office and offered him "safe passage" until it became available. And there was Lou Ann, who terminated an angry and unstable employee with such finesse that he shook her hand and agreed to seek counseling.

Firing is one of the more unpleasant duties of a leader and, as I have often told managers, you should start to worry when it no longer tears you up. *Humanagers*, servant leaders, imbue a life–altering event with self-worth, kindness, and hope.

How Servant Leaders Help Employees Retire

When I retired from an organization after twenty years, I knew I would miss my work and my colleagues. I was well aware that changes would be made in my absence, my pet projects would shift in scope, and managers with different ideas and methods would quickly fill the gap I left. I thought I was prepared.

Nevertheless, the first few months were fretful and off–putting. I was fortunate to have colleagues like Dee and Maureen who understood and were willing to smooth the "change of life" by contacting me periodically, forewarning me of new directions in our work, and tapping into my experience and insights. I sincerely hope that their example of servant leadership will be paid forward when they too retire.

Technically, leaders have no obligation to an employee after retirement. In many organizations, the relationship ends when the figurative gold watch is received: the employee simply and abruptly falls off the radar screen.

Morally, however, the servant leader accepts the obligation to help the retiring employee bring closure to a career. In a culture of *humanagement*, there is a desire to retain the institutional memory and the historical perspective the long–term employee brings. In these organizations, retirement is a process rather than a party; a transition instead of a termination. Some facilities have adopted partial retirement programs to achieve this, easing the employee and the organization into the retirement.

Servant organizations have a duty in the nuts and bolts of retirement to be accurate in pension calculations and diligent in activating benefits. Some institutions take months to deliver the first pension payments, leaving employees in a lurch without income.

In a disturbing illustration, Roger was enjoying his own retirement event with family and co–workers when the Personnel Manager interrupted with news that the employee's retirement eligibility had been miscalculated. Roger still had a year to work before his benefits kicked in! The festivities broke up and Roger returned to his job with great bitterness. In a servant organization, Personnel would have taken responsibility for the error and found a mutually acceptable solution.

Recognition is usually related to a specific accomplishment, but at retirement it is a celebration of an entire body of work. *Humanagers* are mindful that the successes of the future are built upon the successes and the struggles of the past.

I recently walked down a very public hallway where portraits of the last dozen CEOs were hung in commemoration. I thought, "People walk past these photos every day, but I wonder how many look at their faces and consider their impact?" It was a powerful visual reminder that we stand on the shoulders of the leader we replaced, and that someone else will stand on our own. Such is the chain of leadership.

Lastly, servant leaders seek data from retiring employees—indeed from any voluntary separations—through exit interviews. Since these team members have nothing to lose, it is the most honest information possible, and gives the leader a "bird's eye" impression of the organization, to reprise what it does well and repair what it could do better.

> LEADERS ARE NOT THE ONLY—OR EVEN THE MOST IMPORTANT—SOURCE OF PRAISE AND RECOGNITION.
>
> **KELLY TURTURICE**

Reward and Recognition in a Servant Leader Environment

 How important is reward and recognition? Isn't it enough that we are paid for the jobs we do? Theorists (Herzberg, 1968) talk about satisfiers and dissatisfiers, motivators and hygiene factors. While a paycheck is a bottom–line necessity, it is neither satisfier nor motivator. Reward and recognition are both.

Motivation is increasingly personal and situational. Recognition is most powerful when it:

- Matches the reward to the person

- Matches the reward to the achievement

- Is timely and specific

- Is authentic

"Best Places to Work" data (Teclaw, Osatuke, 2015) have demonstrated connections between employees' satisfaction with the amount of praise and recognition they receive and their overall perception of the organization. That recognition can be expressed in many ways, from monetary awards to a sincere "thank you".

Humanagers understand the energy of sincere and simple praise. Many profitable organizations carve out a percentage of budget for recognition. Some businesses plan lavish awards dinners—even weekends—for their top performers. In government, the big event is the Presidential Rank Award, the Emmy of public service. These major accolades are special, but only a comparative few are privy to them and most companies cannot manage the extravagance.

I believe that if we reserve awards only for top performers, the rest will not be motivated to become top performers. I do not ascribe to the "trophy for every team member" philosophy, however there are good, but not great staff who could be encouraged by an award, and those who are solid performers who could be recognized for simply doing their best. Praise and recognition have to permeate every level of the organization. Employees have to earn praise and learn to accept praise. Supervisors need to become more attuned to praiseworthy acts.

Denise tells the story of "Pennies in my Pocket", a mechanism she used to prompt her attention. She put ten pennies in her pocket one morning, with the goal of finding ten acts of service or positive interactions as she made rounds through her facility. To her chagrin, all the pennies were still there at the end of the day. How could she have missed those opportunities to recognize staff? Was it that no acts of service occurred or that she hadn't noticed them? The exercise caused Denise to be more observant, to develop the *habit* of recognition, and to be genuine and spontaneous in her praise.

When organizations are forced to "do more with less", reward and recognition budgets are among the first items slashed. So the practice of non–monetary recognition is becoming an art. People need to feel good about what they do; they want to be noticed. What the leader rewards and praises will be repeated and emulated by others.

Group recognition has the added advantage of coalescing the team. What stands out in my memory are the employee picnics, professional recognition days (almost every occupation has one), receiving turkeys at Thanksgiving, chair massages after a stressful project, ice cream sundaes served by leaders on the night shift, a birthday card and cup of coffee from the CEO, company–wide holiday celebrations, etc. Leketha and Linda cooked breakfast for their office mates once a year and served it at their desks.

Even more important, however, is individual recognition. Singling someone out for praise creates momentum: for an accomplishment or work excellence; a good deed or a kind word; serving a client or helping a colleague. These can be observed in private or in public; can be planned or "on the spot". In fact, they should be all of the above.

Personal recognition can include a prime parking spot, an employee of the month designation, a time–off certificate, nomination for a major award, selection for a prestigious educational program, acceptance of an innovation or suggestion, appointment to a committee, a chance to work outside one's job description, credit for reaching a milestone, acknowledgement of a non–work–related achievement, appreciation for extra effort—the list is endless.

It is also personal. Servant leaders know what kind of recognition is pleasing and acceptable to the individual.

Recognition from colleagues is equally welcome. *Humanagers*, by definition and by example, cultivate a sensitivity for the value of praise in staff. In an organization where gift–giving was frowned upon, Rhonda honored her colleague every Christmas by giving her a little bell she could ring to summon some small service. Lee and Terri presented an engraved nameplate to a co–worker they claimed as a role model. Some businesses sponsor peer awards. In one company, employees salute exceptional teamwork with "praise stars"; in another, work groups honor exceptional service with "shout outs".

Praise and recognition are so much more than nice things to do or a ploy to pacify overworked and under–appreciated employees. In servant leader organizations, celebration not an event but a frame of mind.

A Month of No Cost/Low Cost Recognition

(Stallings-Cox, 2015)

1. Honor employee groups in your department with their own day or week and present them with flowers, treats, etc.

2. Have a monthly breakfast meeting in an outside location. Invite your team, share ideas and recognize at least one person.

3. Put up a bulletin board and post compliments from customers

4. Create a "U Rock" award. Recipients choose who gets it next and pass it on

5. Ask staff to mentor a new hire

6. Send a special message to say thanks or recognize an employee – a song, poem, etc.

7. Serve on the lunch line in the cafeteria

8. Give an employee the choice of assignment for the next week

9. Arrange a special parking space

10. Have a picnic, either indoors or out

11. Submit information of your employee's achievement to the organization's newsletter

12. Create a team yearbook, with pictures & stories of the year's successes

13. Remember birthdays, anniversaries, etc. with a handwritten card

14. Provide "lunch on me" coupons

15. Say, "Thank you."

16. Give a special sticker or pin for the ID badge to acknowledge a good job

17. Encourage employees to give out stickers or pins to peers as well

18. Volunteer to do an employee's least favorite task

19. Let an employee shadow someone in another department for a day

20. Copy senior management on your thank you note to an employee

21. Bring the person a cup of coffee at their work station

22. Invite family to an awards ceremony

23. Deliver ice cream cones to night shift employees

24. Bring an entertainer in to a staff meeting

25. Ask a team member to lead a staff training

26. Appoint a staff member to a favorite committee

27. Have a "guess the baby picture" contest

28. Present an "On the Spot" certificate to award service as it happens

29. Sponsor a group community service project

30. Allow the employee to bring a pet to work for the day

31. Give a day off award

How do Servant Leaders Handle Reorganizations, Mergers, Closures, & Layoffs?

Reorganizations are a fact of corporate life. They come in many varieties, but all create disruption. Sometimes reorganizations improve lines of accountability and communication; frequently they do not; often they are simply a game of musical chairs. Some individuals are deeply impacted by a reorganization, whereas others hardly know it is happening. Perhaps the most important determination for how the reorganization will be received is the impetus for restructuring itself.

Unfortunately, I can name more damaging examples of reorganizing than constructive ones. Recently in my area a racetrack was shut down. The track had been functioning for decades, employed hundreds of workers, and housed dozens of thoroughbred horses. The animals' owners and track staff were told *today* that the facility would be closed *tomorrow*, with no thought to the loss of livelihood or the problem of finding accommodations for horses. Doors were locked, gates were bolted, and both human and equine occupants were left in the cold.

In one national enterprise, an order came down to merge two facilities more than a hundred miles apart. There was a quota to meet—whether the merger was logical or not wasn't on the table. This was expected to result in an improvement of quality, but with a loss of accessibility. Clients now had to travel further, but received better service. Was the trade–off worth it? Questionable. Leadership and staff at each location were resolute in their opposition to the consolidation. Managers at one site were forbidden to consult with corresponding managers at the other site. Duplication of staff and effort were rampant. Years later, only minimal progress had been made in merging the two sites functionally and none in merging them culturally.

On a smaller scale, a program office had an executive position cut from their budget, necessitating an organizational shuffle to accommodate the cutback. The outcome probably enhanced the operation in the long run, but the executive involved was effectively demoted.

I can't forget to note on the positive side the closure of a woolen mill in New England a number of years ago. The owner of the mill understood the impact on staff, families, and the local economy, and continued to pay salaries while helping employees find alternative work. Not all employers have such means, but the servant leadership of this owner rescued a town and restored the faith of its people.

And then there was the medical center which was confronted with the specter of layoffs. Instead of seeing departments boarded up and co–workers given notice, employees elected to reduce their own work weeks and spread the hours among all staff, thus eliminating the need for any reduction in force.

Humanagers can follow some basic principles when faced with reorganization:

1. Be honest about the state of the business, but never use closure or layoff to contrive a "burning pier". A less ethical, more unscrupulous strategy cannot be imagined.

2. Do not wait until all the "t's" are crossed before informing affected staff. Give them sufficient notice to make plans and find reasonable options.

3. On the other hand, people can sense when something is about to happen. If you announce plans prematurely, you will lose employees before you want to. Organizations that cannot meet their commitments to customers have been forced into taking more drastic or precipitous actions than originally intended, when staff fled the "sinking ship".

4. Servant leaders strive to achieve a balance between #2 and #3 above, to the maximum benefit of both the employees and the organization.

5. Mergers should make sense, not just meet a quota or a budget goal.

6. Merging buildings, workforces, and services is hard enough, but the real challenge is in merging the cultures. Avoid a "takeover" mentality, blending the best of each component's culture. *Humanagement* thrives on integration.

7. Layoffs—reductions in force—are always a last resort. If layoffs are truly the only option, there should be a plan. Help affected staff to secure other employment, find ways to tide them over until the paychecks recommence, update resumes, and offer counseling—whatever is needed to "companion" them through the ordeal.

There are many ways to eke out savings that do not cause human suffering or destroy the human spirit. *Find them first.*

Staffing

When was the last time you stood in line at a deli counter, scoured a department store for a clerk, or waited weeks to get a doctor's appointment?

Proper staffing is one of the responsibilities of a leader that is given short shrift in today's workplaces. The attention is so fixated on paring down staff, that the acuity of the client or complexity of the work is neglected. These are critical considerations that affect quality, safety, and service.

In health care, patients are assigned acuity ratings. Not all patients require the same amount of time or assistance as others. For example, a post–operative patient needs 1:1 care for a time, where a patient ready for discharge is fine with an occasional check. Hospitals accommodate that variation by staffing for both the number of patients on a unit and their severity of illness, or _acuity_.

Most businesses have some counterpart to acuity: a severity index, a complexity ranking, etc. But few businesses acknowledge that element when determining how many employees to schedule. For most, a simple and uniform staffing ratio is the norm, even when there are extenuating factors.

Perhaps your organization's complexity can be measured by delays in answering the phone, customer waiting times, people forced to use self–serve options who would prefer full–serve, first available appointments, lengthy encounters, customer complaints, days to case completion, accident rates, rush times, etc.

Each of these has an impact on the customer and on the employee. John and June have ten accounts each, but John's accounts are more intricate, taking him twice as long to close them out. _Humanagers_ make allowances for the variation. With some extra help, John's customers are better served, satisfied, and loyal to the organization. John himself is less stressed, more focused, and not as likely to make costly errors. In organizations that have quality, safety, and convenience at their core, acknowledgment of complexity is crucial.

Key Qualities of a HUMANAGED Workplace

What *humanagers* do is critical, but how they lead is at least as significant. Servant organizations do it with civility, respect, engagement, and enjoyment.

Civility is a baseline expectation of all staff. It's our on–stage behavior, the courtesy we all learned in kindergarten. I don't have to know you; I don't have to like you; but I understand the fundamental rules of acceptable interaction.

The Case for Civility: Business Outcomes

Customer satisfaction
Employee satisfaction
Performance
Safety
Productivity

Sick leave
EEO complaints
Grievances
Recruitment costs
Accident/ Injury
Worker's comp claims

Figure 15

Respect goes a little deeper. This is where honesty, empathy, and ethics come in. It covers listening, eye contact, and putting down the smartphone for a moment.

CIVILITY IS ASKING HOW SOMEONE IS. RESPECT IS WAITING TO HEAR THE ANSWER.

Engagement is the product of civil and respectful relationships in an atmosphere of trust. In this environment, every employee is authorized to act and every employee is accountable for his actions. Data show that only about one third of employees are actively engaged and the rest are just going through the motions.

Servant organizations use engagement as a fulcrum for excellence.

Aspects of Engagement (NCOD, 2015)

Think: Mentally absorbed and immersed in work, focused attention, finds work meaningful

Feel: Enthusiastic, mindful of work, inspired to accomplish things

Act: Energetic, motivated, wants to contribute, shows intense effort

Figure 16

Civility, respect, and engagement are contagious. Established interventions like the Department of Veterans Affair's CREW initiative substantiate the sustained effectiveness of such programs as well as an array of related outcomes. Simply raising awareness of civility increases its presence in the workplace.

Finally, *humanagers* care that the work experience is enjoyable. People need to have fun on the job. Not to be confused with tasteless pranks or horseplay, humor and levity are important for team building and defuse stressful or volatile situations. Intentional servant leaders weave opportunities for laughter into the workday.

<u>Completing the Sentence</u>

Finish the sentence with what is true for you. How would you describe civility, respect, and engagement to a team member?

1. What does civility look like to me?

2. I demonstrate civility by:

3. What does respect look like to me?

4. I show respect by:

5. What does engagement look like to me?

6. I know I am engaged in my work when:

Leading in a Unionized Environment

You may know Oscar the Grouch as a Muppet; I know him as a union president. Many organizations are unionized, particularly skilled trades and governmental operations. The origins of collective bargaining were honorable, the natural consequence of management avarice and hazardous working conditions. Organized labor helped to even the score.

So it seems to me especially incongruous when I see union officials practicing the same management offenses they oppose in institutional leadership. Take Marlin, for example, a strident union president who does not offer his administrative staff basics benefits. Or Chester, who helped himself to union funds. Or Oscar, who wielded his power for power's sake.

But then there are those union officials who use their positions and power to improve the lot of employees and clients: Kelly, who took heat from his union brothers when he worked with instead of against leadership; and Cynthia, a true professional who raised the standards of her profession; and Marty, who partnered with leadership to wipe out abusive practices. Thank goodness that for every Oscar there's a Kelly, a Marty, and a Cynthia.

Many of my more traditional colleagues come into a union environment with an obstinacy—albeit sometimes painfully earned—that they will not work with labor unless they have to; that they will not cede anything unless it is spelled out in the contract. When one CEO was asked why he routinely stonewalled union requests, he responded, "Because I can." Those leaders are throwing down the gauntlet, setting the stage for perpetual conflict. They are also missing a strategic opportunity. We accomplish so much more when we work in concert.

Together, institutional leaders who are reasonable and cooperative and union leaders who are reasonable and cooperative can elevate the organization and every person in it.

I have found some keys to creating that kind of relationship:

- The contract is a guide. If both parties agree to situational tweaks, there is no violation.

- Talk...talk...talk... Let union officials know what you are doing and what you are even thinking about doing. I call this _speaking in draft._ Communicate upfront, encourage input into decisions, ask about the impact on union members. Do whatever you can to create understanding and prevent misunderstandings.

- Find common bonds. I bonded with one union steward over her love of animals; with another, through a mutual intolerance for dishonest behavior. When you find a nub of agreement, you can begin to build on that.

- Realize that you will disagree on some things, and learn to respect that position.

- Establish trust, one interaction at a time, and be careful not to betray it. That trust can get you through disputes without becoming adversarial.

- Search for win/win solutions. Remember that union leaders need to earn credibility with their constituents as much as institutional leaders need to with staff. So help them achieve wins and credit them publicly.

- Find initiatives that you can support jointly. Programs like CREW, which enhances civility, and servant leadership, which empowers staff, are natural partnerships between labor and management.

- If you ask employees' opinions about their workplace, be prepared to follow through. Employee satisfaction surveys are often a source of contention if the union fears reprisal or lacks confidence that corrective actions will be undertaken.

- If there is an impenetrable roadblock in your relationship, take a detour. There is a union hierarchy that can be accessed if all else has failed, just as there is an institutional chain of command. Don't use this gratuitously, but don't allow a good decision to be obstructed unnecessarily.

- If the relationship has stalled, contact someone who can help get it back on track.

And that is what happened with Oscar. Through a few skillfully facilitated dinner meetings, Oscar and I came to a place we could both accept. Friendship was not in the cards, but rather than being constant irritants, we learned to stay out of each other's way.

Labor/management relations are often the most insistent sources of WE/THEY attitudes in the organization. *Humanagers* work to change WE/THEY to US.

The Leader as HUMANAGER

We have covered a lot of specific leadership functions in this section. That's no different than any management text. What is different is the blanket of *humanagement* that overlays them all. You can get the sense that these functions are contemplated and performed from a non-traditional posture.

I can hear the *humanager* cogitating: How well do I know my team? How can I develop deeper professional relationships with them? How do I show genuine care and concern for the people in my life? In what ways have I put the needs of my colleagues and staff before my own? How do I make this a habit? How do I foster joy and pride in my team? In what ways do I show a firm but supportive response when I see undesirable behavior?

In contrast, I remember my first day on a particular job where I heard from my direct reports such sentiments as:

"Are you the new *godfather*?"

"Just tell us how high you want us to jump."

"Hope you'll make as much noise in the organization as our last boss."

"If you fail, you'll take us down with you."

"I check out the bosses' mood first thing in the morning."

"Servant leadership—I'll believe it when I see it."

Humanagement calms the stormy seas and stabilizes an unpredictable organizational climate. Perhaps what employees desire most is a boss who is competent, compassionate, ethical, and honest; who expects excellence and inspires growth. I am surprised at how many of us yearn purely for a little kindness or an ounce of gentleness in the workplace.

People are insulted and demeaned wherever they go; they don't need to be demeaned in their jobs. They are roughed up by the events of the day; they don't need rough treatment at work. They are ill-used and exploited in every walk of life; they don't need to be ill-used by their leaders.

The *humanager's* principal consideration is this: would my decisions change in any way if the most important criterion was to "put people first"?

And if that is the leader's refrain, how does it trickle throughout the organization? Does each department reflect on how it can serve its clients? How they can serve each other?

Servant leadership is not a philosophy: it is a way of life.

Sweet Dreams

LET ME SHARE A PERSONAL EXPERIENCE THAT MAY RESONATE WITH YOU OR NOT. THIS IS AN EXERCISE IN VULNERABILITY! I AM GIFTED AT BUILDING RELATIONSHIPS WITH ALMOST ANYBODY. THE OPERATIVE WORD HERE IS ALMOST. DESPITE MY BEST EFFORTS, THERE ARE A HANDFUL OF PEOPLE OVER MY CAREER WHO HAVE SEEMED IMPOSSIBLE AND RELATIONSHIPS THAT HAVE SEEMED HOPELESS. THOSE SITUATIONS MAKE ME CRAZY. I FIND, HOWEVER, THAT IF I CAN'T HANDLE THEM CONSCIOUSLY, THEY ARE SOMETIMES HANDLED FOR ME SUBCONSCIOUSLY. THIS IS CALLED DREAMWORK. I DON'T PLAN IT AND I DON'T EXPECT IT, BUT SOME VERY DARK RELATIONSHIPS HAVE BEEN BROUGHT TO THE LIGHT IN THIS UNUSUAL MANNER.

Charles was a union president who appeared to be collegial, but blocked every issue. He was a nice man, but seemed amused by thwarting management, shutting down any progress with a smile on his face. Charles pushed all my buttons. I sensed rationality in there somewhere, but could never get past the crusty exterior.

Then I had a dream. Charles and I were in a small chapel. He was sitting in a pew on one side of the aisle and I was opposite him on the other side of the aisle. We did not engage and remained there for a while not saying anything and both frustrated. Finally Charles said, "I'm going to move to the back and let you speak to my twin sister, Charity." A woman I had not noticed before came into view. She looked like a female version of Charles. The barriers broke. There was an instant rapport and we talked until we reached resolution.

Dreamwork: The chapel provided a neutral, yet inspirational setting. It was no accident that we found ourselves on opposite sides of the aisle: labor and management are often described that way. When I was unable to see the humanity in Charles, he brought forward his higher self—*Charity*, as fate would have it. By altering my perspective, by seeing Charles' other side, I was able to reach across the aisle and pull down the wall between us.

Outcome: Miraculously, our relationship improved after that. Though Charles had not had the dream experience himself, my change of heart alone was enough to shift the mood.

In another example, a situation with a family member was unbearable. We had not communicated in a very long time. She had caused me great pain and I was struggling with forgiveness. Then I had a dream. She was elevated on a platform, posed like a Buddha and surrounded by an aura. Many people were bowing to her, and I was one of them.

Dreamwork: In life I had been looking down on my relative; in the dream I was looking up to her. She was no longer the malicious person I dreaded, but an embodiment of goodness. The crowd and I were bowing to that *goodness* in her.

Outcome: The outward relationship has not changed, but the inward one has. Until our issues are resolved on a physical plane, I will continue to greet her in spirit every day.

And here is one more: Bess was a manager whom I mentored and promoted until she became one of my "impossibles". She began to manipulate her staff, shaping her organization in ruthless ways. With employees on the verge of mutiny, I terminated Bess from her position. She promptly filed a wrongful discharge action against me. Until it was settled, I was required to keep her at work. The environment was tense and the forced interaction was intolerable.

Dreamwork: I was with colleagues at a banquet. The atmosphere was festive and relaxed. I was sitting at one of the many round tables with friends when I saw Bess approach. I had not known she was at the event and immediately grew apprehensive. She circled my table several times, staring ominously. Then she came up behind me and, as I waited for a blow, she bent over and kissed my cheek. As my friends looked on, Bess smiled graciously and walked away.

Outcome: That week Bess dropped her complaint and quietly resigned. We parted without animus.

Our minds work overtime to put things right. It is said that the people who give us the most trouble are our greatest teachers. If a relationship seems impossible, we just haven't viewed it from the right angle. If we are exasperated with "problem people", we haven't asked the right questions:

1. Who are you really?
2. What do you need?
3. What can you teach me?

If we remain open, the answers will come. Awake or in dreams, deliberately or incidentally, willingly or not, the universe is programmed for us to learn and grow. And if we don't get it quite right this time, the opportunity to do better will surely come around again.

Practice Period

Humanagement Distinction

Humanagers are called upon to make tough decisions and take firm actions. They have high expectations and hold workers accountable, but they are fair and humane. Even the most arduous responsibilities can be tempered by a servant leader approach.

Think about the situations below. How could you improve the expected outcome by using servant leadership or *humanagement*?

• Terminating an employee who has not hit the mark

• Informing staff that the corporate office is cancelling a popular work–at–home policy

• Announcing a new round of budget cuts

• Floating an idea for department consolidation

• Disciplining an employee for bullying

• Your department did not meet its performance metrics

• Some employees who did not receive annual awards are disgruntled

• The local labor union is opposing all your good ideas

Contrast: Humanagement in a Traditional vs Servant Organization

Management in the TRADITIONAL Organization	Humanagement in the SERVANT Organization
Hire	
• Perfunctory interviewing • Interviews are fair and consistent, often with no feedback • Warm bodies • Probationary period • Selection is a unilateral decision	• Creates an enticing environment • Pairs facts with intuition • Interviews are fair and consistent AND connect with the applicants • Matches candidate with job • Eliminates probationary period • Multidisciplinary panels make recommendations to hiring authority
Onboard	
• Mandatory and mechanical • A one-time event, the shorter the better	• Interactive, engaging, effective, and just–in–time • Periodically reinforced
Retain & Motivate	
• Attrition is expected • Uniform benefits; carrots and sticks	• Finds out what motivates employees to stay • Addresses peoples' high priority needs

Management in the TRADITIONAL Organization	Humanagement in the SERVANT Organization
Promote	
• Inflexible career ladder • Career progression always hierarchical	• Promotes upwards, laterally, and in place • Helps staff members to fulfill promotion goals by alternative means • Uses each person's talents fully wherever they sit in the organization.
Delegate	
• Delegates only "sure bets" • Delegates accountability with the task • Micromanages to be sure it's done right	• Delegates courageously, responsibly, and accountably • Makes certain employees have skills to accept the delegation • Refrains from micromanaging • Retains accountability
Evaluate	
• Evaluations completed per policy, usually once a year • May or may not be discussed with employee • Evaluation is top down only	• Evaluation is continual • Always shared with employee • Evaluation is reciprocal • "No surprises" rule

Management in the TRADITIONAL Organization	**Humanagement** in the SERVANT Organization
Discipline	
• May be used as punishment or to control • Discipline is progressive and uniform. If it isn't documented, it doesn't exist	• Only legitimate purpose of discipline is to improve performance or behavior • Fair and compassionate • Cares enough to hold people accountable and is strong enough to show them mercy
Fire	
• Not always for the right reasons • May be arbitrary • A means to an end	• With grace, with compassion, and for the right reasons • Takes swift action to remove legal or safety liabilities • Faces up to their part in an unsuccessful outcome
Retire	
• No obligation to employee after retirement	• Helps the retiring employee bring closure to a career • Retains institutional memory • Accountable in the nuts and bolts of retirement • Performs exit interviews to gain helpful information

Management in the TRADITIONAL Organization	**Humanagement** in the SERVANT Organization
Reward	
• Reward is often uniform • Recognition centers around pay and bonuses • Monetary awards limited in tight fiscal times • Tends to disregard non–monetary awards • Recognizes both individuals and groups • Celebration occurs at regular events	• Reward is personal and situational • Praise and recognition permeate every level of the organization • Planned and spontaneous; monetary and non–monetary • Recognizes both individuals and groups • Celebration not an event but an attitude
Reorganize	
• Often just a shuffling of the chairs • Uses reorg as burning pier to create sense of urgency • Holds information close until time of announcement • Mergers feature one site taking over another • Layoffs and reductions in force considered a bona fide management tool	• To improve lines of authority or communication • Never contrives burning pier to create sense of urgency • Involves appropriate staff before final decisions are made • Merges cultures as well as buildings and staff • Layoffs are always a last resort

Management in the TRADITIONAL Organization	**Humanagement** in the SERVANT Organization
Staffing	
• Uses minimal workable staffing	• Adds a complexity component to staffing ratios
Key Qualities	
• Civility initiatives are fluff • Work is serious: there is no room for levity	• Civility • Respect • Engagement • Enjoyment
Union Relationships	
• Follows the contract to the letter—or to his/her advantage • Does not give union a chance to derail a decision: announces decisions only when final • Trust is not necessary: we have a contract • Working with the union is a game of one–upsmanship	• Good relationships are a strategic advantage • Communicates upfront; encourages pre–decisional input • Establishes trust • Searches for win/win opportunities

Make Your Own Kind of Music

Try This...

1. With a group of staff, develop a reward and recognition program for your department. Include monetary and non–monetary options and specific criteria for each type of recognition. Determine what behaviors and accomplishments you want to recognize. Be sure to cover peer–to–peer mechanisms as well. The goal is to be consistent, fair, and motivational.

2. Collaborate with the Human Resource Department to eliminate probationary periods for new employees. If this is imposed by regulation or beyond the scope of your authority, consider adopting the "intention", making hiring decisions without the mental safety net of a probationary period. How does this change your thinking about recruitment and selection?

3. Call to mind the people with whom you have had difficult working relationships, personality differences, job conflicts, etc. Identify the advantages, personally and professionally, of resolving them. List three specific actions you will take to accomplish that. Reevaluate after a few months of sincere effort.

4. Incorporate an opportunity for employees to evaluate your leadership during their next performance appraisal. It can be as simple as, "How am I doing?" or as detailed as a 360 degree assessment. How does it feel? What will you do with the feedback?

5. Review your personnel policies. Do they reflect Humanagement? Revise a few that would send a servant leader message to staff. Explain what you changed and your rationale for doing so.

Tune–Up

Your regional manager has received another complaint from a particular customer about poor service in your department. He has forwarded it to you and wants a response by close of business today. Which answer best reflects servant leadership?[*]

1. According to the schedule, Mary was on duty that day, so you issue a response that Mary will be disciplined.

2. You dispute the complaint because this customer is a chronic complainer.

3. You call a team meeting to listen to the staff's frustration with this customer and strategize a more effective approach.

CUSTOMER CARE IS THE STRING SECTION IN A SYMPHONY OF service. Their volume and vivacity carry the concert. The high notes and the low notes, melodious and harmonious, they tie the work together and make it sing. While the other instruments have their moment in the sun, they are often mostly support for the strings. In the hierarchy of the orchestra, strings have pride of place.

And so it is in the servant leader organization. Customer service has pride of place; it is the apex of the upended pyramid. It is the song to which every department and every employee adds their voice; the tune that winds through the disparate tests and tasks to create a masterwork.

Creating and sustaining a Culture of Service is a daunting task. It requires strong, clear leadership, specific and personalized plans, communication, measurement that makes sense, and a shared commitment throughout the organization. A culture of service doesn't just happen; it is intentional. It is also inclusive; every leader and every employee must be invested and engaged. Clients and families must be close partners as well. Everyone is on both the giving and receiving end in a culture of service.

---

[*] ANSWER: 3

Who Is Your Customer?

THE ANSWER IS NOT ALWAYS AS EASY AS IT SOUNDS. DEPENDING ON YOUR business, customers may be accorded a variety of labels: client, consumer, user, patient, partner, member, purchaser, enrollee, subscriber, constituent, or patron.

Some health care and social service agencies reject the word "customer". Medical professionals, for example, can be uncomfortable with the economic implications of the term, disassociating themselves from the billing and marketing aspects of those industries. Being one of them myself, I understand their position, but the language of the commercial sector is more honest. We can coin the cleverest euphemisms, but a customer by any other name....

"Customer" is not a *four–letter word*. Whether patronizing a grocery store or a clinic, we want them to go the extra mile to satisfy us and retain our loyalty; to be served quickly & respectfully; to trust in the quality of the product and the competence of provider; to have our preferences acknowledged and expectations met.

Being a customer is not about the exchange of money; it is about the exercise of choice. Choice is easy to understand when we're talking about a bank or a drug store, but for many businesses the customer is captive: there is no choice. My HMO, the utility company, local garbage pick–up, the IRS, my cable provider, the post office—most governmental agencies and monopolies—all have policies, but the concept of customer satisfaction is just *lip service*. Where else would you go? What choice do you have? What is your recourse?

Even when options are limited though, the consumer still has the freedom to make choices. I can choose to comply with or reject a treatment regimen; to support or slam an agency. I can choose to follow the rules or I can find ways to cheat and deceive ("captives" often find small deceptions the equalizer against a faceless system). I can stir up discontent, blast them on Facebook, write to my Congressperson, or call the media hotline. All of those are choices.

And what effect does a captive clientele have on staff? Think about the last time you phoned a company with a complaint, were left on hold, repeatedly asked for the same information, transferred to a robot, and finally connected with a real person who did not have an answer or could not solve your problem. If leadership doesn't care about service, why should the employees?

Whatever we call them, when we view people as customers who make choices and deserve service, *we treat them differently.*

I believe that every organization has a customer service objective, but things happen along the way. Business realities intervene, staff are disengaged, or leadership takes its eye off the ball. There are companies who are well–meaning, but don't have the structure or framework to carry it off. There are some who speak the jargon and flaunt the slogans, but do not live it. And there are certainly many workplaces that hold onto archaic definitions and concepts of customer service.

The Full Spectrum Customer Experience

The designation of "customer" used to be reserved for the commercial enterprise, but has expanded to service industries as well to connote a philosophy of serving. For our purposes, "customer" will be applied generically, so please think of it in the context of your own work environment. The field of customer service has matured over the years. The model below depicts the evolution of customer service, retaining and building upon previous models, leading to a more systems-oriented, comprehensive, and holistic approach.

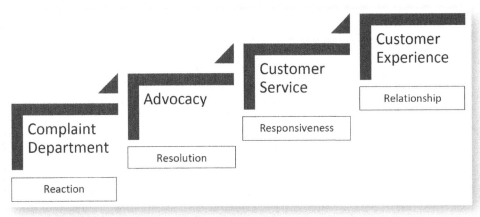

Figure 17

Originally, customer service was characterized by a Complaint Department. The work was transactional (fix the complaint) and isolated (not viewed in the context of a system). Later, an ombudsman function was added. In some businesses this took the form of advocacy;

in others, a call center. This was a step forward in championing the cause of the customer and in designating specific job roles to accomplish service, but the responsibility for satisfying customers was confined to the staff in those roles.

Many ombudsman and advocacy departments evolved into customer service programs, where customer problems were viewed in the context of a system and there was an emphasis on preventing complaints as well as reacting to them.

What we know today is that the fullest and most satisfying customer experience is built on relationships. Developing that relationship requires us to solicit and respond to individual needs, preferences, and goals. It requires listening, changing the conversation, collaborating, and fostering continuity, loyalty, and trust over time. The full–spectrum experience is customer service on steroids!

Here is my formula for customer service:

$$\text{Customer Service} = \frac{\text{Systems Thinking x Mindfulness}}{\text{Empowerment}}$$

Systems Thinking

Customer satisfaction is not a discrete activity—it's part of an overarching "system of service". In organizations, customer failures are often due to system error not an individual's fault; as we have described before: *glitch hunts, not witch hunts.*

Systems theory tells us that everything is connected to everything else. We know that a customer's positive or negative experience in one area carries over to other areas.

And organizational systems are not the only ones we're dealing with. In holistic terms, the customer is a collection of systems—biological, psychological, familial, and spiritual. Sometimes we get so caught up in dealing with systems and sub–systems, we forget about the whole human being.

A customer returns a toaster for the third time. A patient continues to press the call bell to make sure help is nearby, just in case. A user wants tech support to walk her through the basics—again.

It's easy to see the customer as a litany of complaints and demands. We are oblivious to how those complaints may relate to what is going on in the rest of the customer's life. How often do we label people chronic complainers or pains in the butt when what we're really encountering is a plea for validation?

So sometimes a toaster is not just a toaster: it's a call to be noticed. Sometimes an argumentative caller is not fighting you, but her own sense of helplessness. Sometimes people perseverate on material things because they can't say, "My spirit hurts."

Mindfulness

Customer service is a core commitment, not a catch-phrase; a daily–actualized philosophy that puts substance to the concept of "people first". No matter what our role in the workplace, each of us is responsible for keeping service uppermost in our minds, for actually having a plan about what service means in our particular job, and how we'll know if we've achieved it.

Circumstances that seem like business as usual to staff may mean dissatisfaction and frustration to the client, so each of us needs to cultivate a state of mindfulness that's alert to systemic deficiencies and personally accountable for taking action. Each of us needs to be fully present. Mindfulness *tunes us in* to systems thinking.

Empowerment

Empowerment is that part of the equation that transforms it from lip service to heart service. Empowerment is a conscious act. The leader consciously shares power and the employee consciously accepts it. Both can be scary.

When we see power as position, status, authority, resources, or control, there is only so much to go around. In that organizational view, there is always a struggle for power. The operative question is "Who's in charge here?" In that organizational view, the concept of service = loss of power, shared decision–making = loss of power, multi–disciplinary teams = loss of power, elevating the advocacy role = loss of power, implementing models of employee participation = loss of power. That's obviously not the organizational view that nurtures legitimate empowerment.

We want "thinking" staff. I hire the housekeeper for her ability to think as well as mop, and the physician for her compassion as well as her diagnostic skills.

Empowered staff have the obligation to be knowledgeable about the workplace, its programs, policies, rules, and expectations; and once aware of a service dilemma, to "own" the problem through to resolution.

Leaders have the obligation to make systemic and procedural adjustments as necessary to meet the unique needs of customers and clear the way for employees, to support and encourage staff to serve creatively and generously, then turn them loose to deliver *customer care*.

Organizational Elements of Customer Service

We said earlier that one of the reasons customer service languishes is because:

1. the organization does not have a thoughtful framework

While much of serving clients is intuitive, a structure must be established so that it happens by design, not fate.

Which can lead to another problem:

2. the organization uses a cookie–cutter approach

Even when a solid framework is in place, it is sometimes mistaken for a mandate. As in any culture initiative—and customer caring is clearly a culture initiative—the structure is a guideline, a set of parameters meant to stimulate and support. It communicates expectations and assures staff that they are "covered" in their actions. It puts in place those essential components of a climate of service.

The most effective customer service programs are:

*   Unified in the fundamentals across the organization: consistent, coherent, and reliable

*   Customized to the site of service: reflecting the local culture of the facility, department, or office

*   Personalized to the customer (the patient, the user, the client, etc.)

They are dependable, yet flexible; stable, yet not standardized; and orderly, but not regimented. They consider the highest priority needs of the consumer and the capacity of the organization to meet them.

The organizational elements of that kind of customer service can be seen in the table in Figure 18. The following pages give details about each element.

Figure 18

Organizational Elements: Administrate

The goal of this Element is to ensure that the organization's structures are in place. Just as the leader promotes a vision for the organization, a vision for customer service clarifies the expectations. A sample Vision might be: **"Provide a world class customer experience arising from authentic respect and an intrinsic commitment to serve."**

There are as many definitions of customer service as there are customers: good quality, timeliness, convenience, a warm demeanor, choices, an emotional connection, an uplifting experience, quick responsiveness, etc. Because of that variation, leaders need to be simple and clear in their definition. One of the best I've seen is, "**_Serving others as they want to be served._**" That broad a definition requires that we _ask_ how the customer prefers to be served.

And here is a model Policy Goal: **"To ensure seamless, exceptional service, defined by and exceeding the expectations of the customer, and experienced at every touch point."**

Principles include the instructions upon which customer service is based. For example, a principle of "Customer First" helps employees determine a course to follow when customer needs and organizational processes conflict: a patient works weekdays, but the clinic is not open on weekends. Or a refund can only be made by a manager, but the manager is off duty. A "Customer First" principle authorizes the employee to act and assures that he will be supported in his action.

Performance measures reinforce accountability for customer service at every level of the organization. They can contain simple data such as compliments and complaints to more sophisticated measures like innovation and process redesign, and should be commensurate with the rank of the employee. It's important that measures be not only numerical, but include culture change achievements as well.

Consider whether your organizational structure sufficiently supports customer service efforts: do you have a Customer Service department? Does it include both proactive and reactive components? Where does Customer Service report in the organization? Is customer service reflected in the governance structure? Designated departments or directors have the most impact when they report directly to the CEO or other C–Suite executive, and when the governing board receives regular information about customer service efforts.

Finally, be sure the structure, processes, and programs related to customer service are in alignment with each other.

ADMINISTRATE WORKSHEET

Thinking about your organization…

1. What administrative aspects are already present? Where is there a gap?

2. Which aspects will we target for development?

   - Goal?

   - Specific actions to be taken?

   - Who will be responsible?

3. What is the specific result desired?

4. What resources are needed?

5. What is the outcome to be measured?

Organizational Elements: Educate

The goal of this Element is to ensure that all staff receive relevant training in customer service at various points in the employee's life cycle. Leaders often make the mistake of relegating customer service to the continuing education department. While training is essential, it is only the tip of the iceberg.

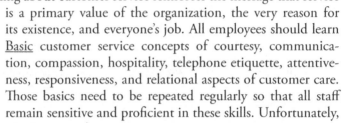

Teaching about customer service reinforces the message that service is a primary value of the organization, the very reason for its existence, and everyone's job. All employees should learn Basic customer service concepts of courtesy, communication, compassion, hospitality, telephone etiquette, attentiveness, responsiveness, and relational aspects of customer care. Those basics need to be repeated regularly so that all staff remain sensitive and proficient in these skills. Unfortunately, many organizations stop here.

Servant organizations look deeper. Professionals may have more intense and intimate encounters with customers and so require provider–specific content in effective interactions, teamwork, partnering with clients and families, accessibility, timely and therapeutic communication, etc.

Try some novel approaches. Use stories to connect emotionally to teach the importance of service at every touch point. Bring in a customer or two to share their experience with staff—what it felt like at the other end of the encounter and what changes or improvements they'd like to see. Customer insight is invaluable. Or use trainers outside the classroom as "coaches on the ground" to assist staff in navigating educational resources and ramping up their skills.

Customer service starts at the top. Customer service education for Leaders emphasizes the leader's role in creating an environment that is conducive to service and weaving it into the culture of the organization. Both current and developing leaders are pivotal to attaining this culture. I always feel that indoctrinating Prospective leaders (the supervisors and managers of the future) reaps huge results. But neglecting to bring existing leaders up to speed as well makes it more difficult for staff and leadership–hopefuls to reach their service potential. Organizations must incorporate customer service content into all corporate and local leadership development programs.

The message of *service* is never more critical than during new employee orientation or onboarding. In fact, in intentional servant organizations it begins before that: in the hiring process. Onboarding is where the *values* discussion takes place, expectations are reiterated, and enthusiasm is generated. This is where the *customer service adventure* begins!

EDUCATE WORKSHEET
Thinking of your organization...

1. Which educational aspects are already present?

2. Are they as successful as we'd like them to be?

3. Can they be enhanced?

4. Does the data show any educational gaps?

5. Which area of education will be targeted for development or improvement?

   • Are there existing educational resources in this area?

   • Specific actions to be taken?

   • Who will be responsible?

6. What is the specific result desired?

7. What resources are required?

8. How will we measure effectiveness of this training?

Organizational Elements: Sustain

The goal of this Element is to ensure that robust system supports are in place. All systems and process components of the organization must be constructed as launching pads for service. If they are not, service and systems will be in constant discord. In traditional organizations, "systems" generally win out over "service". In servant organizations, service prevails; it is given precedence.

Leaders need to evaluate all workplace systems in light of the "sustain" imperative, however human resource, financial, and data practices surface most often. These areas are largely governed by corporate policy or regulation, but there are opportunities to spotlight and strengthen their impact on customer service.

For example, some HR departments promote "fit" interviewing and use customer service-related performance–based interview questions to help determine how service-oriented applicants are. Selecting employees with customer service skills up–front is critical and cost effective. Promotional actions and reward and recognition are outstanding occasions to highlight service. All employees should be aware of how their _customer caring_ will affect their advancement and acknowledgement opportunities.

Fiscal functions often hold themselves apart from service considerations. They rarely see the customer or are confronted with customer grievances and, after all, things cost what they cost. Drawing fiscal practices into the service arena is not as hard as you'd think. Help business office staff to see themselves as service providers, both indirectly and directly. Let them see the customer's face from time to time and teach them the skills to finesse service problems. Finance people are pragmatic, so showing them the budget advantages of satisfied customers is persuasive.

Enhancing customer service feedback systems ensures that actions are data-driven. There are a variety of proprietary, real-time customer feedback options available and many organizations develop their own:

- ✓ Patient rounding
- ✓ Exit survey kiosks
- ✓ Online reviews
- ✓ Satisfaction questionnaires

Data sources are most valuable when they combine "point of service" (real–time) results with longitudinal statistics (collected over time).

Data is worthless, however, unless it is used. This is true whether measuring internal or external customer opinion.

And don't forget the power of observational data. You may consider making customer service rounds, arranging regular opportunities to speak directly with the consumer, and to ask staff how systems and processes can be improved. Including customers on company councils and committees is also a practical source of information.

So your organization has a functional program and a commitment to service, but what about those times when we fail? Every organization does, so it's not a matter of "if" but "when". The process of *getting it **very** right the second time* is called <u>Service Recovery</u>. Service Recovery programs acknowledge that we don't always meet customers' expectations and they forge an opportunity to regain client trust.

For many customers, a simple acknowledgement that we missed the mark is sufficient. There is a knack to apologizing without admitting wrongdoing. The organization's legal advisors will be quick to caution employees not to accept blame. But if the organization is truly at fault, I believe an honest admission is the only ethical recourse.

The Department of Veterans Affairs *extreme honesty* policy is a case in point. All health care facilities make mistakes, but most work hard to keep patients from finding out. The VA (and some other systems I've found) not only admits its errors, but works with patients and families to remedy the situation.

Happily, most customer satisfaction glitches don't rise to that level and can be handled with some attentive listening, empathy, and pinpointed resolution. Statistically, those who complain and are left dissatisfied are more disloyal than those who didn't complain in the first place. Unhappy customers often expect a dispute, so "I'm sorry that you had a disappointing experience with us," is enough to defuse many irate interactions.

Servant leaders clarify the parameters of their Service Recovery program so that no employee is left wondering where the limits of their authorization lie. Employees need information on the range of actions they can take. At some sites leaders make personal phone calls to affirm their commitment to better service next time. CEO Randall installed an "Aspirin Line", a direct customer link to his office. Others utilize cafeteria coupons, "concierge" attention, and follow-up contacts to ensure satisfaction. One facility issues service recovery lapel pins that move the customer up to the head of the line; many have determined dollar amounts that staff can access to "recover" a problem.

An organization's dedication to customer service is evident in the waitress who comps an unacceptable meal, or a hotel clerk who reimburses for a lost pair of eyeglasses, or a clerk who writes off a bill. Those actions, performed by frontline staff of their own volition and without first seeking permission, bespeak an empowered workforce and a pervasive culture of service.

Service Recovery can be very creative and very effective. And, contrary to conventional wisdom, customers rarely take advantage of such programs. They merely want the situation rectified and, more significantly, they want to *feel heard.*

Intentional servant leaders use their systems knowledge, HR processes, data, and service recovery successes to spread best practices across the organization. They don't hide their lights under a bushel; they use them to inform and inspire further success. They continue to raise the bar of service excellence.

> THE SINGLE BEST PREDICTOR OF LOYALTY IS WHETHER OR NOT A CUSTOMER HAD A PROBLEM AND HOW IT WAS HANDLED.
>
> **JOHN A. GOODMAN**

SUSTAIN WORKSHEET

Thinking of your organization…

1. Which aspects are already present?

2. Can they be enhanced?

3. Which aspects will we target for improvement?

   - Goal?

   - Specific actions to be taken?

   - Who will be responsible?

4. Are there existing resources or best practices in this area?

5. If HR and data policies are developed on a corporate level, what actions and improvements can we take to add value here?

6. What additional resources are needed?

7. What is the specific result desired?

8. What is the outcome to be measured?

9. How will effectiveness be measured and monitored?

10. What will success look like?

Organizational Elements: Enculturate

The goal of this Element is to ensure that customer service is linked to other programs and initiatives leading to a healthy organization. A transformational organization is one in which principled and progressive leaders support engaged and invested employees in the delivery of safe, quality, and relationship–centered service.

Workplaces participate in many service–related priorities. Often they are not labeled as such and are perceived as discrete and unrelated activities. For them to be seen as more than "fly–by–night" pursuits or trends of the moment, they need to be wrapped in a common theme, one that is relentless and enduring. Service can be effective as that common theme.

Customer service is allied to and inherent in civility and respect, safety, continuous quality improvement, high–performing teams, process redesign, patient centered care, a Learning Organization, ethics, servant leadership, and other corporate efforts. Customer service winds its way around, through, among, and between those initiatives. These are the cohering factors of a healthy organization. Enculturation underscores their connectedness without which they become fragmented, isolated, and transient.

Demonstrate the links between service and civility, service and safety, service and learning, service and ethics, etc. Discuss their interconnectedness at every opportunity. Soon staff will begin detecting those linkages themselves, experiencing "aha" moments when the hodge-podge of responsibilities comes together; when they comprehend that there are not multiple priorities, but one: service. All the assorted program domains are simply expressions of that service.

These initiatives are pursued simultaneously, not sequentially, in order to impact all aspects of a healthy organization. They build upon, support, sustain, and synergize each other to *embed* a culture of service. In such a scenario, they transcend program/project/training tags to become "the way we do business".

Organizational culture is principally dependent upon the person at the top. If service heads the priority list under an amenable CEO, what happens when the executive moves on? When service becomes enculturated, it is not so easy to dislodge; it is not contingent on leadership permanence because it has become a fact of organizational life. It has been internalized.

Servant organizations search for ideas that will strengthen and entrench their service culture. Many businesses have carved out a Chief

Experience Officer or Chief Customer Officer on the theory that if someone is not accountable, no one is accountable.

One facility recruited Service Champions to discern and alert colleagues to missed opportunities for service throughout the workday. Another enterprise funded Service Scholars who studied both classical and quirky service environments to identify service traditions elsewhere, adapt them to the company's environment, and measure outcomes. They compiled a catalog of effective practices over the course of the program that is still being used.

Then there was the medical center that inaugurated a "Caught Caring" award to recognize amazing service—even as it was being performed! Yet another started a "kindness initiative" in the belief that kindness is the foundation of great service and a welcoming workplace.

Culture is established by repetition of words and actions; by purposeful blending, intertwining, and integrating of aligned initiatives. They balance past, present, and future to systematize and personalize the values and mission of an organization in a way that is not dependent on any one person, but is shared by all employees across time.

ENCULTURATE WORKSHEET
Thinking of your organization…

1. In which programs/initiatives leading to a healthy culture are we already engaged?

2. Does the data show any cultural gaps?

3. Are there additional cultural initiatives that would enhance internal and external customer service?

4. Which area will we target for development?

5. What resources will we need to access?

6. What specific actions will need to be taken?

7. Who will be responsible?

8. What is the desired outcome?

9. How will it be measured?

Successful Customer Service Communication

Customer service starts at and is communicated from the top. Leaders create a vision for service and communicate expectations for service at every level of the organization. Leadership messages flow throughout the organization; managers and supervisors interpret and reinforce them to staff.

When leaders aren't explicit in their communication, misunderstanding can occur. To avoid this, messages must be consistent and repeated at every opportunity. Examples of commendable customer service are publicly recognized and rewarded. Linkages are verbalized, connecting customer service to organizational priorities like relationship–based service, quality outcomes, and access; and to healthy organizational behaviors such as teamwork, accountability, and civility.

The message is a critical, but not complete, strategy. Leaders convey their commitment most effectively by personal modeling of customer service behaviors. Communicating values by acting on them is powerful. Communicating values without modeling them erodes credibility and trust.

Communication is bi-directional. Feedback from staff and customers is a rich source of information about service strengths and opportunities. Listening sessions, direct observation via customer service rounds, and survey data are all useful methods of gaining intelligence and insight from those closest to the line of service.

An environment of truth-telling supports customer service by encouraging honest, open dialog and psychological safety, even when the message is not what leaders want to hear. Conveying information regularly, liberally, and transparently is fundamental to an atmosphere of trust.

Leaders who share customer service plans, strategies, actions, and measured outcomes help all employees become engaged and invested in authentic customer care.

Practice Period

The Experience of Care

Think about a time you or a loved one received exceptional customer service.

What specifically made it rise to that level?

How did it feel?

What are the characteristics of excellent customer service?

How can you apply those characteristics to your own work? Your own leadership?

Now remember an example of outstanding *internal* customer service.

Are there similarities?

Share your story.

Customer Service, Inside Out

THIS IS WHERE *HUMANAGEMENT* BLEEDS INTO CUSTOMER SERVICE. What if we treated each other as well as we treat our external customers? Colleagues, staff, and other departments are internal customers. They are the people who ask for help or a minute of our time; who want to feel welcome and respected. Do we tell them we're glad they're here? Do we understand their needs and likes? Do our actions reassure them of their worth and do we go beyond their basic expectations? We would do all of that for our "customers", so why not each other?

Ask a company that has a reputation for great customer service. Those organizations recognize the value of a stellar customer experience and they know that serving their employees well is a linchpin of that experience. Service—good or bad—rolls downhill. When I see staff that are oblivious to a customer, I infer that leadership is neglectful of staff. When an employee clobbers a patron with officiousness, I conclude that management is imperious. And when I witness a truly caring interaction with a client, it's evident that this institution prizes *heart service*, not *lip service*.

Servant leaders use the tools of *humanagement* to create a culture of service that faces in both directions. They appreciate that good customer service doesn't happen without employees who feel valued, invested, and empowered to deliver it. Leaders who provide that environment send a loud message to staff about expectations of service. Intentional servant leaders reward service, inside and out.

It is up to the leader to set the stage for internal customer service and to model the behavior. Then it becomes every employee's role to serve their teammates. Customer service can be turned inside out by remembering a few simple precepts: (Graff-Reed, 2014)

1. Think of co–workers as VIPs! Respect and assistance go a long way.

2. Treat them as you want to be treated. Show an interest, cut people some slack, and forgive them when they disappoint you.

3. View interruptions as opportunities to serve. Your time is precious, so giving a moment of it to help someone makes a statement.

4. Exceed their expectations. Don't just say, "It's in the manual." Take the manual to them. Instead of giving a new employee directions to the Personnel Office, walk with them.

5. Make your internal customers look good. Find ways to support the success of your colleagues.

6. Say thank you, acknowledge good work, notice the small niceties, and express appreciation.

When leaders and individuals become passionate about service, teams and departments are challenged to discover new ways to serve their counterparts. I have found organizations that make this a quest! Here are some innovative examples:

- The HR department that did small errands for clinicians who had to work overtime

- The housekeeping department that used aromatherapy to freshen institutional odors

- The accounting office that offered to assist colleagues with tax preparation

- A food service team who turned a cafeteria meal into a dining experience

- The organization that provided dry–cleaning and package pick–up for staff

- A canteen that delivered lunch orders to employees' desks

- A business center that offered free copying and faxing to co–workers after hours

- A volunteer department that displayed artwork in previously sterile hallways

- The security office that accompanied staff to their cars after dark

- An IT department that furnished simple tech support for employees' home computers

Let your organization be ablaze with service! Intentional servant leaders light the match, fan the flame, and watch it spread. They convert every employee into, as one work unit puts it, "a server with fervor"!

The Customer Service Experience: Key Principles

Building on the Organizational Elements and best practices of successful customer service programs, the following are *key principles* leading to a brilliant Customer Experience. Consider them overarching guidance for a program that is <u>unified</u> to the organization, <u>customized</u> to the workplace, and <u>personalized</u> to the customer.

1. Servant leaders create and model an attitude of serving.

Customer service thrives in a culture of trust, connectedness, and accountability. Servant leaders build the culture by consistent modeling and messaging over time. By modeling serving behaviors toward both internal and external customers, leaders set the expectation and give permission to staff to serve customers and co-workers with abandon!
- *Culture of trust*
- *Consistent modeling and messaging*
- *Set expectations and give permission*

2. Expectations of serving flow throughout the organization.

Service is coordinated and aligned throughout the encounter. The leader adopts a unified approach to service that is customized to the site and personalized to the client. All employees develop competence in customer service through onboarding and training, in basic or specialized skills, appropriate to the position and professional discipline.
- *Coordination*
- *Alignment*
- *Training*

3. Expectations of serving are measured throughout the organization.

Customer perceptions of service are tracked via real-time and longitudinal data, providing useful and comparative information for continuous improvement. Leaders regularly review satisfaction and complaint data to forecast potential systemic service problems, and implement "early alert" procedures to ensure customers receive the support and attention necessary *before* challenges become overwhelming.
- *Real-time data*
- *Direct observation*
- *Longitudinal data*
- *Regular review to forecast potential systemic service issues*

4. Courtesy, competence, and quality are baseline.

Customers have a basic expectation of courteous, competent staff and high quality service. Meeting those expectations does nothing to *delight* the customer, but failing to meet them becomes a significant dissatisfier, eroding the customer's confidence and trust. Courtesy is not a "wow factor", but a minimum requirement.

- *Meeting basic expectations is NOT a satisfier*
- *Failing to meet basic expectations is a significant dissatisfier*
- *Deliver service on the customer's schedule, not yours*

5. Every interaction leaves an impression – positive, negative, or neutral.

Leaders ensure staff are "service ready" at every touchpoint and at every visit. One negative interaction requires at least five positive interactions to restore trust. What may seem a routine interaction to staff, can be a defining moment in the consumer's well-being, safety, and confidence. Employees build these experiences into *service relationships*.

- *Trust*
- *Keeping customers is easier than winning them*

> EACH EMPLOYEE HAS THE POWER TO AMAZE, ANTAGONIZE, OR LEAVE NO IMPRESSION AT ALL
>
> **VIRGINIA MASON HOSPITAL**

6. Hire for attitude; train for skills.

Recruit, hire, develop, and retain staff for the right "fit" to guarantee customer service excellence. Ensure HR processes, interviewing tools, leadership development models, and reward and recognition schemes reflect the characteristics of and commitment to customer service. Provide training in competencies necessary to perform the work, and anticipate and meet customer needs. It is unacceptable to be technically proficient without the ability to effect *healing* relationships with internal and external customers.

- *Put the right person in the right job*
- *Need to be both technically and interpersonally proficient*

7. Empower and support employees to do whatever it takes.

Motivate employees, train them, care about them, and make winners of them.

If employees are treated well, they'll treat customers right, and if the customers are treated right, they'll come back. Given suitable hiring, clear expectations, and appropriate training, employees are trusted to make sound service decisions. Leaders instill a sense of ownership and pride so all staff feel personal accountability for service. Customer service can be implemented superficially by mandate, but achieving a stellar customer experience requires employees who are invested, supported, and empowered to exceed the customer's expectations.

- *You've hired, you've trained; now trust the employee*
- *Every employee needs to know how to handle customer complaints & concerns*
- *Each employee is an entrepreneurial "franchise"; a leader in customer service*

8. Build every interaction and relationship around the customer.

Coordinate a customer service approach across the workforce, keeping mission, vision, and core values at the forefront of delivery. Develop environments conducive to engagement and respect. Design systems to meet the needs of the customer, not the organization. Service is personalized and proactive. The concept of "customer service" is surpassed by the broader "customer experience" and "customer care", which arises naturally from the relationship.

- *Personalized, proactive service*
- *Always make decisions in favor of the customer before the company*

9. Service recovery: getting it VERY right the second time.

Because we may occasionally fall short of the customer's expectations, it is important to have a plan to regain confidence, trust, and loyalty. Define the parameters of Service Recovery. Acknowledging a problem or expressing regret are not the same as admitting error and should be offered without hesitation. Ask the customer what it would take to win back his support. Customers who register a complaint which is subsequently recovered express higher levels of satisfaction than those who did not have a complaint in the first place.

- *What would it take to regain the customer's trust?*
- *Empower staff to do whatever it takes*

- *Provide customer service/service recovery during the visit, not after, so problems can be resolved timely*

10. Deliver service as a single unified experience.

Customer service happens before, during, and after the point of service. If the client's experience in any one department is less than satisfactory, the result may be a poor overall perception of service.

Before: The customer experience begins with the intent to patronize your organization. Early contacts (exploration of services, *window shopping*, telephone encounters, online connections, etc.) create initial impressions of service.

During: Perceptions are intensified at each touchpoint from parking to paying, and reaffirmed by caring interactions, a hospitable environment, ease of navigation, timely information, knowledgeable and comprehensible communication, and quick problem resolution.

After: The customer's estimation of service is enhanced by follow up communication, post–visit satisfaction surveys, and feedback opportunities.

Servant leaders ensure that staff understand the totality of the customer visit including handoffs to other points of service, in order to prevent service gaps. Leaders make certain that all employees are sufficiently versed in the organization as a whole to help provide a seamless and uniformly satisfying experience.

- *Customer service happens before, during, and after the point of service*
- *Receiving fantastic service in one area and mediocre service from another lowers the customer perception of the overall experience*

KEY PRINCIPLE WORKSHEET
[Use one worksheet per principle chosen]

Realistically, all the Key Principles cannot all be addressed at once. Start with a few which will have the greatest impact and reap the biggest benefits in your environment. You can work on the other Principles later. The worksheet below will help guide your thought process and action planning.

Principle Name: _____

Considerations for this organization:

1. How are we doing on this principle?

    • What does the data show?

    • What do qualitative data and observation tell us?

    • If we address this principle, will it positively impact other areas of customer service?

    • How should we prioritize this principle?

2. What specific actions can we take to improve on this principle?

3. How will we do that (action steps)? Who will do that?

4. What resources do we need?

5. How will we measure/monitor improvement?

6. Do we have strengths in this area upon which we can build?

Customer Service Strategy / Plan

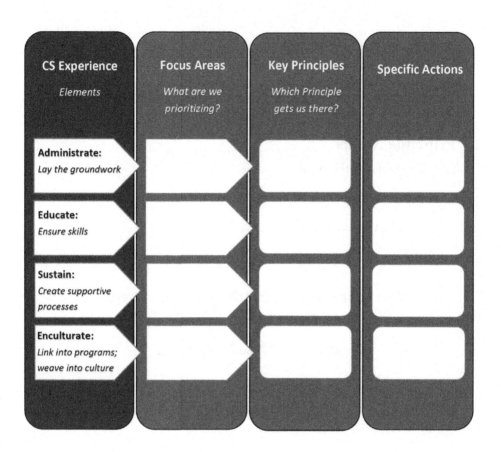

Figure 19

Ambassadors and Advocates

A KEY PLAYER FOR CUSTOMER SERVICE IN HEALTH CARE IS THE PATIENT ADVOCATE. IN SOME TRADITIONAL ORGANIZATIONS, THE ADVOCATE IS "THE COMPLAINT DEPARTMENT". IN SERVANT LEADER ORGANIZATIONS, THE ADVOCATE IS THE CORNERSTONE OF A CULTURE OF SERVICE. LET ME SHARE A PERSONAL STORY ABOUT MY IDEAL PATIENT ADVOCATE.

Jo started out as an ombudsman in the chaplain's office. She was well liked, but to many, patient advocacy was considered a fringe job. Jo didn't have an advanced degree in advocacy, but she had remarkable communication skills and could intuitively analyze complex situations.

She had gift for making patients feel listened to and cared about; she also made the staff feel listened to and cared about. Because of this, Jo was able to coax providers to see a patient's perspective without making them feel threatened.

The patient advocate position was eventually elevated to department status and Jo was appointed chief, reporting directly to the hospital CEO. She was authorized to "stop the line": to make any decisions necessary and commission whatever staff was required to carry them out.

Over the years I saw Jo:

- avert legal action by reconciling caregivers and unhappy families
- melt the resistance of clinicians who tolerated criticism from no one else
- instruct the business office to write off portions of patients' bills (service recovery)
- persuade unhappy patients to give the hospital a second chance

Front-line staff to supervisors sought Jo's assistance in handling thorny patient issues. She was respected by administrators, physicians, and finance managers. Jo brought a smile to everyone's face.

The medical center re-engineered processes and procedures as Jo identified systemic obstacles to service, and because staff and patients trusted her judgment and knew that she had management's ear, she was effective over time in shaping both personal attitudes and the corporate culture.

Jo saw patient advocacy as a mission. She challenged employees and leaders alike, nudging them to new avenues of service. How could we, she posed:

- …make every interaction user-friendly?
- …remain conscious of service in the decisions we make?
- …de-bureaucratize correspondence?
- …make it easier for patients to navigate from one department to another?
- …communicate in ways that are more understandable and less technical?
- …truly involve patients and their families as partners in care?
- …get past thinking of demanding patients as adversaries?
- …remain respectful and courteous even when we're having a bad day?
- …and when we make the inevitable mistakes, how do we recover the patient's trust?

The right "fit" for service couldn't be more apparent. Jo was exactly the right person for the job. I'm left to wonder whether anyone else might have been as effective. Jo was not my ideal advocate because she had the right credentials, but because she had caring at her core. A woman who built a "fringe" job into an unexpected asset became an organizational ambassador, stirring staff to service and patients to devotion.

ULTIMATELY, THE SECRET OF QUALITY IS LOVE. IF YOU HAVE LOVE, YOU CAN THEN WORK BACKWARD TO MONITOR AND IMPROVE THE SYSTEM.

— AVEDIS DONABEDIAN

Putting People First: How Are You?

Think about the last time you had a verbal exchange with someone as you passed them in the hallway. What did you say? What did he/she say? It probably went something like this: "Hi, how are you?" "Good, how are you?" Think beyond this traditional greeting in order to experience more meaningful interactions with others, express genuine care and concern for their well-being, and ultimately, deepen your connections with the people around you. Take a few minutes to write down some different, more substantive greetings, then try them out with a colleague.

Examples:
    "Good morning, Chris. Did you do anything fun last night?"
    "Hey Janet, what has been the best part of your day so far?"

Or to get past a superficial greeting, try asking for an opinion or an idea.

Examples:
    "How do you think the new policy will affect us?"
    "If you could change one thing about this assignment, what
       would it be?"
    "I noticed how skillfully you handled that difficult customer.
       Do you have any hints for me?"

_____

_____

Does a more thoughtful exchange evoke a different response?

How can this enrich your relationships with internal customers?

From Lip Service to Heart Service

Much of what we've discussed in this section is technical and practical. The reason is that many organizations fail in their pursuit of service excellence *because they lack the framework and the structure to enculturate it*. Good intentions are not good enough. Conversely, other organizations fail when they become slaves to structure, neglecting the cultural variables and "homogenizing" the human variables.

Servant leaders focus on resolutions, not complaints. They strive to soften the impact of business environments, health care environments, and technological environments that often frustrate and befuddle the consumer. They struggle to encourage internal customers who feel powerless and exposed, and who may in turn pass that along to vulnerable clients. They endeavor to inspire customer service based not on rules and declarations, but on heart–connections.

Intentional servant leaders *norm* service: it becomes the default position. Anything that does not smack of service falls short of the mark.

We have lots of terms for "customer" and many code words for service. But in the end the customer is just "somebody" and service is simply love. "Somebody" in your workplace needs love right now.

> LOVE IS THE SIMPLE TRUTH AT THE CORE OF COMPLEXITY. WHAT IF THE PERFECT CUSTOMER EXPERIENCE STEMMED FROM AN INTRINSIC DRIVE TO SERVE INSTEAD OF AN EXTRINSIC FORCE TO COMPEL SERVICE?
>
> **L. BELTON**

Contrast: Customer Care in a Traditional vs Servant Organization

Customer Caring in the TRADITIONAL Organization	Customer Caring in the SERVANT Organization
Customer Service Model	
• Complaint Department • Reactive	• Full Spectrum Customer Experience • Builds relationships
Organizational Elements of Customer Service	
• Lacks a thoughtful framework • Uses cookie–cutter approach	• Unified in direction • Customized to the site • Personalized to the customer
Educate	
• Customer service is a training program • Teach courtesy basics	• Training is only the tip of the iceberg • Teach courtesy + service competencies
Sustain and Enculturate	
• Human Resources and data practices governed by corporate policy • Other functions remain distinct and detached	• Human Resource and data practices support customer service • Integrates priorities to avoid "flavor of the month"

Customer Caring in the TRADITIONAL Organization	Customer Caring in the SERVANT Organization
Key Principles	
• The advocate/ombudsman is accountable for customer service • Service Recovery is minimal to avoid admission of guilt • Employees are expected to provide good service within limits • Customer service and how employees are treated are unrelated • Customers cannot always expect the organization to accommodate them	• Customer service is everyone's job • Service Recovery ensures getting it VERY right the second time • Employees are empowered to do whatever it takes • Customer service extends to both internal and external customers • Service is built around the client, not the company

Make Your Own Kind of Music

Try This...

1. Think about creative ways to serve employees of other departments. Is there something your team can do to serve colleagues so that they can better serve customers? This is especially useful in departments that do not provide direct customer service.

2. Incorporate customer service competencies into all leadership training. Create a series of teaching modules about service and the customer experience in various formats (online, in person, written materials) and lengths (half an hour to half a day). Make these available to supervisors and managers for events from team meetings to retreats.

3. Develop a set of Performance–Based Interview questions that ascertain the service competencies and disposition of the candidate, for use in hiring, promoting, and appointing.

4. Appoint customers/patients/clients/users to all major organizational committees and task forces. Or establish customer advisory councils to include the voice of the client in planning and programming discussions.

5. Commission some staff to interview customers/patients to tell their stories. Understanding the customer is powerful. Many have never been asked about themselves, what their service needs are, or what they seek from the interaction. Share those stories in writing or aloud.

6. Go beyond the greeter concept to create a concierge desk to welcome guests. Or start an Ambassador program to help patients navigate the system. Ask each supervisor to volunteer a two hour Ambassador shift weekly and open the opportunity to all staff as well.

Humenvironment

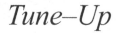

Tune–Up

You are breaking ground for new construction. As a servant leader, how can you add value to the project?

1. Solicit employee input during the planning process

2. Communicate progress fully and often

3. Allow staff to personalize their workspace

4. Rely on the architects to create the most productive design

5. Help employees understand how the changes will affect them

In the symphony of service, a simple, steady drumbeat underlies the busy goings–on of the orchestra. The strings sing, the reeds tootle, and the brasses boom, each elbowing for a place and making their presence known. All the while, the percussion is keeping time; marking the tempo. Except for the occasional thunder and clash to capture our attention, it reliably and unobtrusively maintains the rhythm.

The work environment serves that purpose in the organization. It provides a situational tenor within which operations hum, service resonates, management clangs, and personnel buzz. The sage environment chants softly in the background. When the environment commands the foreground, it signals an organizational SOS.

Environment is important: it sets the stage and cues the performers; it stimulates behaviors and kindles responses. Sometimes environments are purposefully jarring. Think about the DMV (Department of Motor Vehicles) or an unemployment office. They are not planned to be

---

* ANSWER: 1, 2, 3, AND 5

warm and inviting; they are built to be off–putting and impersonal. An austere milieu, self-important officials, demeaning waits, and pointless paperwork are often not indifference, but a deliberate strategy. These are environments where the customer is not *meant* to get too comfortable; that are *calculated* to intimidate. These are environments that embolden employees to be overbearing and rigid; and to be more concerned with procedure than with people. You and I have had those experiences and shudder at the memory even as we read this. We may sometimes be obliged to go there, but they are not environments we choose to inhabit.

No one wants to dwell on these environments, but it's important to recognize that they exist—exist deliberately—in order to understand their effects on both customers and staff.

More often, though, we encounter environments that are deficient by default, not design. Traditional leaders may be insensitive to environmental influences or more concerned with physical plant than environment. *Physical plant is the material aspect of environment; ambience is the transcendent.* The *humenvironment* is both.

If environments can be designed to *dispirit* they can also be designed to uplift. What an exhilarating idea! Intentional servant leaders can create workplaces that engage and inspire; that are productive and congenial; and that elicit our best work and our highest selves.

Employees long for an environment that is humanized—a *humenvironment*—, one that is dignified, healthy, respectful, safe, and conducive to the work. They need assurance that the job, however menial or repetitive it may seem, has worth. They crave a workplace where they can make a contribution and develop relationships. They do not want to be perpetually on guard against traps and deceptions, schemes and personal agendas.

People want to go to work with anticipation and leave work with a sense of accomplishment. A *humenvironment* considers the physical and the transcendent; the personal and the collective. It is the mood, the atmosphere, and the organizational consciousness. A *humenvironment* is the pulse of the servant organization.

IF ONE'S WORK ENVIRONMENT ISN'T ABLE TO PROVIDE INDIVIDUALS WITH MEANING, PEOPLE WILL SEEK OUT ONE THAT DOES.

MARC KIELBURGER

Harmony or Cacophony?

ENVIRONMENTS ARE LIKE MUSIC: THEY CAN BE MELODIOUS OR DIS-
CORDANT; HARMONIOUS OR LIKE FINGERNAILS ON A CHALKBOARD. LOUD IS OK;
HARSH IS NOT. OFFBEAT IS INTERESTING; OFF—KEY IS NOT. ANIMATED WORKS;
FRENZIED DOESN'T.

Environments can vary greatly and still be within the boundaries of
"healthy and happy". They are innocuous enough that we tend to forget
they are there. The environments we do notice are those that fall outside
the margins, to the organization's benefit or detriment.

I remember a nursing home where the environment seemed to col-
lapse in on the people there. Residents were lined up in hallways and
dayrooms. A TV provided some background noise to ramblings of inco-
herent patients, but no one was watching. Rooms were painted gray;
there were few decorations or wall hangings. An odor of urine mixed
with disinfectant lingered everywhere. For residents, this environment
dulled the senses and inhibited connection. For the staff, it prompted
detachment and neglect. The tone was cheerless and hopeless.

At the other end of the spectrum was a lingerie shop where customers walked out of the mall—way and into an experience. Soft classical music and a lightly perfumed fragrance greeted them. There was an
immediate note of pampering. As it often does, the environment and
the service combined to enhance the impression. Merchandise was displayed invitingly. The shop always seemed full, but never crowded; the
clerks were always present, but never pushy. This store had its own sense
of space and time. Purchases were wrapped in scented tissue and secured
with a gold seal. Patrons lingered because they didn't want to leave; they
were in no rush to return to the rat race of the mall.

Then there's the complementary medicine clinic that served lem-
onade and tea in the waiting room. On one wall was an aquarium, on
another an undersea mural, and on another a water feature. The colors
and the movement were stimulating, and the steady trickling of the

water was soothing. Lights were low, but sufficient, and there was a faint aroma of incense. A resident therapy dog settled down in one corner of the room and was available to those clients who wanted to pet him.

Privacy was honored as staff obtained confidential health information. This office provided alternative treatments and so was used to meeting clients' holistic needs, but the difference from the usual doctor's office was staggering. These services were not covered by insurance, but patients who came here for care were happy to pay out of pocket.

From the employee's standpoint, the company that has an *intentionally* inviting work environment does the best at recruiting, retaining, and satisfying their staff. Take a particular office park which accommodated many employers from doctors and lawyers to government agencies and merchants. The facility was located on a tract of land just beyond the city limits. Outside were pastures housing an array of animals including a herd of bison. Parking was plentiful and free. Offices were well–appointed and cared for, and relaxing common areas were sprinkled throughout the buildings. Amenities abounded: cafes and snack bars, day care and elder care, a chapel, a post office, and a fitness center. Occupants could look at paintings, buy handmade jewelry, or have their car detailed. In this environment, workers had their personal and professional needs met without having to leave the grounds.

There are so many other examples of helpful and harmful environments, but what do they show us? Whether we are employees, customers, or *captives*, they announce the "coming attractions" and set the stage for "coming interactions".

From a *business* perspective, the right environment induces commerce. People *want* to patronize companies that make them feel respected and valued; who go the limit to create a shopping experience. From a *service* perspective, the right environment induces caring. Even when it's more necessity than choice—or perhaps because it is—people appreciate an environment that dignifies their circumstances. From an *employment* perspective, healthy environments are   alluring, fulfilling, and growth–enhancing, exactly what a servant organization should be.

Indifferent environments weary our bodies and discourage our minds; toxic environments wither our spirits; but *humenvironments* feed our souls.

> A SOUL-BASED WORKPLACE ASKS THINGS OF ME THAT I DIDN'T EVEN KNOW I HAD. IT'S CONSTANTLY TELLING ME THAT I BELONG TO SOMETHING LARGE IN THE WORLD.
>
> **DAVID WHYTE**

Physical Plant: Home Away From Home

If we think of it that way, it colors our interpretation. Not just bricks and mortar, but a sanctuary for living, breathing human beings. An edifice that encompasses vulnerable people and those who serve them. The building is meant to be intuitive, to be safe, to ensure privacy and create flow, to calm fears and stressors—or at least not exacerbate them—, to invite communication, and to make morale soar. A little anthropomorphism doesn't hurt!

Construction: If I Had a Hammer

Leaders are not usually engineers or contractors, but often have to oversee their work, especially during renovation and new construction. Construction is a dreadful venture, at best annoying and at worst agonizing, until the final perfect result. Only it is never perfect.

Because leaders are not experts, they entrust the technical stuff to those who are. Instead, they need to become partners in the process—indeed, all staff need to become partners in the process—because *humenvironments* don't just happen: they are *intentional*.

New construction and major renovation are opportunities to create a *humenvironment* from the ground up. Many leaders never get that chance, but those who do can leave their mark for years to come. At the risk of oversimplifying a complex undertaking, let me share my personal "punchlist":

✓ Include as many staff as possible in the design process. Let them know that everyone's needs can't be met, but that their input will guide your decision–making. Select an architect that welcomes this feedback; who wants the job to be flawless, not just over.

✓ Listen to your own internal experts. The radiology employee will know if the MRI equipment will fit into the space allotted; the food service worker will understand the physical requirements of a tray line; the pharmacist can advise on the security standards for narcotics. Listen to them now or retrofit later!

✓ Remember that this project will define the future, and leaders after you will have to live with it for years to come. Make it a facility that will accommodate the way business is done, not dictate it. Exercise your servant leader skill of foresight.

✓ That includes building in flexibility. For example, hospitals constructed in the 1950's, a time when health care was burgeoning, were designed for inpatients—lots of them, four to a room. Today's medical centers have fewer beds, mostly private rooms with accommodation for family, and they house technology that was not dreamed of. To the extent possible, providing flex space to adapt for changing standards and demands ensures relevance and viability for longer periods of time.

✓ Be open to revisions. I described earlier the project that was in construction for so long that it no longer served the purpose. When the leader attempted to modify the plans, she was denied by the governing board who felt it would be viewed as a failure. They directed her to complete the project first and then make adjustments. Ego has no place in the *humenvironment*. Deliberately proceeding with an inadequate design is irresponsible, unethical, and costly. *Humanagers* and servant leaders monitor along the way and tweak when necessary.

✓ Which brings us to budget. Every project has a construction budget, and every manager knows that the budget will be overspent. So throughout development, minor (and sometimes major) alterations are required. Servant leaders understand the realities, but do not let budget determine the outcome. The *humenvironment* depends on leaders who know where they can compromise and where they can't.

✓ Instead, let vision, purpose, and stewardship drive the plan. Keep mission and core values front–and–center in the project. Exercise courage and moral authority.

✓ Communicate, Communicate, Communicate. Keep everyone apprised of progress, how it will affect them, and what to expect next. Continue to listen. As the project nears completion and becomes more "real", questions and concerns escalate. Be prepared to inform and conciliate to the *nth* degree.

✓ Orient people to the new facility. Take employees on a tour so they can visualize their work processes, locate equipment, etc. Invite family to see where their loved one will be spending the day. And have an open house for customers to familiarize them with the new milieu.

✓ Don't forget culture. Anticipate the human impact of reassignments and relocations. Find meaningful ways to integrate or re–create organizational cultures.

> POSITIVE WORK ENVIRONMENTS OUTPERFORM NEGATIVE WORK ENVIRONMENTS.
>
> **DANIEL GOLEMAN**

If I Had a Hammer

Create a plan for your next construction or renovation project. Include factors such as how you will:

- ⇢ Solicit and incorporate input from staff

- ⇢ Communicate plans and progress

- ⇢ Adapt the old culture to the new reality

- ⇢ Orient staff and customers to the completed structure

What additional items would you add?

Navigation: You Can Go Your Own Way

Leaders who are not immured in capital construction can find other avenues to humanize the environment. Service begins before the customer or employee enters the building, and navigation starts with parking. Poor parking arrangements can be a significant irritation, getting the workday or the interaction off to a bad start. Organizations have found innovative options to troublesome parking. Some provide a valet service or a van from outlying lots. Organizations in larger metropolitan areas offer a ridesharing or subway benefit. One educational institution routes a special bus around town to pick up students and faculty at no charge. And a health food company encourages employees to bike to work by giving cash premiums.

Once inside the facility, a *humenvironment* calls for a warm greeting. A model customer service organization has a welcome desk and escorts ready to accompany patrons to their destination. Others use ambassadors, volunteers, and docents for this purpose. Waiting rooms should be cheerful and cozy, devoid of institutional décor, but the object is *not to wait*. From the moment a customer walks through the door, the aim is hospitality.

Navigation through a labyrinth of hallways and annexes can be frustrating. I remember checking into a gargantuan convention hotel with two suitcases and a migraine headache. I wandered from one wing to the next, stopped to ask hotel staff for directions (they pointed and spouted a series of right and left turns), and scrutinized the floorplan I was given, but by the time I finally found my room, I had already decided never to patronize this hotel again.

Wayfinding is a goal of *humenvironments*. Wayfinding can be achieved by color coding walls or painting paths on floors, interactive kiosks, maps, and detailed signage. Better yet, have a roaming golf cart to rescue the bewildered. This is particularly important in a health care setting where patients and visitors are frail or in pain. In a servant organization, any employee who runs across a disoriented customer drops what they are doing to accompany them where they wish to go.

Healthy Work Spaces: A Room with a View

Studies have found that surgical patients recuperate faster if their bedside curtains display scenic landscapes instead of a utilitarian beige. And nurses know that a picture panel on the ceiling above an exam table helps the person to relax and cooperate. A *humenvironment* is important for patients and other customers, but it is also critical for staff.

Employees don't live in a vacuum. We spend an inordinate amount of time in conditions that can spark creativity or dumb us down; spur productivity or dull our senses; and isolate us or nurture community.

In some respects we are the triumphs or the casualties of our environments. Think about the place where you work, the spot where you sit, and the department where you go about your business. What would you change if you could? What would improve your productivity or your outlook? And what in your current work space is a blessing?

Space costs money and space must be used prudently. Companies are experts at reducing square footage or not increasing it when staffing rolls grow. People get crunched and processes are collapsed to reduce or conserve budget. But here as in other areas of our discussion, if budget is the sole driver of decision–making, the organization will pay in other ways.

I'VE GOT A THEORY: IF YOU LOVE YOUR WORKSPACE, YOU'LL LOVE YOUR WORK A LITTLE MORE.

CYNTHIA ROWLEY

Consider the advantages and disadvantages of:

- Working in cubicles
- Sharing an office
- Open/group offices
- Virtual offices
- Communal workspace

For many years I worked in an organization that assigned square footage by rank and grade. The boss got the exalted corner office, windows on two sides, and sometimes even a balcony. The next managers in the hierarchy snagged smaller offices, but they were private and had a window. Next came the front–line supervisors—quarters a little smaller and with no windows. At the back were the rest, in a maze of cubicles.

One day, word came down that the square feet allowable had been decreased. Workmen descended upon us, took the cubicles apart and reconstructed them two feet smaller. Now some of the desks didn't fit, so new ones had to be purchased. Staff no longer had room for personal effects; they barely had room to turn around. This decision cost the organization in dollars and in morale, all to gain a few feet.

There are pluses to congregate work spaces:

✓ Staff whose functions relate are close at hand

✓ Equipment can be centralized

✓ The atmosphere may be more social

✓ Open space is more flexible

And there are minuses:

✓ Distractions

✓ Crowding

✓ Picking up multiple conversations simultaneously

✓ Not being able to hear oneself think

✓ Loss of privacy

✓ Problems with confidentiality

Allocating space by rank reeks of privilege and can set up a "*we–they*" mentality. Cramming people into tight spaces impacts productivity, relationships, and job satisfaction. Herding airline passengers into jam-packed seating is a common complaint these days, but passengers eventually disembark. Employees are there for the duration.

Everyone wants a room with a view. Greg was stuck in a cubby, so he created his own view by installing a mural. Over his desk was a sign, "Cubicle Sweet Cubicle". Jill and Ina shared an office. They personalized their own areas, were conscientious of disturbing each other, and left the room when privacy or confidentiality was needed.

A group of techs cohabited a large open space. They agreed to use headsets and earbuds to minimize distractions, grouped worktops in a way that made the most of common space, and even acceded to a "no scent" rule (no food/no cologne) inside the office. And wheelchair–bound employees appreciated the open office because it was barrier–free.

Virtual offices have become more popular with staff and accepted by managers. Virtual space allows for expansion of personnel without capital construction or leasing. Many employees enjoy working from home for a variety of reasons. The lack of interaction is a downside for some and team building is more challenging. In an organization that permits virtual work, the leader must develop opportunities for contact, collaboration, and commitment; and to retain connections that are more reliant on relationships than technology.

And not everyone works in an office. What about large communal workspaces such as showrooms, wards or units, assembly lines, warehouses, etc.? Systems redesign can be useful here to decipher work patterns, traffic patterns, efficiency and convenience, safety and human factors considerations. And don't forget *ambience*, even in areas that are off–limits to customers. Tedious and mindnumbing environments predispose to accidents and errors, and kill motivation and morale.

There is no right or wrong answer here. Even less than optimal arrangements can be made to work. But leaders need to be aware of the tradeoffs and potential shortcomings: competition, overfamiliarity, inefficiency, excessive distances, hostility, horseplay, attitude contagion, isolation, etc. There are times where such an environment is unavoidable or even beneficial. Intentional servant leaders weigh the alternatives and take steps to humanize the environment to the greatest extent possible.

Workplace Musts and No–Nos

A secretary continued to complain about noxious fumes in her office. She had recently moved into an expensively renovated area and immediately began getting headaches and rashes. The supervisor turned a deaf ear to her complaint—no one else was having a problem—until it became a formal grievance. When toxic levels of formaldehyde were discovered, he had no choice but to abate it, but the damage was done. The secretary left his employ and filed a lawsuit.

At a manufacturing concern, business offices were located above the loading dock. When staff began to pass out, it was determined that carbon monoxide from idling trucks was leaking into the offices above. Then there was the suite that housed thirty–some people in an open, cubicled area. Whenever one employee came down with the flu, it predictably spread through the rest of the office.

Crowding, chemicals, and poor ventilation predispose to work areas that actually do harm or at least cause concern. A *humenvironment* does not condone "sick" offices or workplaces. It takes precautions and listens when employees raise the alarm.

Some characteristics just make sense for a healthy workplace:

- Good lighting and acoustics: sunlight where possible and fewer fluorescent bulbs to avoid headache and eyestrain. Supply high–intensity lamps where appropriate.

- Temperature control: I had a boss whose office was freezing in the winter and boiling in the summer. Not a recipe for productivity or job satisfaction!

- White noise: headphones or soothing music to muffle equipment racket and conversations

- Adequate team or meeting space: collaboration and communication will be sidestepped if there isn't a place to accommodate it

- Break rooms: everyone needs to get away from the desk or work area periodically, to congregate with co–workers for a moment of respite

- Availability of food and refreshment: some organizations stock the refrigerator with drinks and healthy snacks to keep the energy up without having to leave the work area

- Workout rooms or physical activity centers: encourage people to move, especially sedentary employees. One company crafted a hiking path around the property and sponsored walking teams during the lunch hour.

- Resources, technology, and virtual connectivity: technology is meant to support the worker. If IT resources aren't secure and up–to–date, they can be trying. Complicated programs can become burdensome. Administrative assistants at one company were required to switch to a time–consuming attendance program. They estimated that it took them more than twice as many hours as the previous system. Another company converted half their staff to virtual employees, but IT connectivity was slow and cumbersome. In cases like these, people develop creative (and not always prudent) work–arounds to make the system function.

WE SEEM TO HAVE FORGOTTEN THAT THE ENVIRONMENT IN WHICH WE MEET (WORK) HAS AN IMPACT ON THE QUALITY OF WHAT HAPPENS WITHIN US AND BETWEEN US AND OUTSIDE US.

PARKER PALMER

- Adequate, ergonomic equipment and supplies: the staff on a nursing unit was upset because they didn't have a piece of critical equipment. They were obliged to race to the Emergency Department on the occasions when the equipment was needed. Another workgroup had some sophisticated office equipment readily available, but were compelled to use a convoluted sign–out process to obtain the supplies necessary to use the equipment.

- Availability of office/clerical assistance: in an era when tech-nology allows staff to do much of their own clerical work, centralizing some functions may be more efficient. In one professional group, doctoral level employees made all their own travel arrangements online, a time–intense and error–prone task. Consolidating this work in a secretarial capacity could have improved proficiency, consistency, and the use of professional time.

- Stress-busters and amusement: there are legendary examples of businesses who excel in customer service and have fun doing it. Places like the Seattle Fish Market, Zappos, and Zingerman's Deli come to mind. Organizations do serious work, but don't have to take themselves too seriously. There are a million ways to help employees reduce stress and enjoy the job without damag-ing a professional image. Intentional servant leaders build those into the *humenvironment.*

- Greenery and esthetics: sterile workspaces do not encourage innovation and relationships. I know people in such environ-ments who count the hours until they can leave it. Plants, paintings, lighting, music, color, décor, etc. affect both physical and emotional health: good air and good vibrations.

- Spiritual or meditative space: in the current national climate, "time–outs" are acquiring a trite and political subtext, but I believe that having a meditative option in the workplace is more than a perk. We are all spiritual beings and servant leadership is at its essence, spiritual work. The pace and the stress of the modern work world can be depleting, and depleted "caregivers" are of limited use. I use the term "caregiver" and I place it in quotation marks because *we are all caregivers*: the lifeblood of the servant organization is caring. Some organizations have chapels, some meditation rooms, and others off–unit quiet areas that accommodate reflection and serenity. I know companies that endorse spiritual practice groups from yoga to prayer, and meditation to AA meetings. Acknowledging and providing for the spiritual health of employees is not just a bonus, but a valuable component of the *humenvironment*.

> WHEN WE MAKE OUR WORKSPACE SACRED AND ENTER IT DAILY WITH RESPECT AND HIGH INTENTION, THEN WE ELEVATE OUR ACTIONS BEYOND EGO AND ABOVE GIMME-GIMME AMBITION.
>
> **STEVEN PRESSFIELD**

Room to Breathe: A Healing Environment

In a class I took years ago on death and dying, we were challenged to locate and adapt a suitable space to inform a family that their loved one had passed away. We explored the building and found a small, warm room at the end of a hallway, removed from most traffic. There were windows looking out onto a courtyard, but none to the inner hallway, so passers–by could not peek in. With the door closed, sounds within the room could not be overheard. Lighting was on a rheostat, so it could be dimmed.

We looked for items of comfort, adding a candle, a Bible, and a box of tissues, and made sure a telephone was available (this was prior to mobile phones). We brought in some comfortable seating and arranged it so people could be close, but not invasive. Notices on the walls were replaced with paintings from nearby offices.

As we closed the door to test the effect, we spotted a poster advertising a drug overdose hotline that had been taped to the back of the door. Had we not shut it, we would not have discovered the poster, a potentially distressful oversight. It was quickly removed, but it prompted us to take another look at the overall effect, this time through the eyes of a grieving family. When we were ready, a panel of our peers evaluated the result.

Select a specific function in your organization and "create" an ideal environment for it. Examples might be: a patient check–in setting; a customer service/complaint area; a client welcome center; or a surgical waiting room. With a small team, mock up the ideal environment. Then ask a user to evaluate your results. Lastly, compare your ideal environment to the real environment.

Safety

We cannot overlook the element of safety in a _humenvironment_. Sadly, safety and security have become more worrisome realities than most of us ever anticipated. As far back as the 1990's, violent acts by disgruntled employees shocked organizations into thinking about security and planning to ensure it. "Going postal" entered the business vernacular.

Employees, as well as customers, have a right to feel safe in the workplace and leaders have an obligation to safeguard the environment. I worked in places that experienced shootings and bomb explosions, so I understand how the innocence of staff can be shattered in the wake of those events. I will not address measures such as armed guards or metal detectors: those are topics for another text and another author. But I remember being surprised when a psychologist told me he always placed his desk by the door of his office, to provide an escape route should it be needed. Helping employees take reasonable steps to feel safe is a sensitivity of the _humenvironment_.

Safety also involves accident–free surroundings. Monitoring incident accounts, worker's compensation claims, hazardous materials reports, etc. gives leaders the data to identify systemic problems that result in breaches of safety. Some organizations also collect information on "close calls" or "near misses" to prevent accidents before they occur.

Safety in a servant organization goes even deeper. Lateral or horizontal violence is perpetrated between peers. Lateral violence can be physical, but more often it is psychological. I recall a dietary department that was "ruled" by an imposing and menacing front–line worker. He had long since cowed his colleagues, and new hires were quickly—and forcefully—put in the picture. When someone crossed him, he made threatening gestures and although they were never carried out, they had the same effect. Even the supervisor was intimidated.

Lateral violence is never acceptable in a _humenvironment_. The emotional consequences to employees and the quality and productivity consequences to the organization are substantial and protracted. But wait, it gets even trickier. Lateral violence covers what are called "exclusionary behaviors", and there is evidence to show that supervisors rank high among the guilty parties. This can include: cliquiness, gossip, withholding of information, not being invited to a meeting that involves you, retaliation, hazing, etc. These are infinitely harder to ferret out and difficult to address, but they are symptomatic of a climate of violence. Exclusionary behaviors diminish productivity and engagement, eat away at the psyche, and erode the human will.

Lateral violence needs to be tackled quickly, firmly, and consistently at the individual level. More importantly, it has to be confronted at the cultural level.

Leaders must communicate and uphold a no–tolerance policy at one end of the scale and assertively promote civility and respect on the other.

And here's one more idea to think about. I once directed a system of maximum security mental health institutions. One hospital was a modern facility with all the bells and whistles: razor ribbon, lock–ups, lock–downs, armed officers, etc. Here staff relied on technology and physical constraints for their safety.

Another hospital was a midcentury property with dozens of buildings and an open campus. No barbed wire, aides instead of guards, and locked wards for only the most high–risk patients. Here staff based their security on forming therapeutic relationships with patients.

Guess which hospital was statistically safer? The second one; the low tech one. This would not have been expected, especially in the current day. It was determined that when we have all the gadgets and martial accoutrements, we become overly reliant on them. The low tech facility knew its patients—it had to. Staff understood who they were, what agitated them, and when they were going to explode. They were familiar enough to interpret the signals; to predict, preempt, and intervene. Because relationships were an important defense, people paid close attention.

We have evidence that superior relationship skills mitigate against aggression and injury, whether it be from disgruntled employees or clients, accidents and mishaps, or episodes of lateral violence. Perhaps it's not an either/or proposition. Modern security measures coupled with strong human relationships may be the best guarantor of safety.

> VIOLENCE IS ANY WAY WE HAVE OF VIOLATING THE IDENTITY AND INTEGRITY OF ANOTHER PERSON.
>
> **PARKER PALMER**

Violence by Any Other Name

{ An unhappy taxpayer shoots up city hall.

A resentful customer drives his car into a shopping mall.

An angry patient bombs his clinic.

{ A surgeon throws a scalpel across the operating room.

A disgruntled employee lets the air out of his boss's tires.

A manager chews out an employee in front of a customer.

{ A supervisor finds out he has been fired by reading it in the newspaper.

A union president deliberately omits his competitors from important emails.

An employee notices that colleagues stop talking when she walks by.

<u>Question</u>: Which of these would you classify as workplace violence?

<u>Answer</u>: All of the above

No one would think twice about labeling the first group of behaviors as violent. They are appalling, inexcusable, and sadly, all too frequent in contemporary society. The horror of these offenses cannot be overstated. This is violence of the first magnitude.

Then what about the next group of behaviors? Many of us would acknowledge them as outrageous and unprofessional, but do we recognize them as violent? These behaviors may leave the body intact, but they do violence to the psyche.

And the third group of behaviors? Unfortunate and regrettable, but haven't we all been there? If you did not identify these as violent, think again. They do violence to the spirit.

Acts of terror have no parallel—they stand alone. Mercifully, most of us will not experience this level of violence personally.

Acts of verbal, mental, and emotional violence may seem trifling by comparison, but if we fail to recognize them as violence, we allow the seeds of hostility to grow and we become complicit. These are the petty slights, attacks, and aggressions that you and I endure every day. Their effects may not be physically apparent, but they result in casualties and inflict wounds. They are called *exclusionary behaviors*:

- Being ignored or excluded by co-workers
- Not included in decisions that affect you
- Not given the information necessary to do your job
- Others are slow to respond to your emails and phone calls
- You experience in-groups or elitism

Over time, many of these behaviors have come to be tolerated as "just the way things are". We are humiliated when a leader reprimands us publicly and we are indignant when we see a co-worker treated that way, but how likely are we to speak up? We excuse the physician who has technical genius, but a poor bedside manner; the public official who is honest, but puts citizens through unnecessary hoops; and the front-line worker who bullies his peers.

When I hear staff say this is par for the course, what they expect, or simply the nature of the work, I am mortified! Somehow violence has become the "new normal".

Violence is an aberrant attempt to restore the balance of power. Servant leadership may or may not have any impact on the madness of violence in a mixed-up world, but it can absolutely impact the pervasive emotional assaults that have become an acceptable part of work life.

Because servant leaders share power, there is no need to seize it.

Because they listen and encourage input, disruptions are not required in order to be heard. Because they tap the potential of all employees, each employee feels special. Because servant leaders are trustworthy, there is no need to prevaricate. Because everyone is offered a seat at the table, elitism is pointless.

What we are calling small violences can do great damage even though it's not immediately visible, and can leave scars for a lifetime. In the long run, a black eye hurts less than a bruised heart or a battered self–image. Label them for what they are—not part and parcel of the job, but gratuitous violence. We cannot afford to turn a blind eye or allow it to pass without comment. When servant leaders engage in assertive, respectful dialog, they begin to teach that the small violences are no longer acceptable. And since we are all leaders regardless of where we fall in the organizational hierarchy, it is up to each of us to do just that.

Here's one more dimension of violence: Thomas Merton (1966) cautions that "too many demands, conflicting concerns, and an unrelenting pace do violence to the spirit and kill the root of inner wisdom that makes our work life truly gratifying and beneficial."

I wonder about the connection between physical, verbal, or exclusionary violence, and Merton's "violence to the spirit"…

> VIOLENCE, WHETHER SPIRITUAL OR PHYSICAL, IS A QUEST FOR IDENTITY. THE LESS IDENTITY, THE MORE VIOLENCE.
>
> **MARSHALL MCLUHAN**

The *humenvironment* is a melding of physical, contextual, and ecological influences. It shifts the organization *as organism* either toward or away from its values and service goals. It enables or blocks its corporate character. Environments don't just toddle along, they take cues from the righteous behaviors of staff and the virtuous decisions of leaders—or the reverse. That is not fanciful. We are not only the products of our environment: *we are the creators of our environments.*

Intentional servant leaders can do more than cobble together a good place to work: they can create healing environments. A *humenvironment* pays dividends in output and efficiency, wellness and innovation, job satisfaction and engagement, teamwork and loyalty, psychological and physical safety. Employees who feel like hamsters on a wheel accomplish about as much.

Work is meant to be joyful. Create an environment that inspires joy!

YOU CANNOT FORCE COMMITMENT. WHAT YOU CAN DO...YOU NUDGE
A LITTLE HERE, INSPIRE A LITTLE THERE, AND PROVIDE A ROLE MODEL.
YOUR PRIMARY INFLUENCE IS THE ENVIRONMENT YOU CREATE.

PETER SENGE

Contrast: The Humenvironment in a Traditional vs Servant Organization

Environment in the TRADITIONAL Organization	Humenvironment in the SERVANT Organization
Environment	
• Deliberate strategy to deter consumer, or environment is unplanned	• Intentional strategy to welcome and support all occupants
Construction	
• Relies solely on external experts • Finishes the project, then retrofits as needed • Project is driven by budget	• Relies on experts who are steered by internal feedback • Remembers that the project will define the future • Project is guided by budget, but driven by service requirements
Navigation	
• Poor parking arrangements are an immediate aggravation	• Wayfinding is planned
Healthy Work Spaces	
• Determined by budget limitations • Allocates space by rank. Fits in as many workers as possible • Provides the basics; the rest is fluff	• Determined by employee welfare and satisfaction, within good budget stewardship • Considers the pluses and minuses of congregate work space • Healthy work areas improve productivity and morale

Environment in the TRADITIONAL Organization	Humenvironment in the SERVANT Organization
Safety	
• Keeping staff and consumers safe means lots of technology and high security measures; loss of privacy and convenience • Lateral violence is objectionable, but endemic in some professions and trades	• Keeping staff and customers safe means appropriate technology and security measures coupled with strong relationships • Lateral violence is never tolerated

Make Your Own Kind
of Music

Try This...

1. Make environmental rounds. Ask staff in each area to suggest feasible improvements to the workplace. Be sure to follow up on suggestions made.

2. Establish a company "civility policy" Be careful to follow a servant leader model. For pointers, refer back to Section 1. *Administructure*: Rules; Policies and Procedures.

3. Begin a "close call" promotion to encourage the reporting of nearly–missed accidents and incidents. E.g. "I almost made a medication error," or "The client came close to tripping on a loose tile, or "I nearly caused a collision in the parking lot." Make clear how you will recognize and reward those who come forward. Make them "safety heroes" to take the stigma and risk out of reporting. Let them know how you plan to accomplish the physical plant or systems fixes required.

4. Tour a selected office suite or work unit. Use the factors in this Section's "Healthy Work Spaces: A Room with a View" and "Workplace Musts and No–Nos" as a checklist. How well does the area stack up? What can you do to improve it?

5. Check your organization's wayfinding competence. Select a person with little familiarity of the building (a new orientee is ideal) and send him from Point A to Point B (you choose the start place and end point.) They may use only existing signage and directional indicators to get there. Note the time it takes for the person to arrive at the destination. Elicit feedback about the exercise. What obstacles did he encounter? What changes can you initiate to make wayfinding more user–friendly?

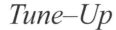

Tune–Up *Your organization is in the midst of a very public crisis. As a servant leader, you:*[*]

1. Initiate corrective measures immediately

2. Explain the situation, but deny any wrongdoing

3. Communicate internally and externally with full disclosure

4. Step down from your position

In the symphony of service, the conductor is the linchpin. The conductor doesn't create the music—he selects the piece, plans the program, and sets the pace. Then he allows it to unfold. He reminds the performers of their purpose, then opens a space for their excellence. He cues them, keeps them on point, averts distractions, and directs the intertwining of instruments to perfection. All the while he is alert to the temperament of the players—to the slightest hesitation or deviation—and silently cheers them on.

At the same time, the conductor senses the mood of the audience. In response, he fine–tunes the performance as it is happening, yet stays true to the composition and loyal to his ensemble.

Each instrument sees only its own line of the music and the spectators know only what they hear in the moment. From the podium, however, the conductor consults the entire score; the integrated components. He communicates to the people in front of him and the people at his back with understated leadership, and moves the musicians inexorably to completion. When the audience rises in applause, he defers to the virtuosos on the stage.

In an organization, the person at the podium is the leader. Leaders are the intersection of "in here" and "out there". "In here", they commission, motivate, and shepherd an ensemble of employees, then give

---

[*] ANSWER: 1 AND 3

them the freedom and trust to prosper. Servant leaders comprehend that it is not they who make the music or accomplish the goals: they supply the venue, the tempo, and the confidence, and they inspire the collective will.

The servant leader is the *maestro,* prompting the sequence and inter-action—service first, now finance, enter environment, rest HR, cue in quality—and linking disparate players in unison with each other and the organization.

"Out there", the person at the podium faces the music, or the reaction to his leadership. He understands that he is observed, judged, and held accountable by his community "audience"; that they are affected by his decisions, dependent upon his stewardship, and ready to help or hinder his efforts.

Leaders see the big picture—a 360 degree perspective. They are sensitive to the needs of staff; they are sensitive to the expectations of stakeholders. The servant leader is the pivot point; the interface between organization and community. The person at the dais is perfectly poised to focus inward (integration) *and* outward (affiliation). Leadership occurs *ex podia:* from this platform.

Integration

The conductor's primary duty is to *lead inward.* We've talked about the component systems of an organization: *administructure,* operations, culture, *humanagement,* service, and environment. But what keeps those elements in working order—what meshes the gears—is how they are integrated; how they are orchestrated.

The intentional leader views the organization as a puzzle. If there is one piece missing, it is not complete. Each part is essential and it is the interrelationships that give it its beauty and its tensile strength. Servant leadership is the great integrator. It embraces customer service, engaged and effective teams, innovation, value and efficiency, and performance excellence.

Organizations are webs of connection. Strands of functionality weave their way until they meet in nodes of commonality; they join and reach out in new directions, establish more nodes, extend and strengthen as they go. These webs of connection fortify the relationships between people, priorities, and programs, and amplify the good works of the organization.

Integration is the enculturation we spoke of in another section. The servant leader uses the *podium* to re–mind employees about the inextricable links among service…and ethics…and productivity…and respect…and solvency…and human resources…and safety… and culture…and relationships…and fulfilment…and personal life.

Yes, everything *is* connected, but I will go so far as to say that *nothing is not connected!* There is nowhere we can go where our impact is not felt.

There are some mechanisms that the intentional servant leader can hardwire into the culture to infuse and sustain integration/enculturation. These are the glue that makes it all stick. Let me highlight a few.

Civility, Respect, and Engagement

We've looked at civility and respect already, so let's concentrate on engagement. Major companies spend significant dollars on improving employee engagement. Several years ago, an international Gallup poll determined that only about one third of workers were fully engaged in their jobs. The Federal Merit Systems Protection Board reported that highly engaged employees achieve better program results, use less sick leave, and stay with their agencies longer (Ballenstedt, 2008). Higher engagement also predicts more positive customer experiences.

Recalling Maslow's Hierarchy of Needs, I would correlate civility with the basic levels, as the ABC's of getting along can affect physiological and safety matters. Respect may come in around Level 3, where relationships become important. Engagement, then, might be seen at the higher end of the order. It is possible for people to be civil and respectful without being engaged. Engagement arises from a more intimate connection to the work, from making a legitimate contribution or being invested in a mission, and from innovation and autonomy.

Employees can "do" civility and respect by rote, but engagement has to be felt. The seed of engagement is intrinsic and can be cultivated through learning and succession planning. Leaders who create that kind of environment do not have to struggle for an engaged workforce: it develops organically.

Practice Period

<u>Terms of Engagement</u>

One aspect of feeling engaged at work has to do with whether we perceive our jobs as meaningful. For many, our duties are determined by someone else, but there are always opportunities to build in meaningfulness. Small adjustments in how we approach work can change the quality of our work lives. Read the story below, part by part, and consider the questions.

PART 1
Paul, who is in his 30's, started a new job a year ago. Paul has an MBA and worked in a startup company in the medical industry for a short time, but came to your organization because he believes in its mission. His position in the business office became increasingly frustrating because he did not have as much freedom to make decisions as he would like and his role did not require much creativity. Paul often remarked that he felt trapped. Much of his work involved fairly repetitive, prescribed tasks.

1. How well has Paul adapted to his job in the Business Office?
2. If you placed five different people in Paul's situation, what range of responses do you think you might see?
3. On a scale from 0-10, with 0 being "Not at all Engaged" and 10 being "Fully Engaged", where is Paul's level of engagement?

PART 2
Determined to make the best of things, Paul sought opportunities to be on every project where he could be creative. He volunteered to review his unit's policies and procedures related to onboarding new hires. While many policies were dictated from

HR, he was able to adjust some procedures to improve the new employee experience. Seeing that he loved to create new products and services, Paul's supervisor asked him to develop an online module to promote a new employee health initiative. This project gave Paul a chance to construct innovative imagery and communicate with a large audience. From that, Paul was chosen to research ideas for best practices and present them at the monthly team meetings. While many of the ideas were not adopted, Paul enjoyed learning about novel practices and sharing them with colleagues. He spends around 1-4 hours a week on these tasks.

1. Why did Paul begin to volunteer time in creative endeavors?
2. How could this change Paul's level of engagement at work?
3. Even though many of Paul's ideas were not adopted, do you think his level of engagement has improved?
4. What role did the supervisor play?

PART 3

Out of his forty hour work week, Paul continued to spend about thirty– six hours in the repetitive tasks he did not enjoy. However the few hours each week he spent creating new products and services seemed to help overcome his frustrations. Paul continued to be grateful for his job and was seen as a high performer by his supervisor and peers. Over time, Paul started to wonder what jobs he could apply for in the future that would allow him to spend more time in innovative pursuits.

1. How did Paul's efforts in the short term contribute to his long term goals?
2. On a scale from 0-10, with 0 being "Not at all Engaged" and 10 being "Fully Engaged", how would you describe Paul's level of engagement? How does this differ from your previous rating? What changed?
3. If you were Paul's supervisor, what other actions might you take? What course of action would you recommend to Paul?

Thanks to Joe Hansel, Rocky Lall, et.al.

A Learning Organization

When Peter Senge raised the concept of a learning organization, many businesses grasped the first idea—that organizations are intended to help employees learn. Inservice training, education and development, skills preparation, etc. got a boost from a perk to a prerequisite. Companies did not, however, always pick up on the second idea: that *the organization itself was capable of learning.*

> A LEARNING ORGANIZATION IS ONE WHICH IS CONTINUALLY EXPANDING ITS CAPACITY TO CREATE ITS FUTURE.
>
> **PETER SENGE**

Studies show that resources (including time and budget), supervisor support, and psychological safety are cornerstones of a learning organization. So let's assume those cornerstones are secure. How do organizations learn as systems?

Communication is vital. A hospital in Texas found a malfunction in an oxygen tank wall–mounting, a potentially life–threatening situation. The equipment had been installed throughout the building by the time the problem was identified by a watchful nurse. She improvised a temporary repair that was safe and serviceable until the proper maintenance could be completed.

Unfortunately, other units in the hospital and other hospitals in the system were not made aware of the malfunction and only after several seemingly isolated tragedies occurred did anyone put two and two together. When the failure was recognized, the organization issued a national alert, negotiated a speedy remedy with the original vendor, and produced an online demonstration video of the temporary repair. In addition, they instituted a procedure to ensure such communication happened *stat* in the future. This hospital became a learning organization.

Businesses use various methods to integrate learning. I love learning maps. Professionally constructed maps employ all the principles of adult learning. They diagram a process or an initiative and how it fits into the larger system. Maps are visually appealing and interactive, often presented in a team setting.

Coaching is another example. The learning organization trains and certifies coaches who in turn become mentors and advisors for others, and the cycle continues. Post–Action Reviews help some businesses to analyze anything from simple mistakes to natural disasters. That learning drives correction and tightening up for the next time around. And it's at least as important to spread the good news. One company hired a retired executive to publish a yearly compendium of best practices and leadership wisdom.

As John Kennedy once said, "Leadership and learning are indispensable to each other." Learning is a natural *integrator*.

An Open Letter...

TO: Leadership Development Graduates
FROM: Your Corporate Director
RE: Managing Upward

Congratulations on completing your training experience! As the company's newest class of prospective leaders, you have learned how to manage personnel, processes, and expectations. You'll come to understand that as you move up the career ladder, you will also have to learn how to manage your boss! I've been asked to give you some helpful hints in that regard. What do I expect of our leaders? Here are some highpoints, in language this group might appreciate:

"Do What You Say, Say What You Mean, One Thing Leads to Another"

- Find the right degree of communication: keep me posted; no surprises, but I don't need all the details. Tell me what I need to know as soon as I need to know it.

- Contribute in meetings: don't save your criticisms or your bright ideas for hallway conversations.

- "Your attitude is showing!" Staff know when you're genuine and when you're blowing smoke: how you really feel about the latest policies and directives, today's corporate deadline, the current reorganization, etc. If you convey a message with a wink and a nod, they'll take the cue.

"We Are Family"

- Let me be part of your creative process: toss out your thoughts, offer suggestions; let me help you see things with fresh eyes. Tell me your triumphs as well as your troubles.

- Never be afraid to say you don't know something or that you need assistance. Mistakes/problems happen: I'm more interested in seeing how you manage them. Be honest, even when it's painful. Trust is the most important bond we'll have.

- "We're Corporate and we're here to help you!" Corporate is not the enemy. Don't withhold information or use Corporate as a *common enemy* to win favor with your staff. No matter how far up the chain of command you go, you're always the cream filling in somebody's OREO.

"R-E-S-P-E-C-T"

- Kindness is not for wimps. Disagree candidly, constructively, and respectfully. Be generous in giving the benefit of the doubt. Tell me when I'm doing something stupid—and when I've done something well.

- Loyalty is important, but it's not blind. Having the *difficult conversations* is sometimes the most compassionate thing you can do.

- Err on the side of inclusivity.

"Going Out Of My Head"

- Don't sing me the "Gimme my Fair Share" refrain (a variation of the "It's Not in my Job Description" chorus). Another department's resource needs may be more critical at the moment. Support your own unit AND the organization as a whole. Pick up that trash, answer that phone, fix that customer problem. If you see something that needs to be done, do it!

- The Lowest Common Denominator approach: "Why should I meet my performance goals/budget, etc. if my counterparts don't?" Satisfy your responsibilities whether or not others do.

- If we agree to something, do it—don't wait for it to go away (or me to forget!) If you can't fulfill an agreement, let's negotiate.

"Taking Care of Business"

- I don't want to mediate disputes with your colleagues—take the initiative. Work out systems issues, collaborate, and find creative possibilities together. Don't bring me problems without prospective solutions.

- Take control of your own environment. Meet deadlines. Make sure reports/briefs/responses, etc. are complete and service–friendly. Assure accuracy and truthfulness of what you say and write. Learn from your mistakes and don't repeat them. Don't give away your control cheaply, and then resent when I get into your business. Don't make me micromanage.

- Be a healthy role model. I don't give points for being a workaholic.

"You Are the Sunshine of My Life"

- Avoid group think on one hand and parochial think on the other. Think systems and expect all your staff to be engaged systems thinkers. Improving our work IS our work. All things are connected.

- Be able to say no, but delight in saying yes.

- Control is an illusion! Use your authority lightly. Remember that any power you have is "on loan" from the people who give it to you. The highest calling of a Leader is to be a Servant.

You are the future of our organization. Be good stewards—we are all in your hands!

Congratulations and Best Wishes,

Adrienne Marshall
Director

Linking and Labeling

Linking and labeling have been mentioned as tools of enculturation, but let's expand on that a bit. I have become quite adept at verbally linking concepts as I speak to groups. Let's say an organization's priorities include: customer–centered service, stewardship, civility, inclusion, and employee development. So I may approach a policy discussion or a didactic presentation by drawing attention to how our priorities tie to that policy.

> *"Based on employee feedback, the new Work At Home policy will surely please a lot of staff. It is also cost–effective since we won't need to lease new office space, so it's good use of our budget. And the dollars saved will be poured directly back into service improvements. This policy is win–win!"*

—Or—

> *"I'm glad you enjoyed the civility training. It does make the workplace more pleasant, but we've also documented less sick time usage, fewer accidents, and better diversity stats. Seems like this program makes HR, Finance, and Customer Service all happy. It's a natural fit with our servant leader initiative."*

Marketing science tells us that people need to hear a message at least six times before they really "receive" it. When the leader repeatedly verbalizes those linkages, staff and colleagues begin to make the connections for themselves. It's always gratifying when employees start using linking language with their peers: they clearly *get it!*

Linking has the significant advantage of signaling what the leader is doing (*"I'm supporting this budget plan because it addresses our mission as much as our bottom line"*) and what the leader is thinking (*"Let's include a discussion of ethics at our quarterly finance meeting"*). Linking priorities potentiates their impact and makes them less vulnerable to budget cuts.

Labeling integrates the device into daily conversation, reinforcing the behaviors a leader wants to reward and replicate.

> *"I know we're short–staffed today, but your pitching in to help is a great example of servant leadership."*

> *"I'd appreciate your thoughts before <u>I make this decision.</u>"*

> *"You handled that problem beautifully; it really reflected our vision of patient–centered care."*

Another angle on linking and labeling is taking the time to develop the significance of the undertaking to each discipline, or what I call "finding the hook". How does servant leadership make the clerk's life easier? Why should the IT tech care about the customer experience? What advantage does the new billing system have for the medical professional? When intentional servant leaders help staff find the relevance to their specific functions and compelling values, they engage them in the work.

Succession Planning

Succession planning is a method of "paying it forward". *Growing more servant leaders* is a core responsibility of every servant leader. But is there a difference—at least a nuanced difference—between the two?

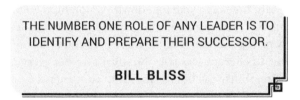

THE NUMBER ONE ROLE OF ANY LEADER IS TO IDENTIFY AND PREPARE THEIR SUCCESSOR.

BILL BLISS

When I started my tenure in one organization, several subordinates at an Associate Director rank were anxious to know what I was going to do for them; what they could expect in the way of career advancement. I was honestly startled that this seemed to be their first priority. I remember telling them something noncommittal like, "I'll work with anyone who wants to move up in the organization." One or two of them bailed almost immediately. The ones who remained told me that they had all been earmarked by my predecessor as "next in line" for promotions. That promise seemed to be based more on "you scratch my back and I'll scratch yours" than readiness.

Later I began noticing more of this "tradition" around the organization. I saw some leaders being pushed aside or not promoted while others were slotted into leadership posts quickly. I won't say they weren't talented—most of them were—but they looked alike, thought alike, and came from similar backgrounds. They were known as "Mel's Mafia". When I once lobbied for a colleague to be selected for an important role, Mel told me he had chosen someone else because "I owe him one".

What does that mean? How does succession planning turn into quid pro quo?

> SUCCESSION PLANNING OFTEN RESULTS IN THE SELECTION OF A WEAKER REPRESENTATION OF YOURSELF.
>
> **PETER DRUCKER**

The quotation above gives us pause. When I am very honest with myself, I can admit to being guilty of this. Years ago I groomed an admirer to replace me when I relocated. She had many of the same values and goals, but was a watered–down version of myself. I knew she was up to the task, but in my heart, I wanted people to miss me; to see that the new person could not fill my shoes. It's embarrassing to put this on paper, but I believe it was true. So did I give her every advantage I could? Did I teach her the best relationship competencies; share all my hints and secrets? Or did I hold back, hoping in some small way that she would not measure up?

I am happy to say that I did not repeat that pettiness again. I learned that just the opposite is true: the person you leave in your wake is your legacy. Instead, look for the stars; the ones that will carry your dream a little further. They stand on your shoulders, build on what you started, and perpetuate your ideals.

So, the truth about succession planning lies somewhere between the two quotes. Succession planning is a legitimate leadership function that ensures the smooth transition of leadership and the uninterrupted transfer of corporate wisdom. It helps to prepare a new generation with the right knowledge, skill, and insight to *steward* an organization.

When we say succession must be planned, we mean it must be long term, beginning early in the chain of command, to provide a diverse pipeline of potential leaders for the coming decades. It must be deliberate in offering both training and experiences that test and *leaven* novices over time. It must be intentional in instilling the finest models of service and leadership right from the start and reinforcing them as the ladder is scaled. Succession planning is not only about preparing the people, but about immortalizing the mission.

But succession planning cannot mean preselecting the people who look like me, or with whom I am most comfortable, or to whom I owe repayment for favors done. By all means tap the rising stars, but don't shut out the candidates that happen to fall just outside your field of vision. And because in servant leader principles *we are all leaders, all the time*, we must plan for the succession—and success—of everyone in our sphere of influence.

Performance

The primary reinforcing mechanisms of servant leadership and the principles of service are the achievements of the organization's leaders. So as with any culture change effort, both the practices and ultimate outcomes of the leader should be measured.

If the goal is to realize the institution as servant, evaluators must take a comprehensive view of performance, setting standards for individual leaders that filter down through the organization to employees at every level. Beyond that, however, and as a learning organization philosophy would suggest, the health of the organization as a whole must be considered. We discussed the pros and cons of evaluation and sample criteria earlier, but as we acknowledge integration and affiliation *ex podia*, standards and accountability are necessary to monitor the overall impact of the leader's actions and behaviors.

Appraising those actions and behaviors is step one, but what changes and benefits do they produce? I have always been amused at how Congress measures itself: by how many bills have been passed. But who looks at the actual effects of those bills?! And so it is with intentional leadership.

Figure 20 shows one company's dashboard to assess a healthy organization. Red/yellow/green labels indicate "stoplight fashion" scoring criteria. Each leader understands in advance what it will take to *get to green.* This is just a model: fill in your own categories and criteria.

MOST PEOPLE DO NOT GIVE TO INSTITUTIONS THE HUMAN CARING AND SERVING THAT THEY GIVE TO OTHER PERSONS.

ROBERT GREENLEAF

In fact, although they are a start, I would advise a few more results–oriented additions like: how do our customers view us and how do we know that? What are our organizational citizenship behaviors and why do we think that? In what ways do our staff go the extra mile? How is compassion shown here? Where do we add value to the community? Numerical indicators are so much easier to assess, but servant leaders get creative in finding ways to measure qualitative results as well.

Organizational Health Dashboard

Category	Green	Yellow	Red
Civility	>50% of leaders have taken Civility Pledge & scheduled a CREW activity	Supervisors have taken the Civility Pledge and met with a certified CREW facilitator	Leaders have not taken the Civility Pledge
Development/ Education	>5 developmental opportunities provided to staff	1-5 developmental opportunities provided to staff	No developmental opportunities provided to staff
Health/ Wellness	At least 1 health or wellness event with no less than 75% participation	1 health or wellness event with no less than 25% participation	No health or wellness events
Engagement	Leader has conducted staff mtg with org health topic discussed	Leader has conducted staff mtg, but with no org health topic discussed	No staff mtg conducted
Leadership	All leaders have taken a servant leader 360 degree evaluation in past 12 months and acted upon results	Only senior leaders have taken a servant leader 360 degree evaluation in past 12 months and acted on results	No leaders have taken a servant leader 360 degree evaluation in past 12 months
Recognition	>10% of staff nominated for award/recognition	<10% of staff nominated for award/recognition	Zero nominations for award/recognition
Communication	>25% of staff and all supervisors receive Org Health newsletter	>10% of staff and all supervisors receive Org Health newsletter	<10% of staff and supervisors receive Org Health newsletter
Servant Leadership	Achieved 10% improvement on Servant Leader scorecard	Achieved <10% improvement on Servant Leader scorecard	No improvement or a decline on Servant Leader scorecard
Culture of Trust	Utilized Culture of Trust tools and engaged in facilitated activity	Distributed Culture of Trust materials	No activities this month to build a Culture of Trust

Figure 20

Affiliation

The leader's secondary duty is to *lead outward*. As the conductor responds to the audience, the servant leader interfaces or *affiliates* with the community. The community is both customer and partner. "Community" is loosely defined. It can consist of local government, media, stakeholders, special interest groups, neighbors, academic institutions, or businesses. "Community" is broad enough to require an array of communication and public relations efforts. The servant leader looks toward the community *ex podia*, never forgetting the primary duty to the organization.

My colleague, Jeanette, was a master at government and media affiliation. She knew that courting those groups could advance her agenda, so she scheduled regular information sessions with them. Jeanette considered this exercise a bank account: if she made deposits, she could also make withdrawals. The practice held her in good stead and garnered her a degree of trust. When constituents raised issues with a Congressperson or reporter, they already had the inside—and accurate—scoop, so were able to clarify misconceptions. Jeanette earned respect and the benefit of the doubt.

Bernie was a CEO who valued community input. Prior to major policy changes or construction that would have local repercussions, Bernie held *listening sessions*. Just the term quieted doubts. Sharing information was only one side of the equation; giving people a chance to react was the other. Bernie gave consideration to much of the input and even when some suggestions were not followed, participants appreciated the sense of inclusion. Listening sessions gave Bernie and his team an opportunity to understand their impact on the community.

I know organizations that take their *affiliation* responsibility seriously and others who just check off the boxes. I found that establishing a Management Assistance Council (MAC) was a practical advantage. (The parent council was called the Big MAC and the sub–councils were called Little MACs!) To make the effort worthwhile, I included wide–ranging and high level representation: Directors of special interest and advocacy groups, Deans of regional universities, legislative officers, local business and health care leaders, and a few consumers. MAC meetings were a combination of their agendas and mine, with plenty of time for sharing plans and progress, feedback, and discussion. Once a year, I sponsored the Fall Forum, a MAC retreat that allowed for deeper conversation and strategic "futuring". It also gave the players a chance to get to know each other differently.

I will never forget a potentially turbulent meeting where I planned to announce a major change in direction. I began by showing a poignant video about our mission and commitment to vulnerable clients, then proceeded to outline the rationale for the change and invited the MAC to come aboard. There were thoughtful questions, but no fireworks. When the meeting was adjourned, one of the Deans congratulated me on a "tour de force".

Affiliation with the community is also modeled to employees. A brilliant example is the partnership between a hospital and a university, where servant leadership is taught and practiced at the medical center, and available to staff from front–line to supervisor. Then there was the office–based work unit that had little interaction with customers. In an effort to remind staff of the organization's mission first–hand, the supervisor granted special leave for employees to attend customer service events: in fact, she required it.

Managing Internal Crisis

One major occasion of community affiliation is *crisis*. The CEO is the public face of the crisis. How leaders handle these events is faith–making or faith–breaking, both inside and outside the organization. We all have our stories. Occasionally we need to step back and consider the systems in which our story resides. From my perspective, that's the realm of organizational health. There is no magic bullet, but healthy organizations—intentional organizations—are better able to prevent, predict, mitigate, manage, and recover from internal crisis.

If we backtrack a bit we can identify precursors to crisis; behaviors that increase the likelihood of trouble:

- Underreporting of errors and near–misses
- "Meet this requirement at any cost" messages
- Minimizing oversight and compliance
- Ignoring shortcuts and workarounds
- Censorship
- Considering some employees to be above the rules
- Writing off complainers as malcontents

Those are traits of a protective culture, where leaders would rather not know about pending problems than have to deal with them. Head–in–the–sand conduct is a crisis in the making.

> IF YOU DON'T CHOOSE TO DO IT IN LEADERSHIP TIME UP FRONT,
> YOU WILL DO IT IN CRISIS MANAGEMENT TIME DOWN THE ROAD.
>
> **STEPHEN COVEY**

Contemporary business lore is rife with examples of the right way and the wrong way to manage crisis. The one that still stands out in my mind as disastrous is Enron. But let's examine instead the one that set the standard for years to come: the poisoned Tylenol debacle.

Tylenol executives did more than manage crisis: they led through it. Their communications were prompt and candid. They could have projected blame on the supplier, the transporter, or the store in which the tainted bottle was sold. They could have called for tougher security measures. They could have denied responsibility altogether. But they did not. They took ownership of the situation, even though it may not have really been their error. They boldly accepted full liability and expressed concern for those affected. Executives demonstrated trustworthiness and caring.

The event could have been catastrophic for the company. Bottles were pulled off the shelves and no one would have been surprised if Tylenol disappeared permanently from the market. On the contrary, Tylenol's honesty and responsiveness, their process and safety modifications, their thorough reporting and resolution, and their compassion for families of the victims reestablished public trust in a comparative instant. I remember thinking that there would never be a safer time to purchase Tylenol products!

Servant leaders can learn valuable lessons from the Tylenol experience. Of course, preventing a crisis is the best option, but there are some basic steps leaders can follow to mitigate a present crisis:

- ✓ Acknowledge the problem; be factual and non–defensive

- ✓ Demonstrate that you are in control

- ✓ Express contrition

- ✓ State your commitment to resolve the situation and how

- ✓ Fix it—even if your organization is not at fault

- ✓ Offer restitution to those who have been adversely impacted

> ## MANAGEMENT IS DOING THINGS RIGHT; LEADERSHIP IS DOING THE RIGHT THINGS.
>
> ### PETER DRUCKER

And what about after the crisis? Learning organizations turn crisis into organizational change by analyzing the antecedents of crisis frankly, rebuilding a foundation of trust, and instituting processes to identify vulnerabilities. Intentional servant leaders transform crises into teaching moments. They depersonalize the event, discuss it broadly and objectively, and generalize the learning to other situations. Don't let the organization become too comfortable with itself: confront the brutal facts. If feedback is a gift, then post–crisis scrutiny is an absolute endowment!

I have discovered some Common Sense Corollaries for crisis. Remember that there are no secrets in a crisis: everything comes out. Don't let embarrassment or fear lead to defensiveness and denial. It's not about assigning blame: it's about reestablishing trust.

Managers are presumed to be corporately driven when bad things happen. So be humane in your words and actions. Let people see your grief, your regret, and your compassion. Don't let the legal watchdogs talk you out of a caring response.

Be alert to the ethical implications of crisis. Everyone is watching. Show the most virtuous side of the organization. And be aware that crisis often takes on political proportions. Elected officials may express "outrage", especially if it will make political points. Be firm in rejecting political solutions that ignore common sense.

The advantage of being *intentional* is to avert episodes of crisis, and there are keys to predicting and preventing it, keys that are rooted in ensuring a healthy corporate environment:

1. Look, listen, and ask the right questions

2. Are employees actively engaged, retired in place, or treading water?

3. Understand the absolute connection between good service and happy staff. If you want a clue, look at your employee bathrooms!

4. Do you reward overwork or workaholism?

5. Are employees advocates for the organization?

6. Do they see the local news channel hotline as the best way to resolve a problem?

7. Do ideas bubble up from the rank–and–file or only from the boardroom? Is the grapevine the most reliable channel of communication?

8. Can the organization course–correct with agility?

9. Do we confront or bury issues? Is there an institutional code of silence?

In the end, we work in human organizations. People overlook important things, they make mistakes, they are distracted by personal concerns, and some few do deliberate wrong. Crisis **will** happen in a human organization.

This is a state of affairs that requires the servant leader to pivot on the podium, supporting and reassuring those inside the organization; informing and instilling confidence for those in the greater community.

Crisis Overview
What Can the Servant Leader Do?

 Build systems/environments that minimize surprises

 Measure and observe

 Plan crisis management before it occurs

 When—not if—crisis happens, act decisively, courageously, and compassionately

 Integrate learning to make the organization stronger and less vulnerable in the future

 Restore confidence and recover stability

 Take care of your staff and yourself

 Be realistic and don't over–react: control is an illusion; there is not a crisis waiting around every corner.

Creating a Crisis Plan

This is not party planning: no one wants a crisis to occur. But the reality is, it probably will at some point. Many organizations engage in disaster planning for environmental events, but few prepare for internal crisis. How to avert, mitigate, and manage crisis is a strategic and public relations plus. Advance planning helps people remain relaxed and purposeful, even in emergency mode. Use the format below as a guide to develop your own crisis plan. Make sure everyone knows the drill and their role.

- ➢ Before a crisis and to prevent crisis my organization will:
- ➢ I will:

- ➢ During a crisis and to mitigate crisis my organization will:
- ➢ I will:

- ➢ After a crisis my organization will:
- ➢ I will:

- ➢ The characteristics my organization will display around crisis:
- ➢ The characteristics I will display:

- ➢ Organizational learning will occur by:
- ➢ The organization will re–earn the confidence and trust of staff by:

- ➢ …Of the community by:

The Institution as Servant

I've told the story of Ed, a Governing Board Trustee of a health care system I once served. And I do mean a system. In theory, this group of medical centers shared resources and a faith–based mission. In reality, that was sometimes a tortuous supposition. The annual budget meeting was a case in point. Members wrangled over which facility should get what percent of the budget, each arguing in favor of the hospital he or she represented. Discussion was getting pretty animated and reaching an impasse when Ed finally spoke up. Softly he said, "Are we not our brothers' keepers?" For a moment no one said anything, then they began to act as a Servant Board should.

> THE MOST IMPORTANT QUALIFICATION FOR TRUSTEES IS THAT THEY CARE FOR THE INSTITUTION, WHICH MEANS THAT THEY CARE FOR ALL OF THE PEOPLE THE INSTITUTION TOUCHES.
>
> **ROBERT GREENLEAF**

This story is worth repeating because it demonstrates the best and the worst in governance. Trustees share the podium with the leader, albeit in a more detached way. They are a link between the CEO and the community; the eyes and ears of the stakeholders; and responsible to both the organization and the public. They must be at once critics and champions of the institution.

The philosophy of the governing body sets a tone for the work that seeps into all corners of the organization. The leader is vital in guiding the Board to the "sweet spot" of governance, and the leader is paramount in steering the employees of the organization to the essence of service. Effective servant leaders are the head cheerleaders, the number one role models, the essential *integrators*, and the masterful *affiliators*. They never forget for a moment that everything is connected and that they are unifiers *ex podia*.

Greenleaf's concept of the institution as servant is a profound one. We spend our energy developing individual servant leaders and that is so important—but it is not enough. Healthy individuals can create a healthy organization. Single servant leaders can build a servant organization. Servant leaders can exist discretely and separately in their pods of benevolence, or they can *choose* to become greater than the sum of their parts. That choice mirrors a learning organization. That choice makes it *intentional.*

Governance

PERHAPS MY MOST INTERESTING—AND FRUSTRATING—EXPERIENCE WITH A GOVERNING BOARD WAS MY FIRST. THE SETTING WAS A SMALL, RURAL TOWN WHERE EVERYBODY KNEW EVERYBODY, AND WHERE BEING ON THE BOARD WAS A STATUS SYMBOL. AS A RESULT, THE LINE BETWEEN ADMINISTRATION AND GOVERNANCE WAS SOMETIMES SHOCKINGLY BLURRED.

Trustees would enter into contracts for snow removal, lawn care, garbage disposal, etc., on behalf of the facility without even consulting the CEO, because they knew the contractor or could negotiate a good price.

At social gatherings, townspeople would complain about their service at the facility or the quality of the food and, over cocktails, the Trustee would commit to having the offender sacked first thing Monday morning. Or a disgruntled employee would demand redress for a disciplinary action and the Trustee would pressure the CEO to remove the supervisor. Worse yet, they would request that a nephew, neighbor, or cousin be hired into a position for which they had no qualifications.

Other Board members would appear in the Personnel Office and peruse staff files, or insist on reviewing purchase orders. I watched several CEO's come and go, each exasperated by Board relationships.

Then it was my turn. As second in command, I was called on to fill a long–term Acting CEO stint. I dreaded my first Board meeting and gave a great deal of thought to how I could modify the harmful behavior, knowing I would have to do it at the outset or forever hold my peace.

I decided to take an interactive approach to the problem, one that was not confrontational, but illustrative. And so I crafted a Monopoly–type game board, complete with familiar situations and options for handling them. For example, a "Cocktail Party" square would pose a scenario and, depending on the Trustee's answer, would result in his moving forward or forfeiting spaces. Some squares would spell out the ideal response, modeling positive reinforcement. Others would mirror actual events that hadn't turned out so well and "send" the Trustee to the County Commissioner's Office (the equivalent of "go to jail; do not pass go...").

You may think this was a simplistic way to proceed or a precarious position to take, and you would be right. But I followed the path I had chosen and presented the game, which I named "On the Spot", at the next Board meeting. I introduced it as *Board education* and prefaced it with remarks about finding the optimal role for Trustees and having thorny conversations in a safe place.

As we proceeded around the game board, some members winced and some members smiled. In most I saw a spark of epiphany: *they got it*. Perhaps because the approach was open, unsophisticated, and non–threatening, or perhaps because they recognized the risk I took, the result exceeded my expectations.

Board education soon became a regular part of every meeting. As I gave them more information than less, their questions and qualms dwindled. Inappropriate use of Trustee influence became largely a thing of the past, and when it did crop up, we were able to talk about it. The proper role of the Board, its function as steward, and its responsibility to elevate service as an institution became the focus.

Since then I have experienced many brands of governance: corporate Boards, religious Boards, government Boards, and non–profit Boards—from both sides of the board room table. Some have been successful relationships and some adversarial.

> THE ULTIMATE GOAL IS TO RAISE BOTH THE INSTITUTION'S CAPACITY TO SERVE AND ITS PERFORMANCE AS SERVANT.
>
> **ROBERT GREENLEAF**

What I do know is that, in whatever setting, governance is formidable and not just in the fiduciary sense. Certainly we are all aware of Boards that are destructive, corrupt, or self–serving. Optimistically, they are the exception, with many more acting nobly and competently in service to the organization and everyone it reaches. Effective Boards set the stage; secure the purpose, the philosophy, and the plan; and safeguard the organization's mission and values from the 30,000 foot perspective.

The best relationship between CEO and Board is often a dance, each challenging and supporting, provoking and inspiring, and keeping the other honest. Boards are only as virtuous as the people who sit on them and organizations are only as relevant as their commitment to serve. Jointly and severally *they are leadership*.

Contrast: Ex Podia in a Traditional vs Servant Organization

Ex Podia in the TRADITIONAL Organization	Ex Podia in the SERVANT Organization
Conducting	
• Leader faces the direction in which he's most comfortable	• Leader is "in here" and "out there"
Integration	
• Misses the connections • Departments fail or succeed in isolation from each other	• Servant leadership is the great integrator • Organizations are webs of connection • Enculturation occurs
Engagement	
• Interested in measuring and coercing "engagement"	• Arises from an intimate connection to the work
Learning Organization	
• Gives employees opportunities to develop within budget parameters and estimation of potential • Learning is localized	• The organization itself is capable of learning • Learning is generalized

Ex Podia in the TRADITIONAL Organization	Ex Podia in the SERVANT Organization
Linking & Labeling	
• Principally unused mechanism	• Useful tools to communicate and reinforce desired behaviors
Succession Planning	
• Selection of a "weaker version of oneself" • Preselection based on personal favorites and loyalty; often excludes other promising candidates	• Develops a diverse pipeline of "potentials" • Plans for the success of everyone in their sphere of influence
Performance	
• Standards set for leaders • Relies on numerical indicators	• Performance expectations help synchronize service • Standards trickle down throughout the organization • Combines indicators that are numerical and results–oriented
Affiliation	
• Minimizes community interaction when possible, unless it's to the leader's benefit • Informs affiliates as needed	• Views community as both customer and partner • Informs and listens

Ex Podia in the TRADITIONAL Organization	Ex Podia in the SERVANT Organization
Managing Crisis	
• May micromanage in order to prevent crisis • When crisis occurs, circles the wagons • Waits out public/media interest • Alert to self–serving expediencies that may present themselves as a result of the crisis	• Ensures an environment that will prevent or mitigate crisis • Errors are admitted and discussed honestly • Leader takes ownership of the problem • Repairs the problem quickly • Alert to ethical implications of the crisis • Regains confidence of staff and public
Institution as Servant	
• Trustees support their own interests • Trustees are either under–involved or over–involved • Board and leaders have conflict-ing goals	• Trustees are critics and champions • Trustees are partners, albeit in a detached role • Leaders are the essential integrators and masterful affiliators

Make Your Own Kind
of Music

Try This...

1. <u>Tracer Methodology</u>. "Follow" a customer's experience through the organization. (This can be done by physically shadowing the person, or by tracking documentation.) As the customer goes from touch-point to touchpoint, can you find evidence of service, teamwork, wayfinding, efficiency, and quality? Do the organization's values and priorities "follow" the customer throughout the visit?

2. How engaged is your staff? Consider using an engagement inventory. Locate the pockets of high and low engagement and try to discern why: what motivates or defeats them? What can you do to raise the standard of engagement?

3. Convene an "after–action review" team around a recent untoward incident or near–miss. Encourage the group to put aside recriminations and defensiveness, and honestly discuss the event. Construct a procedure for applying the learning to future events. Regularly evaluate whether that procedure is effective and share results with staff.

4. Design a "Linking and Labeling" sticker or certificate. (Use an image of a chain, a web, or whatever works.) As you interact with employees throughout the day, watch for actions and behaviors you can "link" to other priorities or "label" as examples of an organizational value, and reward them with a sticker. Commit to distributing a dozen per day (or whatever you deem reasonable). As staff pick up on this activity, you may want to issue stickers for their use as well.

5. Who is on your slate of "leader potentials"? For each, list the skills that impress you and those that need development. Determine what you will do specifically to encourage their development. Now

look at others under your supervision who have not reached your standard of "leader potential". What about them is holding them back? Think truthfully about whether you carry some personal partiality or preconceived notion about these employees that will keep them from advancement.

6. Make a Board Development Plan. Schedule a short educational session for each meeting, highlighting a particular function, department, or topic about which Board members could benefit from a deeper understanding. Consider an annual offsite Board retreat as well.

7. Go back and review each Section in Part II of this book. How well have you integrated them in your leadership practice? For example, do your structure and *humenvironment* mesh, your operations and customer service support each other; or your *humanagement* and culture overlap? Can you identify instances where themes are replicated or carry over from one section to another? Is your leadership this cohesive?

8. Find an event in your community that relates to the mission of your organization, but from a unique slant. For example, if yours is an IT business, have your staff sit in on a senior computer skills class; or if your company constructs public buildings, encourage employees to volunteer at an event there. Getting a feel for your product from the perspective of the participant affords community/stakeholder input and gives staff a greater sense of *affiliation*.

Finale

Sonatina Glorioso

SERVANT LEADERSHIP CREATES A SYMPHONY OF SERVICE WHOSE magnificence is remembered long after the strains have died away. I marvel at Beethoven who couldn't hear his own music or the applause it generated. He gleaned approval and assurance that he was on the right track from body language, postures, expressions; cello bows in unison, and horns up together. He had to intuit the reactions of the audience. Individual players might have made small missteps along the way, but the outcome was certain.

So it is with servant leaders. They live a paradox: even when in command and control mode, service is at their core. They exist in counterculture, their actions and behaviors flouting traditional leadership archetypes. They are quiet revolutionaries, delighting in insurgent feats of love and caring.

To lead with intention is a noble ambition. It requires clear thought, deliberate activity, visionary foresight, and a deep sense of mission. It also takes practice.

Practice is a place where mistakes and failures can be ironed out, nuances and flourishes tested. Perhaps practice does eventually make leaders perfect, but in the meantime it *seasons* them. Our need for practice is never outgrown. If we miss a beat or skip a note, we simply take it from the top. We can rehearse some by ourselves, but we can't hear the fullness of the symphony without the others. If we're singing solo, we've lost the chorus. Servant leadership is an ensemble event.

Leadership has grown up. It demands a paradigm that has also grown up. As Greenleaf surmised, being *servant first*, addressing people's highest priority needs, offering them a seat at the table, and upending the hierarchy contradicts common wisdom. Servant leadership, while preparing us for the hard realities of management, achieves success by affirming the very values and relationships that make our work a calling. Servant leaders know that by serving with *intention,* they make a difference in the lives of everyone they touch.

> THE BEST WAY TO LOSE YOURSELF IS TO FIND
> YOURSELF IN SERVICE TO OTHERS.
>
> **- GANDHI**

I Have Called You by Name

THOSE ARE THE WORDS OF AN OLD HYMN. I HAVE ALWAYS BEEN FASCINATED BY THE POWER OF A NAME.

Do you remember the 1980ish mystery series, "Murder She Wrote"? In perpetual reruns since then, the title character, Jessica Fletcher, has a knack for calling everyone by name—bellmen, cocktail party waiters, parking garage attendants. Somehow she knows all their names and uses them generously. And how they all respond! As if they were people used to blending into the woodwork who were no longer invisible! I watch with fascination the effect it has on their eagerness to serve, going out of their way to do a special favor or look after her.

I think of so many other examples. My colleague Kasey teaches large numbers of employees at a time and remembers every one by name, a talent I envy. Not my forte, I have learned to look at name tags, ask and write it down, or come up with mnemonics. This doesn't come naturally to me; it requires *intention*.

Then there is the elderly man at church who has intermittent memory problems. During a recent service I reached out to him at the appointed time to say, "Peace be with you, Roger." It was pure joy when he responded, "And also with you, *Linda*." At long last he spoke my name.

When I was in nursing school many years ago, we were taught not to call a patient "the gallbladder in room 230", but to use the patient's name. In those days, it was a sign of respect to use the person's last name or title.

I was known by my surname for years as a mark of professionalism and position. I'll never forget the shock when, interviewing for a job in a remote corner of the country, I was addressed by my first name. It seemed entirely too familiar, but as I became ensconced there I grew to appreciate the closer connection it engendered. The name our parents give us—or for some, the name we choose for ourselves—reflects more intimately *who we are*.

In "A Nobler Side of Leadership: The Art of Humanagement," I used names to credit colleagues for a thought or a phrase that found its way into the material. A "Thank you, _____" asterisked at the bottom of a page noted their contribution to my work. This was not a formal citation, but an affectionate recognition; and an attempt to be a servant leader while writing about servant leadership.

So what does any of this have to do with the everyday realities of corporate life? Servant leaders need all the help they can get. Remaining in the "ivory towers" of our offices or our minds, putting space between "us" and "them", staying professionally and positionally aloof, creates a distance that is hard to bridge. Titles are legitimate expressions of esteem as long as we don't hide behind them, don't create artificial barriers of rank, and as long as they don't separate us from one another.

How many people do you have regular interaction with and don't know their names? Do you know the name of the woman who cleans your office, the messenger who delivers your mail, or the fellow who cashes you out in the cafeteria line?

I overlooked the power of that for many years, but now I make a point of finding out and addressing by name those with whom I intersect, even for a moment: the restaurant server, the post office clerk, the assistant at the golf course, the checker at the market, the man who sits next to me in church, the new employee down the hall… The results are remarkable: a link, a bond, an incentive, an inspiration—an instant if momentary recognition of a fellow traveler.

The ring of a name is sweet. It says, "You are worth remembering." It beckons us to a deeper connection. It summons us to personal and profound service. You are invited to *listen* to that voice, and to *be* that voice. If you didn't also believe that, you would never have picked up this book. Whether it is you who are being called or you who are reaching out to call others, the message is, "This is no accident. This is not a fluke. This is *intentional*. You have been called by name."

References and Indexes

Bachman Turner Overdrive. (1973). Taking Care of Business. Mercury Records.

Ballenstedt, B. (2008). Merit Board Links Employee Engagement and Productivity. Government Executive.

Barnes, S. and White, S. (Spring 2011) Organizational Health Newsletter, Vol.10. National Center for Organization Development.

Bliss, B. Coachingforleaders.com/153

Belton, Lawrence. (1984). Communication Behavior in Organizations. Oshkosh: University Of Wisconsin.

Belton, Linda and Anderson, P. (2017.) Servant Leadership —A Journey Not a Race. HealthManagement.org: The Journal. Vol 17, Issue 4, 268-270.

Belton, Linda and Anderson, P. (2017). Servant Leadership and Health Care: Critical Partners in Changing Times. Arkansas Hospitals: Winter Issue. 17-20

Belton, Linda. (2016). A Nobler Side of Leadership: The Art of Humanagement. Atlanta: The Greenleaf Center. 197-198

Belton, Linda. (2017). A Nobler Side of Leadership: The Art of Humanagement. The WORKBOOK. Atlanta: The Greenleaf Center. 76

Cameron, K. and Quinn, R. (2011). Diagnosing and Changing Organizational Culture. San Francisco: Jossey-Bass.

Chapman, E. (1975). Supervisor's Survival Kit. Palo Alto: Science Research Associates. 47, 54.

Claar, V., Jackson, L., and Ten Haken, V. (2014). Are Servant Leaders Born or Made?

Servant Leadership: Theory and Practice, Vol. 1, (1). 50-51.

Coffman, C. and Sorenson, K. (2013). Culture Eats Strategy For Lunch. Denver: Liang Addison Press.

Dispenza, J., (2017). Becoming Supernatural. Carlsbad: Hay House. 296-297

Edmondson, A. (2014). YouTube TEDx Talks

Eisenkopf, G., Hessam, Z., Fischbacker, U., and Ursprung, H. (2013). Academic performance and single-sex schooling: Evidence from a natural experiment in Switzerland. Harvard Kennedy School, Women and Public Policy Program, Gender Action Portal.

Franklin, A. (1967). R-E-S-P-E-C-T. Atlantic Records.

Ganong, W. and Ganong, J. (1976). Nursing Management. Germantown, MD. 325.

Goodman, J. (2009). Strategic Customer Service. New York: AMACOM. 35, 71, 97.

Graff-Reed, R. (2014). Customer Service Inside Out. Organizational Health, Vol.23.

Greenleaf, R. K. (2009). The Institution as Servant. Westfield, IN: The Greenleaf Center for Servant Leadership. 9, 12, 15.

Herzberg, F. (1968). One More Time: How do you Motivate Employees? Harvard Business Review.

Hess, E. (2013). Servant Leadership: A path to high performance. Washington Post.

Jennings, K. and Stahl-Wert, J. (2004). The Serving Leader. San Francisco, CA: Berrett-Koehler.

Katzenback, J. and Smith, D. (March-April 1993) The Discipline of Teams. Harvard Business Review.

Koyenikan, I. (2017) Wealth for All: Living a Life of Success at the Edge of Your Ability. Goodreads.com/quotes.

Lencioni, P. (July 2002). Make Your Values Mean Something. Harvard Business Review.

Little Anthony and the Imperials. (1964). Going Out Of My Head. DCP International.

McCarren, H., Lewis–Smith, J., Belton, L., Yanovsky, B., Robinson, J., and Osatuke, K. (2016). "Creation of a Multi–Rater Feedback Assessment for the Development of Servant Leaders in the Veterans Health Administration." Servant Leadership: Theory and Practice, Vol. 3, (1).

McLuhan, M. (1976). "Violence in the Media." *Canadian Forum.* Volume 56. 9.

Merton, T. (1966). Conjectures of a Guilty Bystander. New York: Doubleday.

Novotney, A. (2011). Coed versus single-sex education. American Psychology Association. Vol 42, No.2, 58.

Palmer, Parker. (2004). A Hidden Wholeness. San Francisco: Jossey-Bass. 6, 8, 34, 85, 169, 171, 172.

Patrnchak, J. (2016). The Engaged Enterprise: a Field Guide for the Servant Leader. Atlanta: The Greenleaf Center for Servant Leadership. 65.

Prosci. (2012). www.changemanagement.com.

Shain, M. (2010) The Psychologically Safe Workplace: new legal requirements and how to address them. Minister's Action on Wellness Forum

Schein, E. (1992). Organizational Health and Leadership. San Francisco: Jossey-Bass. 231.

Sister Sledge. (1979). We Are Family. Cotillion Records.

Stallings-Cox, L. (2015). Thirty One No/Low Cost Recognition Ideas. Organizational Health. Vol. 25.

Teclaw, R. and Osatuke, K. (2015). When High Performance is Rewarded: Praise, Recognition and More. Organizational Health. Vol. 25.

The Fixx. (1983). One Thing Leads to Another. MCA Records.

Van Dyke, H. (1904). Gone From My Sight. www.allpoetry.com.

Veterans Health Administration National Center for Organization Development. (2011). Research Summary.

Wonder, S. (1972). You Are The Sunshine of My Life. Motown Records.

www.azquotes.com/Drucker

www.azquotes.com/Gandhi

www.azquotes.com/Goleman

www.azquotes.com/author/28694-Marc_Kielburger

www.azquotes.com/Pressman

www.azquotes.com/Rowley

www.brainyquote.com/topics/integration/Covey

www.brainyquotes.com/McLuhan.

www.brainyquote.com/topics/workplace/Peter Senge

www.brainyquote.com/authors/david_whyte

www.goodreads.com/author/quotes/1110231.Avedis_Donabedian

www.google.com/search?/Covey

www.google.com/search?q=quotes/Kennedy

www.google.com/search?q=quotes/Senge

www.ideachampions.com/weblogs/archives/2011/01/50_awesome_
quot_1.shtml.

www.lanstudio.wordpress.com.

Yohn, D. (Feb. 2018). Ban These 5 Words From Your Corporate Values
Statement. Harvard Business Review.

INDEX of FIGURES

INDEX of "THINKING BETWEEN THE LINES"

INDEX of "PRACTICE PERIODS"

About the Author

 Linda W. Belton served as a Senior Executive in the Veterans Health Administration for 20 years, as Director, Veterans Integrated Service Network, leading a region of VA hospitals and clinics in the Midwest, and as VA's first Director of Organizational Health. Prior to her work in VA, she was appointed by the Governor of Wisconsin to lead the State Hospital system, and held executive leadership positions at a variety of private sector health care organizations.

Linda earned an R.N. from Jameson School of Nursing, a B.S. from the University of the State of New York, and an M.S. from Columbia Pacific University. She was a Johnson Fellow at Harvard University's JFK School of Government (Senior Executives in State and Local Government), and completed the University of Rochester's program in Leading Organizations to Health.

Belton served on the Board of Trustees of the Greenleaf Center for Servant Leadership, is a Fellow in the American College of Healthcare Executives, and a lay Associate of the Sisters of the Sorrowful Mother (SSM). She has received three Presidential Rank awards for her professional contributions.

Additional works include *The First Shall Be Last: Servant Leadership in Scripture* (2017), *A Nobler Side of Leadership: The Art of Humanagement* (2016), and *A Nobler Side of Leadership: The Workbook* (2017). She has co–authored publications on Servant Leadership, CREW (Civility, Respect and Engagement in the Workplace), Organizational Health, and workplace violence.